AF448119

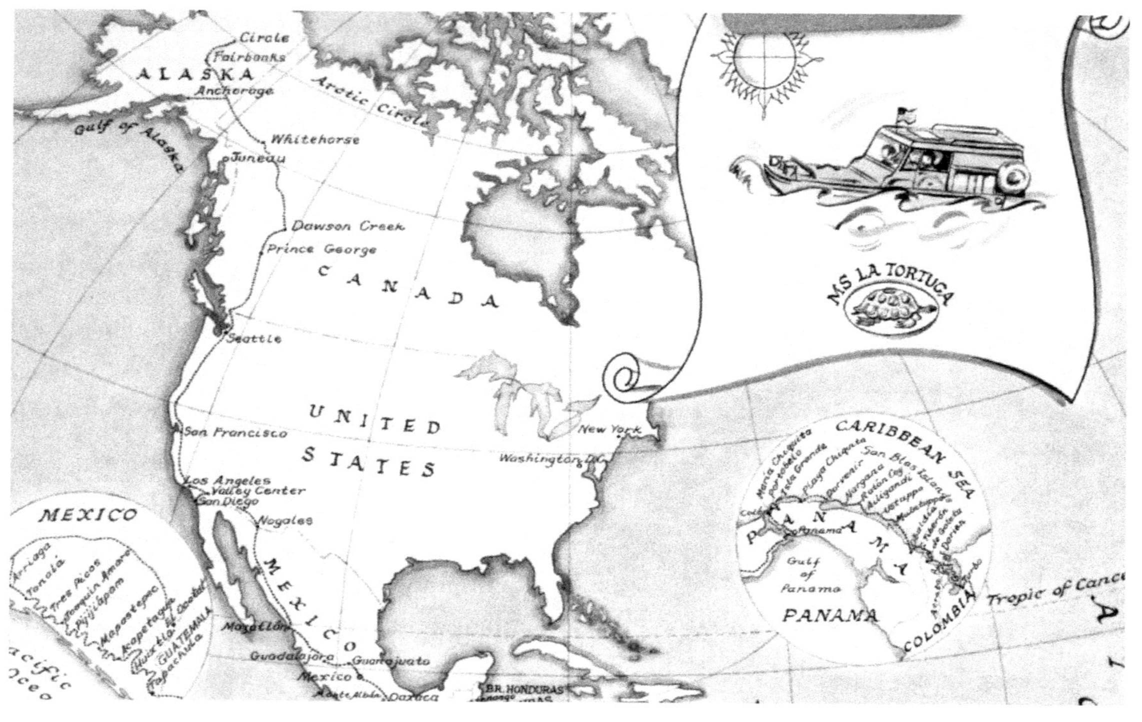

ALASKA
Circle
Fairbanks
Anchorage
Gulf of Alaska
Arctic Circle
Whitehorse
Juneau
CANADA
Dawson Creek
Prince George
Seattle
UNITED STATES
San Francisco
Los Angeles
Valley Center
San Diego
Nogales
Washington D.C.
New York
MEXICO
MEXICO
Mazatlán
Guadalajara
Guanajuato
Mexico
Monte Albín
Oaxaca
BR. HONDURAS
GUATEMALA
Tapachula
Arriaga
Tonala
Tres Picos
Joaquin Amaro
Pijijiapam
Mapastepec
Xapetagua
Huixtla
Ocotal
Pacific Oceo
MS LA TORTUGA
CARIBBEAN SEA
PANAMA
PANAMA
Gulf of Panama
COLOMBIA
Tropic of Cancer
San Blas Islands
Porvenir
Nargana
Ailigandí
Playa Chiquita
Isla Grande
Portobelo
María Chiquita
Colón
Panama

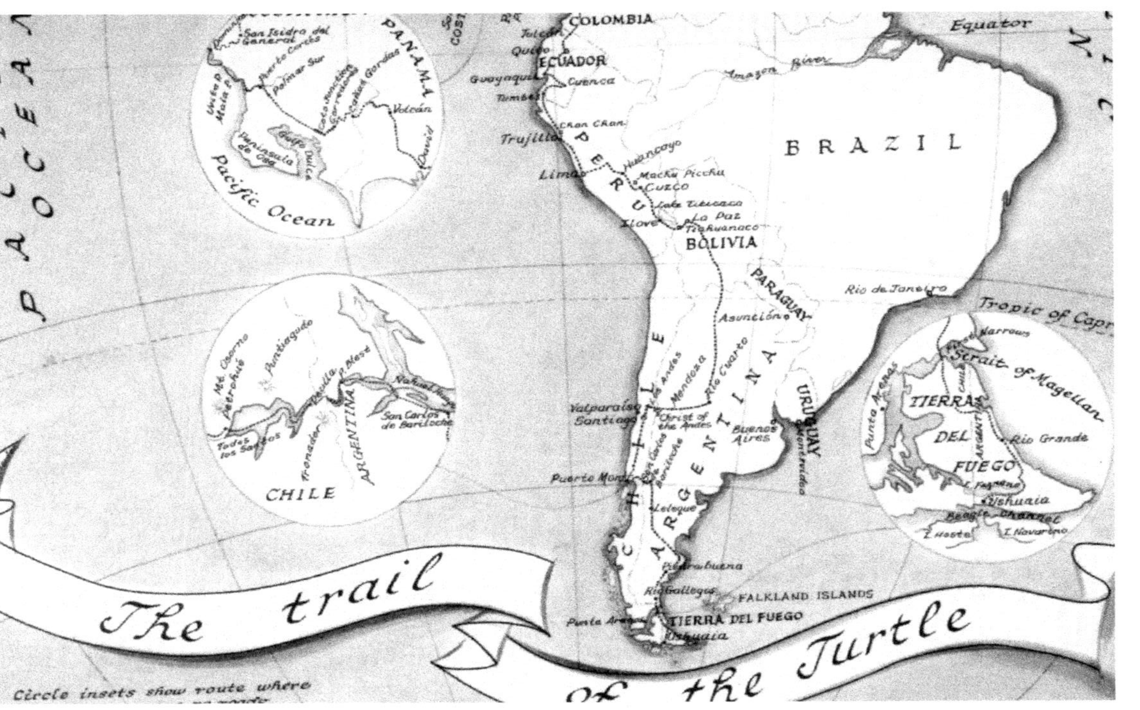
The trail
of the Turtle
Circle insets show route where
PACIFIC OCEAN
COLOMBIA
Equator
Tulcán
Quito
ECUADOR
Guayaquil
Cuenca
Tumbes
Amazon River
Chan Chan
Trujillo
P
E
R
U
Huancayo
Macchu Picchu
Cuzco
Lima
Lake Titicaca
La Paz
Ilo
Tiahuanaco
BOLIVIA
BRAZIL
Rio de Janeiro
Tropic of Capr.
PARAGUAY
Asunción
C
H
I
L
E
A
R
G
E
N
T
I
N
A
Andes
Mendoza
Rio Cuarto
Valparaiso
Santiago
Christ of
the Andes
Buenos
Aires
URUGUAY
Montevideo
FALKLAND ISLANDS
Puerto Montt
San Carlos
de Bariloche
Esquel
Leleque
Piedrabuena
Rio Gallegos
Punta Arenas
TIERRA DEL FUEGO
Ushuaia
Pacific Ocean
San Isidro del
General
Puerto Cortés
Palmar Sur
Cañas Gordas
Volcán
Golfo Dulce
Peninsula
de Osa
PANAMA
Mt. Osorno
Petrohué
Puntiagudo
Casilla Blest
Nahuel Huapi
San Carlos
de Bariloche
Todos
los Santos
Tronador
ARGENTINA
CHILE
Narrows
Strait of Magellan
Punta Arenas
TIERRA
DEL
FUEGO
Rio Grande
CHILE
ARGENTINA
Ushuaia
Beagle Channel
I. Hoste
I. Navarino

20,000 Miles South

20,000 Miles SOUTH

A Pan American Adventure

HELEN *and* FRANK SCHREIDER

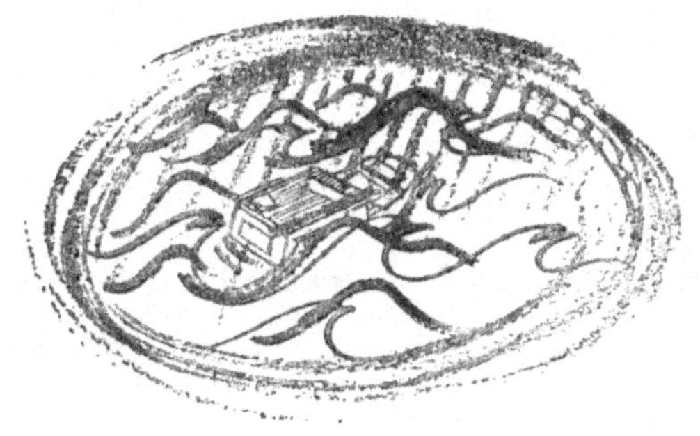

Drawings by Helen Schreider. Photographs by Frank Schreider

DOUBLEDAY & COMPANY, INC., GARDEN CITY, N.Y.

A PATHFINDER BOOK REPRINT EDITION

Complete and Unabridged

Printed in the United States of America

ISBN: 979-8-8691-9281-3

*To everyone, named and unnamed,
without whose friendship and understanding
this adventure might well have had
a different ending.*

20,000 Miles South

Chapter One

IT WASN'T until we met Captain Parker that we were discouraged. Others had told us it couldn't be done, but before it had been easy to rattle off glib answers to their doubting questions. To the ex-Army officer who had had an amphibious jeep sink from under him in a calm bay we had replied, "But ours has a watertight cab." To the sailors in Panama who warned of the *chocosanos* we had answered, "But we won't put to sea when it's stormy." But now, after four days of waiting for the weather to clear, marooned on a tiny island in the Caribbean, with the wind bending the palms horizontal and the sea piled in high mountains and the sand

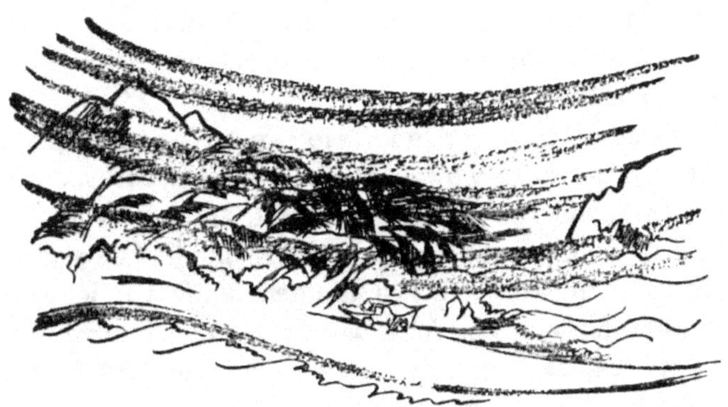

glaring white as salt under a black sky, those answers didn't seem like answers at all.

When a fishing boat took shelter in our cove, we swam out to her, eager for a few cheerful words of English. But what we heard was far from cheering. As I reached for the ladder, a large man leaned over the rail, yachting cap on his head and rat-sized fox terrier perched on his shoulder. In one breath he said:

"I'm Captain Parker of the *Sea Horse*, and I've got ten to one bet ya won't make it. If the storms don't finish ya, the reefs will."

I looked back at tiny La Tortuga parked on the sand spit. Our fifteen-foot amphibious jeep looked mighty small, and I wondered if he was right.

Later Helen and I sat under the whipping tarp by the jeep and thought about what he had said. This was not the way we had planned it. This month, May, was supposed to be the calmest time of the year in the Caribbean, just after the beginning of the rainy season and just before the *chocosanos* were due. The sailors had painted a vivid picture of those short but violent storms of near hurricane force that plague the coast of Panama after the middle of June. The storm around us was bad enough—what would the *chocosanos* be like?

We had allowed one month to bypass the third gap in the Pan American Highway, two hundred and fifty nautical miles from the Panama Canal Zone to Turbo, Colombia, where we could again reach a road. A month had seemed ample time to island-hop two hundred and fifty miles, even in an amphibious jeep. Yet it was already the twenty-fourth of May. A week had passed since we left the Canal Zone, and we had covered but twenty-five of those two hundred and fifty miles. While the rain cascaded in sheets, we again studied the charts, even though we knew almost by heart every cove and reef, every landmark and island in this section of the Caribbean. Repeatedly we stared at the frothing turbulence of Hellsgate at the far end of the island. We had already been turned back once by that channel.

On this pin point in the ocean off the coast of Panama the ten thousand miles that lay behind us and the ten thousand miles that lay beyond Turbo didn't seem to matter. Only the next 225 miles, the next few weeks, seemed important. We knew now that if we didn't make Turbo before the *chocosanos* came we never would.

No—this was not the way we had planned it. In California's Balboa Bay we had cruised confidently in La Tortuga, secure in the belief that we would never put to sea in anything but calm water. Despite her bright gray paint, La Tortuga was an ugly duckling among the sleek yachts. Neither car nor boat, but a little of each, she looked more like a Victorian bathtub with wheels. But, ungainly though she was, we were as proud of our amphibious jeep as the owner of the most de luxe cabin cruiser—or Cadillac. Her bunks were comfortable, her one-burner stove an adequate galley, and when the day's cruising was over we could pull up on the beach to the highway and drive home to the Palomar Mountains of San Diego County, California.

People laughed at La Tortuga. When California "dew" was falling and the streets of Los Angeles were flooded, motorists teased, "I know it's raining, but isn't that a bit ridiculous?" Others hailed her as a scout car from a flying saucer. And one night, a week before Christmas, when we pulled into a Pasadena service station, three attendants just stood and stared. One finally recovered sufficiently to stammer, "Is that for the Tournament of Roses?" Though I couldn't imagine La Tortuga bedecked with flowers, I guess it was a logical question. All Pasadena was busily preparing for the parade of roses that precedes the great football classic each New Year's Day. But when the champions of the Pacific Coast Conference and the Big Ten met in the Rose Bowl on January 1, 1955, La Tortuga was on her way to Nogales, Arizona, and points south.

Four years earlier we had driven that same road in a different jeep. The plans we had made then had not worked out either—the plans that began in 1947, when Helen and I were both students at the University of California at Los Angeles. Married while still lower classmen, we couldn't crowd a honeymoon into the budget of the GI Bill or the busy curricula of painting and engineering, so we talked of a trip after graduation. Since dreams were cheap we could afford the best, and I thought a short jaunt by jeep to South America would make a fine belated honeymoon.

I don't think Helen took the dream seriously until one night when we received a telephone call at the home where we were renting a room with kitchen privileges. Perplexed, she came over to my desk and asked, "Do you know anything about a dirty jeep and a clean Oldsmobile?"

"Oh, that must be the owner of the little jeep I saw parked on campus today. But I didn't say anything about his jeep being dirty. I just left a note, in good used-car parlance, asking if he would like to trade his jeep for a really clean '36 Olds coupe."

"Well it isn't a he, and she said that just because her jeep had a few leaves in it was no reason to intimate it was dirty. She wants to see what a really clean car looks like."

The secondhand Oldsmobile coupe that carried us to

classes was swapped for an equally secondhand jeep, and planning our trip to South America swung into high gear. We wrote to the Pan American Union and to the Bureau of Public Roads, and read everything we could find on the Pan American Highway. We learned that it was still a fable—impassable in many places, they said. There were still three gaps that necessitated transshipping vehicles by rail or sea at any time of year: southern Mexico, southern Costa Rica, and eastern Panama, and two other places that were passable only in the dry season, northern Costa Rica and southern Ecuador.

Undaunted, we expanded our planning to include pioneer equipment and enrolled in a course in Spanish.

About that time we added a third member to our proposed expedition, a huge German shepherd named Dinah who barked fiercely, frightened everyone she met, and allowed children to pull her tail. Not having the heart to leave her alone all day, I brought her to classes with me. She soon acquired the reputation of being the most informed BDOC.

Little by little our plans took shape. We frequented war surplus stores and watched for sales of camping equipment. In the pocket-sized notebooks which we always carried we jotted items as they came to mind, and on weekends practiced driving the jeep over rough terrain. At first the fire trails in the hills near Los Angeles were favorite proving grounds, but soon we needed more varied training. UCLA provided an ideal solution. The campus was having growing pains; everywhere new buildings were under construction. At night, just before dusk, while the campus cops were patrolling elsewhere, we drove the jeep to the construction area. The dense grove of eucalyptus trees around the Greek Theatre became our jungle, and when it rained the broken muddy ground where the law building would someday stand became our swamp. The excavation for the medical school made a fine canyon, and we practiced driving up and down and diagonally along the steep sides. As a practical problem in engineering, I computed just how far we could tip the jeep before it would turn over, but I never could get Helen to drive it at an extreme angle. No doubt she doubted the accuracy of my calculations.

In February of 1951, seven working months after graduation, we started on our belated honeymoon. Four months later we were back, disillusioned and broke. In that four months we had traveled six thousand miles across six countries. For eight sweating days we had struggled with machete through two hundred miles of jungle in southern Mexico to get through the first gap in the Pan American Highway. We had shivered in Guatemalan highlands and "ohed" at the white coffee blossoms of El Salvador. We had bounced across Honduras and Nicaragua, and skidded down muddy ravines in northern Costa Rica. In the south of Costa Rica the road dramatically ended at a wall of mountains where even a mule would have had difficulty. We saw that the only way to reach Panama was by sea.

Having bridged that first gap in southern Mexico, we could not resign ourselves to shipping over the rest of them. Those eight days had done something to us, and driving to South America under our own power had become a very real challenge. We couldn't say why we wanted to do it, but for the first time we understood why men climb mountains.

We sold the jeep in San José, Costa Rica, for passage home, packed our maps and equipment in cardboard boxes, and built a crate for Dinah. Helen's mother must have sensed the change in us. As we stepped off the plane she said, "You're going back, aren't you."

The first few months after our return were a frenzy of job hunting, apartment hunting, and jeep hunting. What we had seen of the mountains of Costa Rica and what we had read of the Darien jungle of Panama had convinced us that going overland through those areas would be impossible. But with an amphibious vehicle we thought it might be feasible to drive along beaches, skirting rock outcroppings by sea. It would, however, have to be a small amphibian to negotiate the jungle trails we had cut in southern Mexico.

In the Pacific during World War II, I had heard of amphibious jeeps, but I had never seen one. They were somewhat beyond the scope of my duties aboard a submarine. After the war, when surplus vehicles were sold, a Los Angeles company bought dozens of the diminutive sea jeeps and adapted them to serve as ice cream wagons. Some of them were still in use when we returned from Costa Rica. Every time I heard the tinkle of bells in the street I ran after the sound, but each one would have sunk in a puddle. I canvassed war surplus lots, but the only ones I heard about had served as ballast in the holds of ships coming back from overseas. They were crushed almost beyond recognition. Finally, after four months of searching, I located a rusted hulk in a junk yard. It had known three owners since the Army declared it unserviceable, and looked as if it had been through the Battle of the Bilge. Full of stagnant water, half dismantled, it wouldn't run. When I asked about it, the proprietor said it was going to be cut up for scrap, and then added, "If you want it, you'd better hurry."

"How much?" I asked.

"Two hundred and twenty-five dollars," he replied casually.

After some rapid mental calculations concerning the price of scrap iron and the weight of the jeep, I concluded that my eagerness must have shown. Rather expensive scrap. I tried hard to be casual too. The price was still $225. But it was the only one I had seen that had any possibilities at all. "I'll take it if you'll throw in some wheels so I can get it home."

Triumphantly I towed the relic to where Helen's family lived near the Palomar Mountains. Its reception was somewhat less than I had hoped for. Aghast, Helen stared at the rusty water trickling from the hull. It had sprung a dozen leaks in just the smooth ride home.

"We can't put to sea in that," she said flatly.

"I admit she doesn't look like much now, honey, but just wait a little while till we get her all fixed up—holes patched, motor overhauled, nice little cab." Then I added soothingly, "And we'll paint it any color you like." I had no idea it would be almost three years before it was in that condition.

The disassembly of the jeep was easy. With a little encouragement it practically fell apart by itself. Leaving the hull with the family, we brought everything portable to the garage of our Los Angeles apartment. One night as I rushed through dinner to get out to the garage, Helen said, "I never see you any more. Why don't you bring that thing inside and work on it?"

That seemed like a good idea. I built a workbench in the kitchen and moved in two sawhorses, from which I suspended the differentials like chicken on a spit. I stood back and surveyed my labor with satisfaction. It made a fine workshop, though it left little room for cooking. I wondered what

Helen would do when guests came for dinner, but I needn't have been concerned. After friends had run an obstacle course around Dinah at the door, Helen's easel in the living room, and part of what would be La Tortuga in the kitchen, we dined by candlelight, with my workbench shrouded under a white sheet.

In the months that followed I became well acquainted with all the automotive stores, war surplus vehicle yards, secondhand stores, and junk yards from Santa Barbara to San Diego. With the motor, transmissions, and differentials overhauled, the jeep was progressing nicely, but we couldn't say the same for our bank account. At the rate we were pouring money into parts, even with no labor charges, it was obvious that it would be many years before we would have enough saved to head south. Just about the time I was ready to begin the transformation of the hull an opportunity came for a higher-paying job with the Army Corps of Engineers overseas. Enthusiastically—and without warning—I presented the idea to Helen:

"How would you like to go to Alaska?" Before she could object I hurried on. "There's an opening for an electrical engineer in Anchorage. And they spoke of a job for you as a draftsman. Between the two of us we could double what I'm making now."

Helen looked around at our new apartment, at the drapes she had just finished, and at the still life she was working on. Sighing, she smiled quizzically. "When do we leave?"

Work on the jeep stopped; there was no time to finish it before we were due in Anchorage, so back to the Palomar Mountains to join the still rusted and battered hull went all the shiny, newly painted parts to await our return. Then the packing began, but that was easy since we were advised to bring nothing but our clothing. Our contract read ". . . two years . . . quarters and eating facilities will be provided." As we sprinkled moth flakes over the things we weren't taking, Helen laughingly held up our swim suits. "I don't imagine we'll be needing these in 'Seward's Icebox.'"

Our first glimpse of Alaska was just what we had expected; a cold sleet froze as it touched the ground when we climbed from an Air Force plane near Anchorage. Pulling oversized GI parkas up around our ears, we slid to the waiting motor pool car and rode to the transient quarters of Elmendorf Air Force Base. Next morning we were assigned to our permanent quarters, and later that same day we picked up Dinah. While we had squirmed in bucket seats of the transport plane, Dinah had flown first class in a Stratocruiser.

The temporary building that we called home for the next two years was a barracks covered with dull black paper. We shared our "tar-paper palace" with ten other couples—in separate rooms, but with common baths. There were apartments available, but our ten-by-twelve room was only sixteen dollars a month. The "eating facilities" provided were family style in the construction workers' mess hall, and, as Helen wrote home, "It's hardly candlelight and wine, but the food's good and there's plenty of it." She said nothing about the bedlam of kitchen rattle and long-arm scramble as everyone ate desperately to get his dollar's worth. After a month, during which time we almost grew into the oversized parkas that had been issued to us, we decided that it would be no hardship to eat half as much and bank the difference. Dinah, however, was of a different mind, and looked forward eagerly to the ten paper bags of meat scraps that were left outside our door each evening by well-meaning barracks mates.

18

Shortly after our arrival, huddled in heavy coats, with thick mittens like boxing gloves on our hands and our breath steaming, we made a tour of Alaska's largest city. Fourth Avenue, Anchorage's main street, once called the longest bar in the world, flashed with competing neon signs like a miniature Times Square. Although we had not counted on the streets being lined with igloos, we were not prepared for the fourteen-story apartment buildings, but we ogled even more the television antenna sticking from a log cabin in the same block. In front of the Northern Commercial Company, Alaska's oldest department store, we froze. But not from the cold. In the window, instead of parkas and snowshoes, we saw bathing suits and water skis in a setting of green paper palms and sugar sand.

With a shiver Helen said, "They must be advertising an all-expense tour to Florida."

But later we found that it was not a vacationer's dream nor even a window decorator's error. It was March 1952, and they were showing the latest mode for Alaskan summer.

With the honking of wild geese, branches spread forth their green shoots and the first iris of spring appeared. By the time the eighteen-hour days of summer came and the purple iris were crowded out by the magenta fire flowers, our illusions about Alaska had undergone a complete reversal. We joined the after-work crowd at nearby Lake Spenard for water-skiing—and its resultant involuntary swimming. But it soon became apparent that there was much more of Alaska than we could see trailing behind a motorboat, so, since Dinah refused to pull a sled, we bought a station wagon. Weekends that followed we spent driving along the jagged coast of Cook Inlet or Turnagain Arm, or camping in the spruce forests of the Kenai Peninsula. And each payday we deposited in the bank anything over our minimum living expenses and payments on cameras and the car.

Although moose occasionally invaded Elmendorf Air Force Base or chased cars through the streets of Anchorage, we wanted to see wildlife in its natural habitat. Our first vacation we spent in Mount McKinley National Park, pitching our tent in the shadow of the highest peak on the North American continent. In the valleys whistling marmots signaled our approach, and porcupines ambled clear of caribou that thundered over the hills. Loaded with cameras, we climbed to dizzy crags where white Dall sheep stood like bearded patriarchs. And we stalked the golden-and-black Toklat grizzlies that padded over the spongy tundra. With no guns allowed in the park, we armed ourselves with a coffee can filled with rocks and followed a huge male that was courting an only slightly smaller female. I had the cine-camera leveled on the tripod and was just ready to release the shutter when I heard the rocks rattling furiously in the can. Angrily I turned to Helen at my side. "Stop shaking that thing. You'll scare the bears."

"That's the idea," she quivered. "Look behind you!"

Less than twenty paces away, and standing upright, was a third bear. Our big male had competition for the affections of his girl friend and we were right in the middle. We concluded our story of the three bears with a rattling good exit.

Winter came, the hoarfrost turned the trees to crystal, and the wind piled the snow in demon shapes. Strapping on snowshoes, we floundered through the white forests to some now deserted trapper's cabin. Dinah adapted herself readily to the deep snow, but I can't honestly say she took it in her stride. More often she took it in *ours*, and her attempts at hitchhiking on our snowshoes always resulted in our being pitched forward on our faces.

Time passed quickly until one gray overcast Sunday in January of 1954. When any sensible novice would have been at home with a book, I was skiing on the slopes of the Chugach Mountains near Anchorage. A combination of drifts, flat light, and overenthusiasm shattered my aspirations of becoming an Emile Allais overnight. After a month in the hospital I returned to work encased in plaster to my hip. Although I was hardly in the executive class, thereafter I enjoyed one of a boss's privileges—I could put my leg on the desk with impunity. But this was little compensation for the dragging months that followed.

At night I occupied myself with books and records, but Sibelius's *Finlandia* brought visions of snow-covered hills and Beethoven's *Pastoral* the green fields of summer. The skis in the corner, the sleeping bags and packboards on the rack near the ceiling, the piece of glacial driftwood, and even Helen's paintings on the wall were sad reminders that our outdoor activities had ceased.

But there was one kind of music that brought me from the past and cheered me with thoughts of the future—the gay guitars of Trio Los Panchos. One evening, about five months after breaking my leg, I was studying a map of the Western Hemisphere. Two places repeatedly caught my eye, Circle and Ushuaia. I wondered why I hadn't thought of it before. Excitedly I interrupted Helen's concentration on her still life. "Why don't we drive north to the little town of Circle and then all the way south to Ushuaia?"

"To where?"

"Ushuaia," I said, pointing to a tiny dot at the tip of South America. "The world's southernmost town."

"But it's on an island," Helen countered.

"That's all right. If we can get through the Pacific to Panama, and the Caribbean to Colombia, we can surely cross the Strait of Magellan."

Helen put down her brush and sat beside me. "It does sound like a wonderful idea, but——"

Before she could finish I continued, "No one has ever driven the full length of the Americas under his own power. What a thrill that would be. Let's give our notice now. Our contract has been up three months, our car and cameras are paid for, and we have almost six thousand dollars saved."

"But, Frank, you're still in a cast."

"But I'll be ready for a brace next month, and I can work on the jeep while my leg is getting strong."

The small town of Circle was as quiet as the broad Yukon that flowed silently beside it. As we watched two Indian children play in the lines of a river boat moored close to the bank, we found it difficult to imagine Circle as it had been at the turn of the century, a roaring tent city bursting

with a conglomeration of men from all parts of the world, all after one thing—gold. When the madcap flurry was over, Circle settled back to enjoy the only distinction left to it, that of being on the Arctic Circle. But it was deprived of even that distinction: a later survey showed it to be slightly south of the polar meridian. Now nothing remains but a cluster of Indian huts, a few caches, and a Northern Commercial trading post. With the opening of the Alaska Highway, however, a new distinction was given it—Circle became the farthest north point in the Western Hemisphere that can be reached by connected road.

On June 21, 1954, from Circle, our second attempt to drive to South America began. At Eagle Summit, a few miles south of Circle, the longest day of the year was drawing to a close. The rolling treeless tundra was bathed in a pink mist, crimson streaked the sky, and the orange sun arced down in a long sweeping curve. Near the horizon it moved horizontally. Briefly the giant ball touched the rim of the world and then began to rise. Twilight, night and dawn fused into one; yesterday became today without the separation of darkness. When Alaska's midnight sun rose again, it was the twenty-second of June, our seventh wedding anniversary. Helen was twenty-eight, I was thirty, and Dinah was seven years old.

South from Circle the Steese Highway to Fairbanks followed the route of the early mail run, when dog teams were the only means of communication. Old log roadhouses, where prospectors once rested on their way to the gold fields, now had a sixty-year growth of grassy whiskers on their sagging sod roofs and served hot berry pie to the tourists. Near Fairbanks gold dredges sat like giant toads spreading warts of tailings on the virgin landscape.

From Fairbanks the Alaska Highway led through greener country, the yellow red of tundra gave way to stands of shimmering birch, and in marshy ponds moose splashed among yellow water lilies. When we crossed the Alaska-Canada border, nearly twenty-eight months had passed since we had stepped from the transport plane and pulled the GI parkas up around our ears. In that time we had come to love the wildness of Alaska and to feel its strength, and had developed an almost chauvinistic attitude that rivaled any Texan's love for Texas.

At Whitehorse we saw the great Yukon River again for the last time. Below the rushing Whitehorse Rapids faded unused stern-wheelers were pulled up on the banks. Once the lifeblood of the Yukon Territory, they now lay eclipsed by the float-equipped planes that landed on the water beside them.

Signposts were common along the road, but at Watson Lake there was a concentration of them, a reminder of the days when the Alaska Highway was new. During World War II thousands of men working together had opened it in a record eight months. Someone, perhaps a bit nostalgically, put up a sign pointing to his home town, and others had followed suit. The one sign grew to a wild pincushion of boards pointing to all parts of the world. We added ours to the scores of others—a bright red-and-yellow sign that said "Cape Horn 17,000 miles."

While I reveled in the pleasure of bending my knee and timorously flexing my ankle, Helen dodged chuckholes in the wide gravel road and moved well to the side to allow other cars and trucks to pass that were in more of a hurry than we. On the open stretches I spelled Helen at the wheel, but for the most part I sat watching clumps of alder and aspen and scattered tamarack roll past—what I could see of them between passing cars. When Uncle Sam transplanted the Dust Bowl farmers to Alaska he must have brought all the dust with them and used it to surface the Alaska Highway.

Sporadic bursts of rain gave respite from the dust and restored the brilliance to the fire flowers that lined the road. In bustling wheat-belt Dawson Creek the Alaska Highway ended at Milepost Zero, and we turned southwest over the Hart Highway through pine forests to Prince George. Trees were larger, the country more rugged as we wound through the deep scar of the Fraser River Canyon to Vancouver and across the U.S. border.

Along the rocky coast of Washington, Oregon, and California the Pacific pounded the cliffs, its foam scouring every hollow. Though Helen had little to say, I knew what she was thinking. What would it be like out there? Would the jeep really be seaworthy?

The assembly of the jeep was somewhat more difficult than its disassembly—in the three years I had forgotten how it came apart. Beginning with the obvious, we dragged the hull from under the tree, where it had gathered three crops of walnut husks, and diligently flaked off the rust, patched the holes, pounded out the dents, had it sandblasted, and gave it an undercoat of red rustproof paint. Then, with the hundreds of parts and thousands of bolts spread out on the floor of my father-in-law's well-equipped workshop, we proceeded to fit together the puzzle, which was akin to getting a ship inside a bottle or a jeep inside a fifteen-foot boat. As each part was bolted into place, the space inside the hull grew smaller, and I had to amend my optimistic statement that I could work on the jeep while my leg was getting strong. I should have added, if Helen was handy to extricate me from some pretzeled position inside the hull or under the hood.

At the end of six weeks the jeep was as it might have been when it came from the Ford assembly line in 1942. Designed during the rush of war, the amphibious jeep was strictly a compromise—conventional jeep motor, chassis, steering gear, and six-speed gear boxes set in a steel tub. With two differentials and four wheels hanging from springs outside, power was transmitted by drive shafts through holes in the hull that were closed by heavy rubber seals. A propeller and a bilge pump driven from the rear of the transmission, a rudder connected by steel cable to the steering wheel, and a power-operated capstan winch on the bow turned the jeep into a boat. To cool the engine on land or in calm water, air entered through a hatch in the bow deck, passed through the radiator and out through a smaller hatch on either side of the windshield. In rough water all three hatches could be closed from inside the cockpit and, by means of an ingenious system of ducts, air was taken from under the dash, passed through the radiator, and then out through a fourth hatch behind the windshield.

All in all, it was a very clever little vehicle, but it had certain undesirable traits. Originally planned as a command car for squadrons of its big sisters, the amphibious "ducks," the sea jeep soon fell out of favor with some officers who objected to leading their troops from the rear. Not only was it slower than the "duck," but it had the unpopular habit of sinking with no more provocation than a ripple. After only a few thousand had been built they were discontinued.

With a shape that would turn a naval architect green, the

sea jeep plowed through the waves rather than over them, and, with practically no freeboard, a few buckets of water over the side was enough to swamp it. But if we enclosed the open cockpit with a watertight cab and counted on the jeep's low center of gravity to keep it right side up, we felt—or I should say I did—that the jeep could take a moderate sea, which was the only kind I had any intention of being out in.

Making the jeep seaworthy and providing for extra fuel and water was only half the problem. Since our budget would allow us to stay in hotels only in the big cities, the jeep would have to serve as our home as well, and this entailed the additional requirements of sleeping and cooking facilities, and protection against heat and insects. Furthermore, we had but three months to complete the transformation. If we could leave no later than January 1, 1955, we could travel without hurry during the dry season and still reach Panama by May, the calmest time of the year in the Caribbean.

With oak and plywood we framed the cab, extending it a foot and a half over the rear. The stern of a boat was not an ideal place for a cantilever structure, but the extra length allowed room for two full-length bunks. To assure that the doors were watertight we wanted to make them as small as possible and still provide easy entry. After clamping wooden slats to the gunwale to form a mock frame, I called Helen, and we practiced getting in and out. We squirmed in feet first and crawled in head first, but the technique used for climbing on a horse worked best. After a half hour of practice we could swing smartly through the mock door, only seldom bumping our heads. But one thing still bothered Helen. The bottom of the door had to be above the water line, and since that was three feet from the ground how could she get in and out in a skirt?

I was concerned with more pressing problems, so I left that one up to her and concentrated on finishing the jeep. Stretching the days and working well into the night, we saw the jeep slowly take shape. For extra fuel and water, on the sides of the cabin above the water line, we mounted racks that held a total of eight five-gallon Jerry cans, two for water and six for gasoline. These, with the sixteen-gallon main tank inside the hull, gave us a forty-six-gallon capacity, enough for an estimated six hundred miles by land or a hundred and fifty miles by sea. While afloat, however, there was no way to transfer fuel from the Jerry cans to the main tank, and we would be limited to forty-five miles of water travel at one stretch. But since we planned to beach-hop, coming ashore each night to camp, we considered this no handicap.

For better traction we mounted oversized 7.60 x 15 tires on specially built wheels, selecting a conventional tread, which was more desirable for operation in sand than the mud-and-snow type. To reduce weight we converted the electrical system from twelve to six volts, eliminating one battery and exchanging the heavy generator for a lighter one. After a few miles of road test we decided that a heater would not be necessary even in the coldest Andean highlands. All we had to do was open the hatch behind the windshield to have all the hot air we wanted. It was more difficult to keep the cab cool, but insulating the fire wall helped some. The road test also showed the jeep to be underpowered, with a top speed of about forty-five miles per hour.

By the middle of December the jeep was complete. Inside the varnished cabin Navy-surplus blue-striped spreads covered the sleeping bags and air mattresses. Clipped over the windows and the emergency exit in the roof were detachable screens to keep out insects. Our main storage space was beneath the bunks, and above them were two cabinets that ran the full length of the cabin. These, along with the wedge-shaped space in the bow, comprised our ship's holds. For mountain curves we installed a blasting horn and for crowded streets a less obtrusive doorbell. For navigation (although we never intended to be out of sight of land) we mounted a small compass. In the sandwiched roof deck there was a two-inch blanket of rock wool insulation topped by a sheet of aluminum and a station wagon rack to complete the confusion. With light gray paint and red wheels, and her name and destination clearly marked on her doors, our seagoing jeep was ready for her salt water test. Christened with a Coke bottle, La Tortuga, the sixty-horsepower, two-and-a-half ton turtle, was born.

Our awkward hybrid caused considerable consternation that day, a week before Christmas, when she rolled down the small-boat ramp into Balboa Bay. One old sea captain pushed his hat back and scratched his head in disbelief. "Well I'll be damned!" he exclaimed. "It really floats!"

After three years of waiting for that moment, that was our reaction too.

While Dinah stood bewildered on the deck that was the cabin roof, we chugged around the harbor observing all the maritime rules of the road. We had little difficulty in keeping within the speed limit; when we clocked La Tortuga over a marked course, her top speed was just under six knots, and in reverse her progress was almost imperceptible. After maneuvering cautiously for a time we recklessly negotiated tight turns and deliberately ran through the wakes of the biggest cabin cruisers. Many skippers undoubtedly thought the side of a boat was a strange place for a spare tire, but one wag recognized La Tortuga for what she was. As he drew his launch alongside he shouted, "Why don't you get a sea horse?"

Though the test was a complete success, we were by no means ready to leave. There was still the matter of packing, and the notebooks we had been keeping were brimming. It would have taken a dozen jeeps to carry all the things we had thought of in seven years. Helen's great-uncle, a world traveler for fifty years, was contemptuous of all the paraphernalia we planned to take along.

"When I went over the Andes on a mule," he said, "I carried nothing but a pocketknife and a change of underwear."

"Yes, I know, Uncle Breck," I replied, "but it will take more than a boot in the rear to get this mule running again if she quits in the middle of the mountains."

Helen's father, an old hand at traveling himself, was more reasonable. He suggested a compromise. "Why not make three piles? In one put all the things that are essential, in the second put those things about which you can't make up your minds, and in the third, the items you would like to have along but can do without."

We tried his suggestion, but everything went into the essential pile. But it was still a good idea, so we tried again.

"We can prepare our meals on the jeep's bow." We discarded the folding table.

"After riding all day we won't want to eat sitting down anyway." We rejected the camp stools.

"What about this lantern?" Helen asked.

"We'll go to bed early." After working eighteen hours a day on the jeep the thought of lots of sleep was very appealing.

With little storage space and a wide range of temperatures to prepare for—requiring everything from a turtle-neck sweater to a Bikini—clothes presented a bit of a problem. Though we planned to be gone a year, we had to settle for no more than we would take for a weekend. For the cities we decided on a suit apiece and whatever else we could squeeze into two small suitcases, and for traveling whatever we could cram into one of the cabinets along with our pocketbook library. We had visions of some peaceful tropical island where we would sit under a waving palm and while away the hours with the *Odyssey* or the *Oxford Book of English Verse*, or perhaps we would feel adventurous and sail the stormy seas with Horatio Hornblower, or live vicariously Ahab's quest for Moby Dick. And for lighter moments there were the *Thurber Carnival* and the poems of Ogden Nash. There were a few practical books too—a Spanish dictionary, a dog-eared copy of the Bible that had been with us since we were married, and an Armed Forces publication with the portentous title *Survival on Land and Sea*.

It took three days to stow everything in La Tortuga. As each item was jammed into place Helen checked the list:

PORT CABINET—
 traveling clothes, library, sewing kit, first aid kit, folder of maps and folder of documents (passports, inoculation records, police clearance certificates, Dinah's health certificate, and jeep-ownership certificate).

STARBOARD CABINET (*ship's galley*)—
 one-burner paratrooper stove, coffeepot, dishes, and canned stores.

FORWARD BOW COMPARTMENT—
 spare parts, tools, machete, ax, shovel, anchor, rubber life raft, winch cable, and hand bilge pump.

suitcases and three weeks' supply of emergency rations sealed in taped coffee tins including walnuts, dried fruit, powdered eggs, powdered milk, chipped beef, vitamins, and dog meal for Dinah.

When we were finished everything was stowed neatly out of sight except for the camera cases, typewriter, and portable radio on one bunk where they would be protected from road shock. We stored our photographic film in a large campers' icebox with silica gel for humidity control. But there was still one thing we had found no place for. I held up the life preservers. "What can we do with these?"

Helen, still skeptical, didn't hesitate. "We'll use them for pillows until we need them."

Dinah, with no such problems about what to bring, was waiting at the jeep several hours before we were ready to leave. Clamped between her teeth was the one thing she prized most—her green rubber dish. As we climbed into La Tortuga I noticed that Helen had no difficulty: she was wearing denim culottes.

Chapter Two

A PORTLY man in a shabby green uniform and sporting a thick Stalin mustache greeted us as we drove over the border from Nogales, Arizona, into Mexico. Taking our identification and automobile registration, he led us to a tiny cubicle, where we proceeded to answer the questions of an even portlier man with an even bigger mustache. After he had written our names, birthplaces, and professions in the large book that covered the top of his desk he asked:

"Your destination, please?"

Unthinkingly I replied, "Ushuaia." His mustache twitched and I hastily corrected myself. "Mexico City," I said.

"Type of automobile?"

At my answer, "Amphibious jeep," his mustache twitched again and he reached for the telephone. There was nothing in his rule book about amphibious jeeps. I knew that if he called his superior it might be hours before we were cleared through customs. Again I explained. "It's just a regular jeep with a different type of body." That seemed to satisfy him, and then came the moment we had been dreading. He asked us to bring in our bags.

We had had nightmares over the thought of unpacking the jeep at borders. I thought of all the things in the cabinets and of the suitcases at the bottom of the hull under the bunks. I stretched a point. "But everything is in compartments."

"Compartments?" he repeated suspiciously. "Amphibious jeep? Ushuaia? This is all very strange. I must look into this matter myself."

That was the last thing I wanted. I was certain he would go through La Tortuga from bow to stern. I could see tools, spare parts, dishes, clothes, and cameras piled high in his office, but there was nothing to do but follow him to the jeep.

"This looks like a boat!" he exclaimed.

"Well, it is, more or less," I said. I showed him the propeller and the capstan winch on the bow, the bunks and the overhead hatch. He was so intrigued by the idea of a floating jeep that he forgot all about the inspection. He issued us our tourist cards, and with a cheery "*Que le vaya bien*" wished us a pleasant journey and sent us on our way.

Many of the cars that swished by us that first day in Mexico bore American license plates. Fishing poles protruded from the windows as sport fishermen drove to Guaymas to try their hands at the huge marlin and sailfish. It all seemed so familiar: adobe dwellings, shades of pink and sun-baked yellow spiked with elementary blue, mother and child one in striped shawl, burros barely visible under their loads of fodder, centuries-old churches with neon crosses and cloistered archways edged with violets, modern tractors in front of mud hovels, and buzzards floating over half-devoured carcasses beside the road.

That evening when no one was in view, we eased from the road and wound through the sage to a clearing where the tall organ cactus of the Sonora Desert pointed to a reddened sky. We had barely stopped when Dinah reverted to her old custom of scouting the area. Then, apparently satisfied that the camp was to her liking, she lay on the warm sand near the jeep to await her meal of canned dog food.

Our campsite was completely hidden from the road. Too many times on the previous trip we had awakened to find ourselves surrounded by faces, noses flat against the windows and eyes ringed by fingers.

While Helen stacked the cameras and typewriter in the middle between the bunks and turned back the sleeping bags, I lifted one of the five-gallon water cans from its rack and lit our small stove. In a few minutes coffee was bubbling. We dined sumptuously on fried chicken and fruitcake, cheese, chocolate chip cookies, and shortbread. Despite the banquet there was a mood of sadness. At home there had been no good-bys, and as we finished the last of the goodies pressed on us by family and friends, it was as if we were severing that last tie.

"This hood makes a fine table," I said, trying to be cheerful.

Helen went along with my attempt at conversation. "And we don't need stools. I'd rather stand anyway."

While Helen and I washed the dishes, Dinah made a last-minute patrol. We heard a surprised yelp, and she came running to us with an apple-sized cluster of cactus spines stuck in her nose. She had forgotten that in the desert it was sometimes painful to be too inquisitive.

Less than an hour from the time we pulled from the road the three of us were climbing into the jeep for the night. Dinah, as usual, was the first one in and was already making herself comfortable on my bunk. "Oh no, Dinah, that's your bed only in the daytime and only when *your* blanket is on it. At night you sleep there." I pointed to the right-hand seat and Dinah moved reluctantly from the bunk.

"Camping in La Tortuga is almost luxurious," I said as I stretched out on the air mattress.

"It's certainly a great improvement over the first jeep. How I dreaded undressing outside in the Guatemalan cold." As Helen reached for the light overhead, Dinah was still trying hopelessly to make herself fit on the seat. "We don't need pillows. Let's fill the gap between the seats with the life preservers. Then Dinah can stretch out too."

Through the open rear window came the chill desert air and the tranquil noises of the night. I reached for Helen's hand over the pile of things that separated us and Dinah gave a contented sigh.

Almost a week later we checked into a hotel in Mazatlán. The occasion? A bath. In our room overlooking the beach happy sounds came from the shower.

"You're doing much better," I said. "On the last trip you insisted we check into a hotel after only three days."

"But I'm a hardened camper now," Helen laughed.

I recalled her first bath in Mexico four years earlier, when she was wetter from her tears than from the shower. There had been a freak snow and we had been cold for days. As we passed a sign advertising a new motel boasting hot water, Helen pleaded, "Can't we forget the budget just once?" When we stopped she could hardly wait to get under the shower—she was already undressing when I went out for the bags. I came back and found her quietly sobbing under a trickle of water. "It's cold," she cried. But I knew that it was more than the shock of the cold water and the fact that she missed her two baths a day. She was homesick.

36

There was plenty of hot water in the hotel at Mazatlán, however, and we showered once to get clean and once again just for the fun of it. The next morning we had had enough luxury to last another week and we drove to Camarones Beach, a few miles from town, to pay a call on an old friend, a Jamaican Negro named Manuel.

Manuel ran a small cantina near the beach. His kinky hair was a little grayer but his gold-toothed smile was as bright as ever. Near the cantina were palm frond canopies and he invited us to set up camp.

Along with his business of dispensing beer and soft drinks Manuel made drums. When business was slack he transformed bits of metal and hardwood into bongos or congas, diligently polishing them and tuning them with a sensitive ear. Afternoons, music-loving teen-agers congregated on the shaded patio with their instruments—guitars, trumpets, maracas, and bones. While they played, Manuel beat out the tempo on his drums. Little Armando, Manuel's son, who had been only a baby when we'd seen him last, broke into a mambo Arthur Murray would have envied.

Helen made me a present of a pair of the small bongos and I tried to learn to play them, but my efforts were disappointing. Patient Manuel tried to teach me. After several hours with no results he turned the task over to his son.

Six-year-old Armando began with an enthusiasm which quickly dwindled. Standing between my knees, he guided my hands in the basic beats—the bolero, the ranchero, conga, tango, and mambo, and then stood aside.

"Now you try it alone," he instructed. I did try, but he just shook his head. We went through it again, but as soon as Armando removed his small hands from mine the rhythm left me as completely as if I'd never heard it.

He looked up at me with sad brown eyes and said, "There is no hope, there is no hope."

Every time I heard a mambo or bolero I picked up my drums, but I was as lifeless as an Aztec idol. I kept trying. A few days later a ranchero was moaning from the loud-speaker and the bongos were clamped between my knees. When the music stopped, Manuel grinned approvingly and Armando danced with excitement at my progress.

"There is hope, there is hope," he shouted gleefully.

The paved highway from sub-tropical Mazatlán turned inland from the coast and wound through steep jagged cliffs so formidable that even the conquistadores bypassed them. We drove leisurely, waving to bus and truck drivers who nodded appreciatively at the name La Tortuga printed on the side of the jeep. Their own vehicles were decorated with painted scalloped curtains on the windows, curlicues on the fenders, and proudly named El Toro or Hurricán or, more affectionately, Lupita. The mere fact that we had bothered to name La Tortuga seemed to make us members of that great fraternity of *choferes*, a highly respected profession in Mexico.

There had been a mild interest in the jeep the one night we had parked in front of the hotel in Mazatlán, but we were not prepared for the reception she received in Guadala-jara. On the outskirts of the city a child let his hoop roll unnoticed down the street and shrilled, "A boat." Pushcart vendors halted by the curb and drivers slowed their mad pace to ours and followed us to the same small hotel where we had stopped before. When we went out to the jeep for Dinah and our bags it was surrounded. Fathers were holding their children up to the windows, little boys were jumping on the roof, and two would-be mechanics were opening the hood. It was then we established the precedent that was to hold for the rest of the trip. Like Minos, I hid the monster in the labyrinth of a local parking garage.

In the hotel we asked for the same room. To my delight, the plumbing still worked. On our first visit to Guadalajara I contracted the usual, the *turista* disease, and for days I dared not leave the room. Afterward Helen never let me forget the eloquent speech that I so sincerely delivered while my condition was critical, "God bless them for the plumbing, God bless them for the plumbing."

Through the wrought-iron grillwork of the balcony window poured a medley of street noises—bicycle bells, horns, the squeal of brakes, and the shouts of lottery-ticket vendors. It was a discordant medley, but it was also part of the music of a new experience, and we were beginning to get in step. The Spanish we had forgotten was coming back, the drone of voices in the restaurants seemed less strange, and we mingled with more ease among the people in the streets or in the markets.

The tempo was easy. There was no hurry, and *momentito* could mean hours. It is said that the only thing that starts on time in Mexico is the bullfight, but in Guadalajara there was something else. At two o'clock sharp the bells in the old cathedral boomed, the stores closed, and the siesta began. Outside the restaurants the *mariachi* orchestras assembled, and the customers settled back to enjoy a two-hour repast.

Each day Helen and I tried a different café. In most places women were conspicuous by their absence and men looked up from their tables as we entered. Although we couldn't eat all six courses, the meal of the day was still the least expensive way to order, and we enjoyed lingering over dinner and listening to the music. One afternoon as we returned from lunch in a nearby restaurant we heard some exceptionally fine *mariachi* music coming from the hotel dining room. Through the open doors we saw an eight-piece band playing for a lone diner, who, from the number of empty glasses before him, was apparently taking his nourishment in liquid form. The musicians, resplendent in silver-brocaded sombreros, spangled jackets, and tight black trousers, stood in a semi-circle around their *patrón*.

"Let's not miss this," I said to Helen. "You go in and order some coffee and I'll go up to the room and check on Dinah."

As I came down the stairs I thought I was too late—the music had stopped. But as I approached the open door I saw that the entertainment had just begun. The fiddlers, guitarists, and trumpeters stood waiting while the gentleman who had hired them raised his glass in toast to Helen. The first musician was walking over to her table. Amused, I stepped back. This, I thought, is a good opportunity for her to practice her Spanish. I have to admit, however, that if her admirer had been young and dashing instead of fat and fortyish I might not have been so willing to further her linguistic endeavors.

The first musician reached her table and bowed. "My *patrón* requests that the charming lady make a selection."

Helen looked up from her coffee and smiled. "Please thank him for me, but I have no request." I thought she had handled that very nicely and was just about to enter when I saw that the gentleman was not to be brushed off so easily. There was a whispered conversation and the musician returned to Helen's table.

"*El señor* insists that the señorita make a selection."

Helen hesitated. Apparently all Spanish song titles had escaped her—all except one, that is.

It was an unhappy choice. The *patrón's* eyes brightened. He was obviously a firm believer in the very prevalent idea that American women are easily approached, and he took the song title as a direct invitation. Wobbling in Helen's direction, he beckoned to the *mariachis* to follow and the room filled with the strains of "Amor." Not satisfied with the vocalists, he took over the serenade personally, and with each line leaned a little closer.

Terribly upset at having been so grossly misunderstood, Helen moved farther and farther into the corner. Even in the guise of a Spanish lesson I couldn't justify my entertainment any longer. With a straight face I took the chair beside her and nodded to the startled *patrón*. "Please continue," I said. "It's our favorite song."

Every morning of our week's stay in Guadalajara we awakened to the whisk of the street cleaner's broom and began our daily wanderings through the city. Sometimes we rode in a horse-drawn carriage while the clippety-clop of the hoofs rang through quiet side streets. We caught glimpses of radiant gardens behind sterile walls or watched children leave for school, blue and white uniforms neat and books like knapsacks on their backs. Or sometimes we walked to the central market, where the commercial heart of the people beat its unchanging rhythm under the steel ribs of a block-square concrete building. With the crowd we pushed between shaded stalls outside, past the saddles and bolts of bright cloth, the sandals made from tires and the tinsmith hammering ladles from old cans. We watched a boy scrape the insulation from wire and a girl weave the wire into a basket. Nothing was wasted except time. On the corner a street magician chanted his patter to an indifferent audience while nearby an old woman shrouded in her shawl slept by the wares no one bought, her gentle snores accompaniment to the unceasing pat-pat of hands making tortillas. Through the iron gates of the market poured an overwhelming dissonance of smells. Meat, covered with flies, hung in strips, thick wheels of yellow cheese overpowered the fragrance of adjoining flower stands, and next to them vegetables formed high pyramids on the floor. Stems of bananas swayed in one corner and one giant variety was new to me. I asked its name and smiled at the answer. Another reminder of Mexico's emphasis on man.

In the church across from the market candles flickered on dark figures in front of a soot-grimed statue of Mary. Helen and I stood quietly and listened to the murmur of voices in prayer—until two tourists entered talking loudly and all eyes turned, expressionless, yet revealing.

Afternoons, when the cathedral bells pealed and the city returned to work, we sat in the parks near the fountains. It was a tranquil period, a time to assimilate the sights and sounds and the emotions of the day before the evening commenced with its new set of associations. Then, when the swift twilight turned to night, we strolled through the streets again, stepping around the outstretched feet of people sitting in doorways, past a man with puppies for sale, or a vendor of sugar-coated peanuts who swore kindly at the children who climbed on his cart. Paper cones of pink cotton candy echoed the neon of a Carta Blanca beer sign and a charcoal fire blazed where popcorn roasted—the dancing flames casting weird shadows on the face of the old crone who tended them. In the lee of buildings scrape-enveloped shapeless figures huddled to sleep till morning, and in the dimly lit parks lovers made a single form.

Each night we returned to our room mentally exhausted, our emotions as mixed as the themes of Orozco's murals. The gay music of the *mariachi* band on the corner drowned the other sounds from the street but some still remained in my mind—the cry of a child, the whisper of a beggar, the scraping of the cripple who crawled on his hands and knees. When the musicians put away their instruments and the voices from the cafés dimmed, only the whistle of the watchman was heard as he signaled to his companion on the next street.

At the end of three weeks in Mexico our turtle was living up to her name—we had covered only eleven hundred miles. But our progress was not measured in miles nor our travels in days—at least not at that time. Instead we geared our itinerary to whimsy, our time schedule to fancy, and when the little town of Guanajuato was described as seldom visited, as well as picturesque, we plotted our course to Mexico City to include it.

Barely half of the less than two hundred miles from Guadalajara to Guanajuato were behind us when we reached another small town, San Juan de los Lagos. Crowds thronged the narrow streets, and at first I thought it was merely the local market day when the people from the surrounding countryside came for their weekly barter and banter session. At the outskirts on the other side of town, however, there was something that indicated it was much more than that. A stockily built youth was being led, blindfolded, down the road, his head crowned with thorns and his bare chest studded with cactus spines. Then a young woman, black dress gray with dust, inched forward on her knees while an older man laid blankets on the ground in front of her. Makeshift camps lined the highway, livestock stood listlessly, and people sat shaded from the sun by blankets or under the bellies of donkeys.

Farther on a solid mass of people blackened a field of at least two hundred acres, and through the pall of dust we saw the high feather headdresses of an Indian ceremonial dance. Parking the jeep, we uneasily worked our way through the crowd toward the center of the field, uncertain as to how the mob might react to strangers. The hard-baked earth burned through our shoes and the dust from thousands of feet filled our nostrils. Suddenly the crowd surged, and then parted, like the Red Sea before Moses, as two dozen Indians danced through the breach. Wooden spears clattered against wooden swords, pink and blue and brown feathers waved over silver papier-mâché helmets as spangle-caped Aztecs fought breast-plated Spaniards in a mock battle of the conquest. Behind them slowly walked a white-robed priest leading a medieval procession; drooping in the still, dry air, brilliant banners proclaimed the annual pilgrimage of San Juan de los Lagos. Women fell to their knees, faces wet with tears and caked with dirt, men crossed themselves as a glass-enclosed image of the Virgin of Guadalupe was carried past, followed by scores of young girls in once white confirmation gowns. And then came a cross section of Mexico—black-suited businessmen with a week's growth of beard, aristocratic women under veils of lace, blank-faced mountain Indians wearing short skirts over their knee-length pants, and bringing up the rear were the old, riding burros or carried on litters. All were barefoot, and all sang the same slow monotonous chant.

The pseudo Aztecs and Spaniards continued the battle in a queer shuffling dance—two steps forward and one back—whirling to the plink of tiny stringed instruments. Helen and I were carried along with the crowd as it rolled like a wave on either side of the procession. And then, as if at a prearranged signal, the mock battle ended, the procession broke up, and the crowd dispersed. It was time for the afternoon siesta. Soon smoke from hundreds of fires curled upward into the cloudless sky, and people sat in groups taking pieces of meat from blackened pots and deftly rolling beans into tortillas with one hand as easily as a cowboy rolls a cigarette. Over each group, like a Lions Club convention, flew the home town flag. Some of the people had walked as far as a hundred and fifty miles.

The sight of the meat and beans reminded us that we had eaten nothing since early morning. Making our way back to the jeep, some two miles away, we continued toward Guanajuato, keeping our eyes open for a likely-looking wayside restaurant. Our daily traveling habits had changed somewhat. Instead of preparing three meals ourselves we had become accustomed to stopping for our large meal in the middle of the day and having simply coffee, fruit, and sweet rolls in the morning and at night. The change was partly due to the fact that Dinah's supply of canned dog food was running low and we had to stop every day at the market to buy her fresh meat. At the same time we filled our wicker basket with mangoes, oranges or bananas. But, more than that, we enjoyed stopping in the small eating places where we could practice our Spanish.

That afternoon it was too late for the meal of the day when we reached a nondescript restaurant on the outskirts of a tiny village. Pink geraniums grew in painted oilcans and a few chickens pecked hungrily in the doorway. As we entered I whispered hopefully to Helen, "With our dusty clothes and sunburned skins maybe we can pass for a couple of pilgrims today."

In the corner was the usual basin and a huge bar of blue soap. After washing we walked, hands dripping, to a table. The waiter, who needed a shave even more than I, quickly flipped his soiled apron to the other not so soiled side, grabbed a fly spray, and filled the air with DDT. Then, after rotating the tablecloth so that the soup stains were away from us, he said, "Now, what may I serve our American guests?"

Though we were disappointed at having been recognized, our appetites were undiminished. I pondered. Shall we have eggs *a la mexicana* or steak *a la mexicana?* Both were fried with onions and tomatoes, which would take the edge from our desire for fresh salads. Then I remembered the strips of meat in the market and the chickens in the doorway. I decided eggs might be the wiser choice.

"*Huevos a la mexicana,*" I ordered.

Helen nudged me. "Ask him not to make them too spicy," she said. We had vivid memories of previous occasions when all the cold drinks in Mexico couldn't cool our fiery mouths.

"*No muy caliente,*" I instructed.

The waiter hesitated a moment, then shrugged his shoulders and headed for the kitchen. There was a surprised protest when he gave our order to the cook, and a woman who obviously enjoyed her work squeezed into the doorway. They both studied us, looked at each other, and then shrugged their shoulders simultaneously. I laughed.

"They're probably thinking, Crazy Americans, they don't like chili peppers."

46

The aroma of frying onions floated from the kitchen, making us hungrier by the minute. We waited. Other customers entered, ordered, and were served, and still we waited. After a half hour the waiter placed two plates in front of us. At the first bite I put down my fork.

"These eggs are cold," I said. "And they're just as spicy as ever."

The waiter looked confused. "But that's what you ordered. 'Not very hot,' you said."

At the next table a man smiled and broke into the conversation. "If you will permit me," he said. "In Spanish *caliente* refers only to temperature. We say *picante* when we mean spicy."

Yes, we enjoyed eating in wayside places. And the Spanish we learned was seldom forgotten.

From the restaurant it was only a short distance to Guanajuato, but since it was almost evening we decided to save a night's lodging and made camp on a side road a few miles from town. After a none too restful night during which Dinah and a company of overly inquisitive burros joined in a symphony of barks and brays, we drove down the narrow main street of the city that was the birthplace of Mexico's war for independence. Guanajuato was a bowl of sun-drenched adobe cliff dwellings, of red tile roofs that made modernistic patterns of intersecting angles, of squares of flamboyant colors where clothes hung drying amid green cactus gardens.

A hotel had been recommended, but one look at the imposing castle-like structure that dominated the whole hill on one side of town was enough to convince us that our pocketbooks would flatten less quickly at almost any other place. We decided upon a more modest hostelry overlooking the tiny triangular main plaza at the bottom of the bowl. The only drawback, after we found that Dinah would also be a welcome guest, was that there appeared to be no quarters for La Tortuga, and news of her arrival had already spread in the few minutes she was parked in front of the hotel. When I asked about parking space, the manager was crushed.

"But, señor, this is a modern hotel. We have fine parking facilities."

Thus reassured, we checked in, and the accommodating manager sent a boy named Pedro to direct me to the entrance of the parking area.

"It's a bit difficult to find," he explained.

It was. The boy led me down the main artery, a zigzagging one-way street, until I was sure I was on my way out of town. All the while he shouted, "This way, this way," and people popped their heads from windows, as excited as if the circus had arrived and the elephants were being paraded through the streets. We made a sharp right turn and headed in a different direction down an even narrower one-way street while burros scrambled up onto the high sidewalks. I was just about to tell the boy that the "fine parking facilities" were much too far away when he stopped, breathless, in front of the entrance to a courtyard.

"Here we are," he said triumphantly.

I was thoroughly confused. "Where's here?" I asked.

"Why, this is the back of the hotel," he answered brightly. By that time half the town was in the undersized alley giving conflicting directions as to the best way to maneuver La Tortuga into position. I looked at the doorway. It was just wide enough for a string of horses to pass through single file, which I presume was what it was intended for. But some ingenious stonemason had used his head. Three feet

48

ABOVE—To combat the relatively mild winter temperatures (—40 degrees Fahrenheit) around Anchorage, Dinah gained ten pounds and grew her own parka. Helen enthusiastically endorsed the Eskimo custom. This fur seal parka is trimmed with wolverine and reindeer fur. LEFT—Huddled in his wolfskin parka, this young Eskimo of Nome, Alaska, is completely oblivious to the temperature, which sometimes drops to 60 degrees below zero Fahrenheit.

ABOVE—The area around the Knik River and Pioneer Peak near Anchorage, Alaska, was a favorite tramping ground during Alaskan summer. BELOW—For seventy miles our route followed the Fraser River Canyon through British Columbia.

ABOVE—La Tortuga comes ashore after her first salt water test in Balboa Bay, California. (Los Angeles Times photo) RIGHT—In the markets of Guadalajara, Mexico, everything is for sale, including Pisa-like towers of bird cages. BELOW—Business was slow in the Guadalajara market, but this shrouded old woman made no attempt to liven it up.

ABOVE—Rough going on an oxcart trail in southern Mexico. LEFT—Helen examines the intricate stone mosaics of Mexico's Mitla, Zapotec City of the Dead, in the state of Oaxaca. BELOW—Frank takes time out before clearing one of the many obstacles from the oxcart trail in southern Mexico.

ABOVE—Guatemalan Indians swing censers of burning incense on the steps of the 400-year-old church of Santo Tomás in Chichicastenango. BELOW—The wind lashes the brown water of Lake Nicaragua near the Nicaraguan-Costa Rican frontier.

RIGHT—Frank inflates the rubber life raft in preparation for La Tortuga's maiden voyage in the Pacific Ocean near Dominical, Costa Rica. BELOW—On a bulldozed trail through the jungles of southern Costa Rica.

RIGHT—Helen and Frank receive La Tortuga's ship's papers from admeasurer Walter H. Hebert in front of the port captain's office in Balboa, Panama Canal Zone. (Panama Canal Company photo) BELOW—Balboa port captain, Captain Abe Lincoln (in white suit), watches on in amusement as La Tortuga enters the Panama Canal above the Pedro Miguel Locks in a rather unusual way for a licensed ship. (United States Navy photo)

BELOW—La Tortuga steams out of the Gaillard Cut of the Panama Canal. Sitting on the "bridge" is Canal pilot Captain R. G. Rennie. (United States Navy photo)

TOP—Captain Rennie pilots La Tortuga past the ship *Haparangi*. (Panama Canal Company photo) CENTER—La Tortuga transits the Pedro Miguel Locks of the Panama Canal. (United States Navy photo)

LEFT—Rear Admiral Milton E. Miles, Commandant of the Fifteenth Naval District, Panama Canal Zone, and Helen and Frank wait while the water floods from the Pedro Miguel Locks lowering La Tortuga thirty-one feet to the level of Miraflores Lake. (United States Navy photo)

from the ground, about fender height, he had chiseled away
the sides of the entrance so that it looked like a cartoon I
had seen of a doorway designed for a bowlegged cowboy. It
would have been all right if he had also cut a place for a
ten-gallon hat since La Tortuga's projections, the gas can
racks, were higher than the fenders of a car. While everyone
chattered at once I unholstered my tape measure. By removing the padlocks on the racks we were just able to squeeze
through. With a relieved sigh I stabled La Tortuga in one
corner of the courtyard. As Pedro helped me with the bags
he said winsomely, "I'm a guide too." We normally did not
employ guides, preferring to wander by ourselves, but we
were taken with ten-year-old Pedro from the first. When he
showed up the next morning, his face scrubbed so it shone

and his hair slicked back like a black skullcap, we hired him.

With him we climbed to the top of the town along cobbled streets that rushed precipitously toward the valley, past fountains where women drew water in earthenware jugs like Biblical Rebeccas, and over the old stone road where burros once trod carrying the silver that built Guanajuato. Once second in importance only to Mexico City, Guanajuato faded into relative obscurity with the closing of many of the mines. Now it maintains its colonial atmosphere with pride, resisting the intrusion of contemporary architecture. Only a few of the streets were wide enough for vehicles; built for burros and foot traffic, they would always remain so.

Here, on September 16, 1810, Father Miguel Hidalgo gave the historic signal, El Grito de Dolores (The Cry of Pain), that started Mexico's revolution against Spain. The Alhóndiga, a large rectangular structure in the center of town, first a granary, then a fortress, later a prison, and now a museum, played an important part in Mexico's war for independence. Pedro related the story of the town's hero, a miner named Pípila, who, by carrying a flagstone on his back as a shield, set fire to one of the doors, making it possible for the revolutionists to take the building. Later, when the royalist forces recaptured it, the heads of Hidalgo and three other insurgents were hung from the iron hooks on the four corners of the building.

The thing we liked best about Pedro was his unfailing good humor. Each morning he appeared at the hotel while we were having our Mexican breakfast of sweet rolls and a spoonful of coffee essence diluted with hot milk and told us what he had planned for the day. On our last day in Guanajuato he was a little late. With an impish grin he said, "I have saved the best for last."

I couldn't imagine what he had in mind. He had already shown us his favorite streets, the Street of the Leaping Monkeys, the Street of the Croaking Frogs, and the Street of the Kiss, an alley where the balconies on either side almost touched so that lovers were purported to kiss across the gap. And we had seen all the public buildings, the parks, and the dam at one end of town. "What is this wonderful sight that you have saved until last?" I asked.

"Today I will take you to the cemetery."

Helen and I were not disposed toward cemeteries, but at Pedro's insistence that this was a very special cemetery we agreed to go along. When we reached the iron gateway in a high walled area Pedro didn't hesitate but, leading us through the crosses and headstones, he headed for a large concrete crypt where he pointed to a tiny spiral stairway that led down into a black hole. "We go down there," he said mysteriously.

Helen must have recognized the gleam in Pedro's eyes as being the same as we had seen in the eyes of a wrinkled old man who had shown us the catacombs under another cemetery four years earlier. Like Pedro, he, too, had had a sense of humor. With only a flickering candle for light, he had led us through a dank tunnel, all the while mumbling incessantly about the founding of the church in the sixteenth century. At the end of the tunnel he ceremoniously raised the cover of a box and invited us to look. Glaring from within, as if angry at us for disturbing its rest, was a horrifying mummy. "This," the old man said, "is the founder of our church." We declined his invitation to see other treasures of the church and climbed out of the dark cavern as fast as we could. But the old fellow wasn't through with us. He insisted that we see the choir loft, a dimly lit balcony over the altar. There we became so engrossed in a beautiful hand-illuminated choir book that we momentarily forgot about the old man. Suddenly he cackled, "Look, there's our founder." Helen and I both dropped the book expecting to see the hideous mummy come clattering across the floor trailing its moldy wrappings behind. The knarled old fellow laughed insanely and pointed to a lifelike wooden image sitting in a carved choir chair against the wall.

Remembering all this, Helen said, "I think I'll wait here, thank you."

This pleased Pedro immensely. "You're scared," he said positively.

I was of the same mind as Helen, but after that I had no choice but to follow him down into the pit. There at the end of a long corridor, under feeble shafts of light from above, was something that rivaled Picasso's Guernica for its horror. Standing upright against the wall, their contorted faces grimaced as if in pain, were several dozen cadavers. Brown parchment-like skin covered the bodies, black stringy hair hung in wisps, lipless mouths disclosed yellowed and crumbling teeth, and vacant eye sockets stared into the gloom.

Pedro explained. All the bodies were natural mummies, preserved by the strange chemical composition of the ground. Because the cemetery was small, burial space was rented for a limited time only, and when that time was up the bodies were exhumed. Those that had mummified were stood at one end of the catacombs while the bones of those that had not were stacked neatly at the other end—leg bones, arm bones, skulls, etc., all in separate orderly piles.

"Aren't you just a little scared?" I asked Pedro.

"Course not," he scoffed. "They can't hurt me." But I

noticed that he was the first to climb the spiral stairway to the flower-scented cemetery above.

Mexico City's wide Paseo de la Reforma was jammed with traffic moving at race-track speed. Driving in the capital was difficult at best, but in La Tortuga it was nigh impossible as demented drivers did a double take at our strange boatlike apparition. On the narrower streets La Tortuga's bow projected so far in front that we were halfway across the intersections before we could see if all was clear. After being trapped in a traffic circle and spending ten minutes on the merry-go-round before we could duck out, we decided to leave the jeep at the Willys agency and went on foot in search of a hotel. But the life of a pedestrian in Mexico City was not without hazard either. "He who hesitates is lost" was most appropriate and our motto became Stop, Look, and Run.

The hotel where we had stayed before was under new management. They would not permit dogs. After trying several other hotels and meeting several other unreasonable managers, we resorted to a taxi. The driver knew of a place that met all of our needs—the manager liked dogs, there was a nearby park where we could walk Dinah, the rates were reasonable, and it was near the center of town. With that Shangri-La in mind, we asked him to take us there.

Off we sped, the driver looking neither to left nor right, around the Monument of Independence like a ball on a roulette wheel, and down the Paseo as if our taxi were the only car on the street. After several near collisions I asked him what his secret was.

"Oh, it's no secret, señor. I just make sure I don't hit the car in front of me. If someone runs into me it's his fault."

With that illogical answer I concluded that the little image of St. Christopher affixed to his dashboard was on twenty-four-hour duty.

When we finally screeched to a halt in front of the hotel I didn't agree with the driver's conception of "near the center of town," but since all the other virtues were as he claimed we checked in.

Mexico City was our last big-city stop before the first gap in the Pan American Highway and Guatemala, and there were several important details to attend to. There was the jeep to service, including the reinforcement of her already sagging springs, provisions to purchase for the rough stretch ahead, and a visa for Guatemala to procure. Since many of the countries put expiration dates on their visas, we had decided to get them as we went along rather than before leaving home. But first there was mail at the U. S. Embassy and we spent hours reading it again and again over cool crisp salads in Sanborn's, Mexico's mecca for Americans.

Within a week our business was taken care of and we had seen the National Palace with its murals by Rivera, the Palace of Fine Arts, the Thieves Market, the new University City, and most of the other things tourists are supposed to see. On our last day we had nothing special planned, and Helen suggested we take Dinah for a walk through Alameda Park. Dinah thought that was a fine idea, hurriedly gulped her dinner, and ran to the door with her leash in her mouth.

The Alameda was bustling with afternoon activity. Clouds of balloons floated over their vendors, an organ-grinder played a tune while his monkey, in a tiny sombrero, danced, and the park photographers huddled under black cloths and pointed the eye of their cumbersome boxes at fidgety children. Dinah sniffed every flower around the

Juárez Monument, ate a *taco* given to her by a vendor, and broke canine diplomatic relations with a dog of dubious ancestry who was a staunch advocate of the Good Neighbor policy. But the end of Dinah's stroll through the Alameda came when we were opposite the Palace of Fine Arts. Helen spied a sign proclaiming a new exhibit.

"But it's too late," I protested. "We don't have time to take Dinah back to the hotel."

"Let's take her with us. She looks like a seeing-eye dog."

"That's real feminine logic. What would anyone with a seeing-eye dog be doing in an art museum?"

"Well, let's try it anyway. We won't have another chance to see the exhibit."

With that dispute settled, we entered the marble foyer and climbed the curved staircase to the galleries. No one paid any attention to us and I was beginning to believe I was wrong in objecting to Dinah's coming in. She heeled beautifully through the corridors lined with sculptures by young Mexican moderns and lay quietly while we studied the frescoes by Orozco and Siqueiros and the paintings of Tamayo. We were on the third floor before Dinah gave any indication that something was amiss. Apparently the *taco* had not agreed with her. She looked desperately for the nearest exit.

"What can we do?" Helen said in despair.

I wasn't sympathetic, but said, "Let's get her out of here."

We were *not* unnoticed as we flew down the stairs to the street. We reached the mezzanine, but she couldn't wait any longer. While an impeccably uniformed guard looked on in shocked amazement, Helen and Dinah made a beeline for the corner, where our mascot neatly deposited the remains of the *taco* in a gleamingly polished brass spittoon. With a sheepish but relieved expression she heeled and the three of us slunk back to the hotel and started packing.

To avoid the menacing traffic—or being a traffic menace —we left Mexico City during the early morning hours. Mexico's fine Pan American Highway took us across the green farmlands of the central plateau, past the still volcanoes, called by the Indians the Sleeping Lady and Her Watching Lover, over a ten-thousand-foot pass where pine forests crowded the asphalt, and then down to drier country of cactus and sage.

In Oaxaca, under shades of glaring white cloth, Zapotec and Mixtec Indians displayed for the tourists gaudy serapes and tiny clay idols of dogs, birds, and frogs. But eight miles away was a better example of the once advanced Zapotec culture, Monte Albán, already flourishing when the Renaissance was born. When we reached the top of a winding dirt road that climbed two thousand feet in but a few miles we found this burial place of priests and kings deserted. Some of the tombs had been excavated and had yielded treasures of gold and jade while others still lay beneath five centuries of dirt and scrubby growth. Alone, we wandered through the quiet pavilions and sunken courts, climbed the terraced pyramids, and poked our flashlights into dark caverns. On the walls Zapotec life lived in stone: shallow bas-relief depicted dancing girls, astronomers, and surgeons with their patients. Added to these rounded forms of Zapotec art were the angular inscriptions of their conquerors, the Mixtecs. These allies of the Aztecs represented the defeated Zapotec upside down. With a thrill almost as if we had discovered them ourselves we crawled on hands and knees through subterranean passageways that twisted between altars and pyramids, but the illusion was abruptly shattered when we passed under a glass and concrete skylight and popped, mole-like, into the bright sun to be greeted by a guide.

About twenty-five miles south of Oaxaca was another Zapotec site, Mitla, City of the Dead. Built as a resting place for the spirits, the temples and open courts were constructed of stone blocks weighing as much as twenty tons. The temple walls were embellished with mortarless stone mosaics in deep relief, horizontal rows of recessed geometric patterns in contrast to the representations of life that we saw at Monte Albán. Less fortunate than Monte Albán, Mitla had been known to the Spaniards. In keeping with their usual practice, they plundered and then erected a church on the remains of the temple. Beneath the main pavilion, in a dark underground chamber, stood a large stone cylinder, which, according to local legend, when embraced has the power to foretell life expectancy—the gap between the finger tips indicating the number of years one has yet to live. What a popular oracle this could be among twentieth-century gourmands.

Continuing south from Oaxaca, we headed for Tehuantepec, a coconut palm and sugar cane town at the edge of a brown river that flowed to the Pacific, about twelve miles away. Tehuantepec was on the proposed route of an overland canal where ships were to be carried by rail across the narrow isthmus that separates the Atlantic and the Pacific, but with the opening of the Panama Canal the plans were abandoned. Even before that, however, Tehuantepec had been important as a stop for caravans transshipping cargo from Spanish ships that plied the two oceans.

When we stopped to buy meat for Dinah and fill our basket with tropical fruit we found a fiesta in progress. In the sandy streets of this matriarchal town Amazons jabbered in

Zapotec—even barefoot the Tehuantepec women looked seven feet tall in their pleated and starched white headdresses. According to one story, this custom originated when a ship carrying a load of baby christening gowns was wrecked off the Pacific coast. Not knowing what to do with them, the Indian women put them on the only place they would fit—their heads. Perhaps it was the added height of these headdresses that gave them their feeling of superiority. In any event, these almond-eyed Zapotec Ziegfeld girls walked proudly in their square-cut velvet blouses and flowing gypsy skirts. They completed the regal illusion with velvet ribbons braided in their hair, earrings of Spanish coins, and chains of gold around their necks. With flowered staffs in hand and an authoritative manner they stopped us. They were conducting a sort of community chest drive, but instead of a red feather they gave us each a brand on the cheek. The red dye took days to wear off.

The market, also run by women, was literally a no man's land. Though I paid for the meat, the butcher lady ignored me completely, wrapped it in a banana leaf, and handed both the package and the change to Helen. I took the not so subtle hint and decided to wait outside while Helen finished the shopping. Stepping over three-foot iguanas that lay trussed on the floor, I threaded my way to the entrance between baskets of gardenias and roses and stacks of pineapples, papayas, and mangoes. Outside I leaned against a column under the eave of the building. That was apparently the correct thing to do, for I had company while I waited. A young Zapotec staggered over and thrust a bottle of murky yellow mescal, fermented cactus juice, at me and hospitably insisted that I have some. After one swallow I coughed and blinked back the tears; it couldn't have burned more if it

had been molten lead. I wasn't partial to his choice of liquor, but I was very interested in his choice of conversation. He was in a mood to expound the virtues of Tehuantepec's matriarchal society, which, according to him, boiled down to this: We don't really mind if the women run things. They're so beautiful, and they're probably more efficient than we are. Besides, they outnumber us.

As Helen and I left the market, I wasn't surprised to see a pedestaled bronze statue of a woman centrally placed in the plaza, no doubt erected by the town mothers as a daily reminder to the men.

For a short distance out of Tehuantepec the road led through more palms and sugar cane, past whitened salt marshes, and then as it turned inland again the sun-baked land became the color of straw and heat waves made the horizon dance. Since Mexico City, La Tortuga had been riding high on her new springs. The extra leaves in the front and rear made her take the bumps like a tank, but the extra road clearance they gave her would be essential if we had to repeat the same route taken in 1951 to enter Guatemala.

Mexico claimed a completed highway from border to border. Guatemala made the same claim and, while both claims were true, there was still no connection by road between the two countries. Their respective roads touched the Mexican-Guatemalan border on opposite sides of a mountain range. The normal way to enter Guatemala with a car was to follow the road we were on some seven hundred miles from Mexico City to Arriaga and load the vehicle on a flatcar. From there a railroad ran for a hundred and fifty miles along the southern slopes of the mountain range to Tapachula, where a road continued south into Guatemala.

At Arriaga, in 1951, we had made our first departure from

the normal route. Instead of loading our jeep on a flatcar we had continued another fifteen miles over a narrow dusty road to Tonalá, where we were flatly told that that was as far as we could go. As we sat on the edge of Tonalá and studied the map of Chiapas, one of the least developed states in Mexico, oxcarts clattered through the streets. One in particular attracted our attention. Driven by an old man, the cart was piled high, apparently with all his possessions and with his whole family riding on top. As we watched it disappear through a tangle of matted growth, the same thought came to both of us—there might be a cart trail to Tapachula.

Enthusiastically we had followed the cart over a pair of dust-filled ruts and asked the old man where the trail led. "Tres Picos," he replied. We checked the map again. Tres Picos was the next little town along the railroad. Hopefully we continued. Soon we learned never to ask for the trail to Tapachula—that was too far away. Instead we inquired from village to tiny village, developing an instinct for which path to follow when the pair of muddy ruts turned into a web of tracks. There were trees to fell, swamps to bypass, mudholes to fill with branches, and high centers left by four-foot-diameter cart wheels to cut down. At night, in the stifling heat, while mosquitoes whirred outside our screens, we had climbed into the jeep too exhausted to eat and fallen asleep to the sound of Dinah's heavy panting. Although it was only 135 railroad miles from Tonalá to Tapachula, we had traveled 220 miles in eight backbreaking days to get there.

As we left Tehuantepec the memory of those eight days was still vivid, and we had no desire to repeat them if there was another way. While in Mexico City we had heard encouraging rumors that Guatemala was working on a new highway to connect with Mexico's at El Ocotal on the north side of the mountain range. Before heading for Arriaga we wanted to see if there was any possibility of getting over the new route. Bypassing the branch road to Arriaga, we continued an additional two hundred miles to the border.

The drive took us north of the Sierra Madre range, home of the handsome, light-skinned Chamula Indians. Many of the men trotted beside the road wearing their ancient dress of short pants and broad-brimmed, flat-crowned hats of

thick straw festooned with streaming colored ribbons. We heard two stories as to the significance of the ribbons. Some said they indicated the number of sons the man had, while others said that the ribbons declared the man was a bachelor. Perhaps they are both right.

At El Ocotal there was no sign of a highway into Guatemala. The Mexican road, paved right to the border, stopped at a barrier of heavily forested mountain. Two Guatemalan border guards told us that construction was progressing from the other end, and that there was still a twenty-five-mile gap. We could see that there was nothing but a footpath, and the guards added that even a motorcycle had been forced to turn back a few months earlier.

With some misgivings, but with no alternative, we retraced our way along the main road to the cutoff that led to the lowlands and Arriaga. We made camp on a dry plateau amid the squawks of parrots, incongruous in the barren land of spiny cactus and stunted trees with only a few stemless gourds affixed to their naked branches. While I lubricated the jeep, Helen transferred the coffee tins of dried fruit and nuts, powdered milk and eggs and other concentrated foods from under the bunks to the cabinet above.

Arriaga, a town of blinding whitewashed adobe, was only slightly above the level of the Pacific, fifteen miles away. The air was heavy with humidity, and the Chinese storekeepers stood fanning themselves in front of their stalls. Arriaga had not changed in the four years since we had last seen it. Insistent railroad workers followed us through the streets—as they did any vehicle alien to the town—wanting to load us on a flatcar. The only visitors Arriaga ever had were those who were shipping to Tapachula by rail.

Tonalá had not changed, either, despite the fact that where before there had been merely a rude trail from Arriaga there was now a rough gravel road. Before hitting the oxcart trails again Helen and I stopped for a cooling *refresco*. The temperature was 110 in the shade, and children played naked in the street. But the old lady who ran the open-air cantina evidently had delusions of grandeur. She disdainfully refused to serve us until Helen put a jacket over her sunback dress and I exchanged my knee-length shorts for a pair of soggy long pants.

While Helen sipped a lemonade and I took lingering swallows of good Mexican beer, La Tortuga was subjected to her usual inspection. One man, about thirty-five, wearing khakis and a ten-gallon hat in place of the usual straw sombrero, noted with interest the license plates. Ordering a beer, he pulled up a stool and in only slightly accented English said:

"I see you're from the States. I used to visit Texas once in a while. Where're ya headed?"

"Tapachula," Helen answered.

"You're in the wrong town. Arriaga is where you load your car on the train."

I explained that we were not planning to take the train, that we were going to follow oxcart trails to Tapachula.

"Ha, that's a laugh." After gulping a long swig of beer he pushed his hat back and said, "Well, kids, see ya in Arriaga."

We watched him swagger away. "He must have done more than just visit Texas," Helen commented.

Chapter Three

Four years before, in the same town and in much the same way, we had been told the same thing: "You can't drive to Guatemala; the only connection is by rail." We knew now that, in a regular jeep, it could be done. But La Tortuga was a little higher, a little wider, a little longer, and had considerably less road clearance than a regular jeep, and size was all important.

With clouds of dirt billowing inside the jeep and branches crackling beneath the wheels, we again followed the pair of dust-filled ruts through brown underbrush. It was near the first of March, the height of the dry season; for months there had been no rain. And yet there was evidence everywhere of the four rainy seasons that had passed since 1951. The six months of tropical downpours each year had wrought a great change. Nothing seemed familiar.

The trail led into more open country, over arid hills and down into barrancas where the ruts were deep from erosion and countless generations of oxcarts. For a while we wondered if we were on the right path. When the trail forked, our only guide was the knowledge that we were north of the railroad, and that the trail should turn in that direction somewhere near the next village. Once we lost the tracks completely at the top of a rise where the sun-baked earth was like granite. Backtracking to another fork, we came upon one of the high-wheeled oxcarts lumbering along behind two immense hump-backed beasts, their driver sound asleep. As we pulled up behind him, he raised his head wearily and squinted his sun-wrinkled eyes. We had learned before never to phrase a question so that it could be answered simply "Yes" or "No." Instead we asked, "Where does this trail lead?"

The wizened old man had the uniformity of age; he could have been the same man we asked four years before. Scratching his grizzled beard, he thought a moment and then slowly answered, "Tres Picos." As we thanked him, he prodded his oxen up on the bank so that we could pass, and called, "*Que le vaya bien* [May things go well with you]."

The going was rougher as the trail led again toward the railroad down to lower country, through a dry river bed where green bushes lined the steep sides. In the rainy season it would have been impassable even to oxcarts. Of each person we passed we asked the same question to make certain we were still on the right path. One friendly coppery-skinned native on foot was going in our direction so we invited him to ride with us. Although Pablo could have made more progress walking he seemed to enjoy jouncing over fallen trees and around stumps in our "boat-car," as he called it. Repeatedly he assured us that we were "*muy cerquita,*" very near, Tres Picos, but we recalled the time we had traveled for three days in this same area looking for a town which was supposed to be "*muy cerquita.*" Twenty minutes away, they had told us, but they neglected to say it was twenty minutes by train. After two hours of Pablo's "*muy cerquita, muy cerquita,*" when we came to a clear stream we decided to make camp. Pablo continued on foot.

The sun was low in the sky as we nosed La Tortuga down

a steep embankment to a moon-shaped gravel bar. On the other side of the stream overhanging branches reflected yellow green in the water and tiny fish flashed to the surface after insects. Brushing the accumulated dust from the rear window, we set up camp while Dinah waded aimlessly in the stream, changing it from a liquid gold to a murky brown. After almost two months of living in La Tortuga we had our camping procedure well organized—in less than an hour we had bathed in the tepid water of the river, the bunks were ready, the screens were clipped over the windows and top hatch, and we were eating our supper of packaged mushroom soup, powdered coffee, and dried fruit topped off with salt tablets, vitamins, and Aralen for malaria. Over the insect noises we heard the creaking of oxcarts as white-clad natives came to bathe. They nodded and went downstream around a bend in the river while their oxen drank thirstily. Then in the purple twilight, with their black hair still dripping, the men stopped to chat, politely, almost casually inquiring where we were from, where we were going, and why. The first two parts of that trilogy were easy to answer, but how could we explain the "why," the challenge, when to them it was challenge enough to exist, or that we liked to travel when many of them had never been ten miles from their homes? But it made no difference to them that we couldn't answer that last question; as each one left he waved and bid us sleep well.

Early the next morning the same creak of oxcarts awakened us and the same white-clad figures came again to bathe, greeting us with a bright "Good morning." We were feeling very cheerful—we had traveled fourteen miles in only five hours the day before. While Helen was making up the bunks and taking down the screens, I was debating what to fix for breakfast.

"Let's try our powdered eggs," I suggested.

Accordingly, I opened a can, poured the yellow powder into a bowl, added a little water, and whipped it into a foamy lather. Once it was in the frying pan we soon had the most appetizing-looking omelette anyone could wish for. "How's this for camping out? Come and get it," I called with culinary pride. Helen and Dinah both answered my summons.

"Hmm, this looks good," Helen said, taking a hearty mouthful. Her mouth puckered disapprovingly. "Have you tried it yet?" she asked.

After that reaction I hesitated, but felt obligated at least to take a bite. My fine-looking omelette had the consistency of an old inner tube. "Well, never mind," I said. "It will be good nourishing food for Dinah. Here, girl."

Dinah looked on suspiciously when instead of her usual tidbit I ladled the whole omelette into her rubber dish. She sniffed it cautiously.

"Go ahead, Dinah, eat your breakfast," I coaxed. Trustingly she took a bite—and promptly spit it out, looking at me with an expression that clearly said, "It shouldn't happen to a dog." As we ate our substitute breakfast of dried cereal and powdered milk I wondered what I could do with the equivalent of nine dozen eggs.

As it turned out, Tres Picos was *muy cerquita*—less than a mile away—but it took almost an hour to get there. News of our coming had preceded us, especially news of Dinah. Bare little boys ran after us as we rolled between the two rows of grass huts that comprised the town.

"Reen Teen Teen," they shouted in unison, "Reen Teen Teen." There were no theaters, no movies; how they knew of Rin Tin Tin I have no idea, but to them Dinah was Reen Teen Teen and they wanted a good look at her. We obligingly stopped the jeep and opened the door. Dinah put her front feet on the back of the seat and grinned just as if she were Rin Tin Tin acknowledging the homage of his fans.

"Hola Reen Teen Teen," they cheered, but when Dinah jumped to the ground they clambered up a nearby tree, hanging and chattering like little brown monkeys from the branches. At our assurance that Dinah wouldn't hurt them, one by one they climbed down and stroked her gently, murmuring all the while, "Reen Teen Teen."

From Tres Picos the trail headed again toward the foothills of the mountains, where the country was more open, and for a time the going was a bit easier although our speed never exceeded five miles per hour. There were always rocks to clear from the path and lightning-struck trees to bypass, and in the arroyos Helen stood like a tank pilot in the hatch to direct me when the long bow of La Tortuga cut off the view of the ruts. The jeep became a furnace. Our thermometer registered 120 degrees Fahrenheit inside. The floor boards became so hot that Dinah whimpered when she touched them as she was thrown from the bunk by a sudden jolt.

Back and forth we zigzagged over grassy hills where hidden stumps battered the bottom of the jeep and where sometimes we lost the trail completely, backtracking, finding it, only to lose it again. By midafternoon we were heading toward the lowlands once more. Close to the railroad the ruts fell into deep ravines or climbed tortuously up steep banks. With one wheel in a rut and the other on high center we crawled forward in the lowest gear, slipping sideways into erosions and straining even the safety factor I had included in my calculations of the tipping point. We crossed the tracks for the first time, bouncing over them and down the embankment, cascading the contents of the cabinets to the floor of the jeep. On the other side we plowed like a tank through dense growth where branches dragged across the top of La Tortuga, dropping hordes of stinging ants inside. And then the digging began. The still heat hung like a blanket. We cut down high centers and filled in ruts, rubbing our hands in the dirt to keep the handles of the shovel and pick from slipping from our grip. By nightfall we were still digging. With the jeep hemmed in by tall wiry grass, we mounted the screens and sprayed the inside with insecticide. Without even a thought to food we stripped off our sodden clothes. We had covered only ten miles since Tres Picos.

By midmorning of the next day we had dug our way along another mile. Leaving Helen to drive slowly behind, I walked ahead clearing away boulders too big to pass over and whacking down limbs that blocked the trail. With each step the forest became denser. Long snakelike vines hung from umbrella-top trees, translucent blue butterflies flitted ghostlike over elephant-eared plants, and frequently as I leaned over to pick up a rock I was startled by a slithering in the undergrowth or by the beady eyes of an iguana doing pushups on a rotted moldering log. To everything clung the dank smell of decay. And then, with no way to bypass it, the trail became a narrow canal, an eighth of a mile of steaming marsh. Where I could reach I prodded with a stick. The water was about eight inches deep, but the bottom seemed firm enough. With four-wheel drive engaged we eased into it. After twenty feet the jeep came slowly to a halt, all four wheels spinning futilely. Quickly, before they could dig in, I put La Tortuga in reverse and backed out. We tried it again, hitting the mud as fast as we could, sending the thick black water streaming to the sides. Twenty feet, forty feet, and then, our momentum gone, relentlessly the jeep began to sink. We watched helplessly as the axles were covered, then the tops of the wheels, the black ooze creeping toward the doors until only the buoyancy of its boatlike body kept the jeep from sinking still deeper.

"What do we do now?" Helen asked hopelessly. "Wait six weeks for the rains to float us out?"

"This is what we have a winch for," I answered encouragingly, though I knew it was never designed for anything like this. There were several trees within reach of our two hundred feet of half-inch-diameter Manila rope. With one end securely lashed to a trunk I took two turns around the cap-

stan. "Engage the winch gear," I called to Helen in the driver's seat. As the rope tightened, the jeep moved forward slowly, pushing a wall of mud before it. Straining against the rope, I kept it taut so it couldn't slip on the capstan, and inch by inch La Tortuga crawled ahead. We had moved only a few feet when the rope snapped and I fell backward, sprawling into the dark mire. I thought it was only a weak spot in the new rope. I spliced it. We tried again, but it broke in another place. Again and again the rope parted, and again and again I spliced it until my fingers ached. Perspiration burned my eyes; black slime covered my clothes. Each time I moved the slippery rope to another tree ahead it became a greater effort. With each splice the rope grew shorter until after four hours it was reduced to less than three fourths its original length and we were only halfway through the swamp.

I tried doubling the rope. It held but continually snarled as the two strands piled up on the capstan in a hard ball and I had to cut them free. Pulling, cutting, splicing, with painful slowness we moved forward, the rope becoming shorter with each foot of progress. A hundred yards, fifty yards, then with barely enough rope to reach to the closest tree we were within fifteen feet of solid ground when the right wheels rode up on a submerged log.

"Cut the power," I yelled. But it was too late. Sickeningly the jeep leaned over, the jelly-like mud coming nearly to the door, where Helen sat operating the winch and throttle.

"Jump," I shouted. Relieved of her weight, the jeep tottered a bit, slid off the log, and then straightened out. Helen scraped the foul-smelling mud from her jeans and climbed back in to engage the winch while I leaned against the rope for that last fifteen feet. Weak and shaken, we reached firm ground once more. As I coiled the remnants of the rope and threw them on the bow, I felt neither elation nor relief, only a numbness at the thought that there might be more of the same ahead.

It was late afternoon and we continued only far enough to get away from the clouds of insects that swarmed over the swamp. We stretched full length on top of the jeep, trying to avail ourselves of every bit of air. I barely moved my head when Helen told me someone was coming.

A white-haired man walked along the trail whistling, as is the custom in Chiapas when approaching a stranger. The old fellow doffed his hat, and the usual questions and answers followed. When Helen asked if there was a river nearby, he shook his head.

"No, not for many leagues. But I have a well and I live only one league from here in Joaquin Amaro. You may bathe there and spend the night with me."

As inviting as was his offer, even after two days without a bath, the thought of traveling the additional three miles to his home was too much when we had covered but a little more than half that distance all day. We thanked him, and he went on his way.

Dinah slept outside that night, seemingly preferring the mosquitoes to the hot interior of the jeep. As we lay on the damp bunks we dimly heard through a pink haze of exhaustion the omnipresent singing of insects, the discordant squawk of parrots, the rustle in the undergrowth as some small animal scampered away, and toward the mountains the cry of a jaguar and the frightened jabber of a monkey.

We slept late the next morning, and as we were getting up we heard the same tuneless whistle and a soft voice calling our names. It was Señor Cabrera, the old man who had been so kind the evening before.

"You must not leave your dog out at night," he warned. "Several cattle were killed by *tigres* a few nights ago near my village." He waved his hand in the direction in which we were headed. "I have told my wife to expect you," he continued. "My house is the first one on the right side as you enter Joaquin Amaro. Please refresh yourselves before you go on."

Thanking him, we eagerly accepted his invitation. He joined us for a cup of coffee and a few pieces of dried fruit, and, after repeating his warning about mountain lions, went on his way.

The three miles to Joaquin Amaro were made in record time, considering the speed we had averaged the last few days. Slightly larger than the other villages through which we had passed, Joaquin Amaro was situated on the edge of a salt water lagoon several miles from the Pacific. It was a

tropical Venice; long dugout canoes were being poled over the tranquil water. White fish nets draped from bleached poles like a Eugene Berman stage set. The green of the surrounding jungle was accented by pink shrimp drying in the sun, orange hibiscus, and purple bougainvillaea that grew along the sides of grass huts. We stopped at the first dwelling on the right, where spread on the bushes to dry was a white flounced petticoat. Even before Señora Cabrera stepped from the doorway we knew she was a Tehuana woman. Her brown face seemed even browner under her silvery hair, and although her ribbons and square-necked blouse were faded she still walked with an air of assurance.

"I have been expecting you," she smiled. "My husband told me you would like to bathe."

It was nice of her to say that before she took a good look at us. Covered with mud, we were certainly in need of a bath. We followed her to the bathhouse, a three-sided palm-thatched stall, shoulder high, with a stone table and a tin pail from which we ladled water with half a gourd. While I formed a one-man bucket brigade between the well and the bathhouse, Helen scrubbed off the dirt industriously with an *estropajo,* a fibrous vegetable sponge that soon brought a rosy luster to her skin. Then Helen took her turn at carrying water for me while I scrubbed. Musical accompaniment for our ablutions was provided by the metallic ringing of water in the pail and the happy snorting of two fat pigs that wallowed luxuriously in a soupy mudhole nearby. I knew just how they felt, but I hadn't derived the same pleasure.

Much refreshed after more than an hour of cool water, we put on clean clothes. Along with the children who had been watching us curiously all the while, we joined Señora

Cabrera under the overhanging eave of her home. Like the other huts in the village, it was of mud and thatch with no windows. The dirt floor of its one room was swept clean, from the walls hung several hammocks, and in one corner were a few rolled reed mats. Across the room was a tiny blue shrine with a lighted candle flickering in front of a picture of the Virgin of Guadalupe.

Helen and I swung in a hammock in the shade of the eave outside where the señora was making tortillas, grinding the limewater-soaked corn on a large flat stone, flattening the meal between two banana leaves, a Tehuantepec custom, and lining the inside of a bowl-shaped clay oven with the round flat patties. When they were done she handed us each a hot crisp tortilla and a handful of dried shrimp. For the first time we realized how hungry we were. We had eaten nothing but powdered milk, coffee, and a little dried fruit since Tres Picos. As we sat there cracking the shells of the shrimp between our teeth, savoring the little bits of white meat, we answered the eager questions of the señora about Tehuantepec. Only a hundred and fifty miles away, she hadn't been back there since her marriage forty years before.

Lazily enjoying the idleness, we swayed back and forth in the hammock for a while. More children came, shyly looked, and left. The only thing that kept us awake was the antics of a scrawny chicken that flapped to the table top intent on a kernel of corn, only to be thwarted by the señora. I almost forgot that there were still almost two hundred miles ahead of us to Tapachula. Though Señora Cabrera invited us to spend the night, there remained several hours of daylight in which we could travel.

"Thank you for everything, and please give our regards to your husband."

76

"*Que le vaya bien,*" she called as we drove off, and then hurried to shoo away the chicken, which had taken advantage of our distraction to land in the earthenware crock of corn.

The rest of that afternoon and the days that followed were one continuous nightmare of digging and cutting until blisters formed, of more swamps where our rope grew shorter and shorter, of fording rivers, of hacking down trees and levering out rocks that had lain undisturbed for centuries. Scouting ahead of La Tortuga, we searched for a path through tall grass, where ticks covered our clothes and, despite our precautions, many mornings we awakened to find some of them, bloated and gray, clinging to our bodies. And there was the dulling heat that drove from our minds everything but the thought of the next obstacle and water. We looked forward eagerly to the type of vegetation that indicated the presence of a stream, many times only to find it clouded with mosquitoes and covered with green scum.

But there were interludes when we found clear-flowing streams, and, stretching full length in the shallow water,

we let it play over us, for a time bringing relief from the heat. Lying with only our faces above the ripples, we watched flocks of parrots or long-tailed birds of glistening blue or yellow in the canopy of trees that overhung the bank. Elongated leaves, like huge African war shields, flicked from side to side, changing color from blue to yellow green as abruptly as the reversing of a venetian blind. Purple morning glories bloomed from tangled masses of vines, and if we looked intently we could usually see a tiny green lizard sunning himself on a vein of a giant heart-shaped leaf. Dinah, completely in harmony with the jungle fantasy, peered from between feathery ferns like a Rousseau lion.

The rivers, where we could bathe and wash our clothes and replenish our supply of drinking water, were as important to us as they were to the people who lived there. Our river camps became a meeting place of two cultures. While I serviced the jeep surrounded by curious natives who had left their oxen and horses to drink in the river, Helen washed our clothes amid amused but friendly women. They looked askance at her two-piece bathing suit; although they worked bare from the waist up they would never think of exposing their legs. But Helen's attire was no barrier, and the women patiently tried to instruct her in their efficient but none too gentle methods of washing clothes. Standing knee deep in the water, long skirts clinging to their ankles, they whacked the clothes resoundingly on the rocks while Helen, attempting to imitate them, produced only a feeble squishing sound. They demonstrated the finer points, kneading together balls of homemade black and white soap in the proper proportion according to the degree of dirt and rubbing soiled spots vigorously with a handful of grass. The native women, rather than carry each piece to the riverbank as it was washed, coiled the clothes on their heads, allowing the cooling water to trickle down their faces and backs. The last time Helen tried this she dropped the soap, and with clothes piled on her head she waddled unsteadily downstream to retrieve it. The comedy ended, and so did her efforts to acquire this very practical art, when she slipped on a mossy rock and tumbled headlong into the water. The soap and several of my socks drifted on to the Pacific.

While the women scrubbed their clothes and spread them to dry on nearby bushes they shared their mangoes or papayas with Helen and chatted, always asking the inevitable questions—where she came from and where she was going. But more, they asked about her family and her home. Once, laughingly, Helen pointed to the jeep and said, "That's our home. We're gypsies." An old woman looked at her with compassion. "You have no home?" she said. "Then you must come and live with me."

When their work at the river was done the women bathed and combed their long black hair before piling the gleaming white clothes on their heads and returning to their village. The men on their way home from the fields always left with us a cluster of bananas, or coconuts, a pineapple, or thirst-quenching stalks of sugar cane. Then, alone at the river, we bathed and watched the sun redden and sink behind sleek tall trees.

Sometimes when we were digging out stumps or filling in ruts we were only a few yards from the railroad tracks. As the train passed we waved to the engineer and looked longingly at those who sat reading in their vehicles aboard the flatcar. Mirage-like, we remembered the billboards that lined the California highways with the Southern Pacific slogan "Next time try the train." And sometimes as we jacked up the wheels to clear a rock we couldn't move, puzzled natives asked why we didn't drive over the rails as the oxcarts did when they couldn't pass. It was difficult to explain to them that to us that would be the next thing to putting La Tortuga on a flatcar.

As discouraged as we became at times there was always something to buoy our spirits. With the sun high in the sky and our water cans hot to the touch, we were digging our way along a ravine at the bottom of the railroad fill when we heard the put-put of a tiny rail car pass us. Then we heard it coming back again. Loaded with seven or eight smiling railroad workers, it stopped directly above us. One of them jumped off and slid down the embankment, bringing with him half of an ice-cold watermelon. Nothing I can remember, before or since, ever tasted as good as that icy bit of pink and green ambrosia.

And there was the time when a few minutes of unseasonal rain bogged us down again in a small swampy area with nothing within reach of our short remnant of rope. All our digging, piling brush in the mud, and letting air from the tires accomplished nothing but sank us deeper. I had decided to leave Helen and go in search of some oxen when six men, their clothes fresh and clean, walked by on their way home from a bath. Without a word they plunged into the mud to push. When La Tortuga was clear they would accept no payment, but with a *"Que le vaya bien"* they returned to the river to bathe once more.

Meeting Tomás again was a real boost to our sagging determination. We had met him for the first time on the previous trip when at dusk we had been unable to find our way around a marshland. Returning to a cluster of grass huts in a jungle clearing, we had asked an old woman for permission to camp there for the night. Making us welcome, she offered us food, water, and hammocks, and that evening we met her oldest son, Tomás. He was about my age, slender and dark, with bright smiling eyes. He told us that there was no trail to the next village, but after hearing our story he said, "Well, I know of a river bed. Perhaps we can make a way."

At dawn we had followed behind Tomás as he cut a path through grass and reeds, through dense growth, felling three-inch-thick trees with seemingly effortless blows of his machete. Down a steep bank and along a dry river bed he guided us, and up the other side, where the earth gave way and the jeep almost tumbled over backward. We inched behind him as he sliced through vines making a tunnel in growth so thick the sky above was hidden. By evening we had detoured five miles around the marsh to reach a trail again.

This time we met Tomás on the trail several miles from his home. Proudly he told us of his wife and new baby, and then just as proudly said that the path he had cut around the marsh was now a regular cart trail.

"You'll come with me to see my mother and my family, won't you?" he asked.

I looked at the threatening sky and hesitated.

"Yes," he said understandingly, "the rains will be early this year. We expect them in a few days. You must not delay. I will go with you again over the trail."

For the second time we followed Tomás as he lopped off new growth that La Tortuga couldn't clear. At the end of the five miles, while Tomás was washing his hands in a small water hole, I said quietly to Helen:

"I wish there were something we could do to show our

appreciation. The last time he was offended when we offered him money."

Helen thought a moment. "You're about the same size. Why not give him one of your shirts?" She reached into the cabinet and pulled out the gray-and-white knit sport shirt she had given me for my birthday. When I handed it to Tomás his face clouded.

"Is this in payment?"

"No," I answered. "It's in friendship."

Thoughtfully he unfolded the shirt. Beneath his big straw hat his eyes brightened again. "Then in friendship I accept it."

After leaving Tomás we continued to jolt over the crude oxcart trails, moving rocks and fording rivers, under the constant threat of darkened skies, knowing that even one day of rain could keep us from getting through. At the end of nine days we had covered but two thirds of the distance from Tonalá, but we knew that if we could make it to Huixtla, some twenty miles away, there was a fair truck road from there to Tapachula. Helen had been quiet the last few days; I thought it was just fatigue.

When we inquired in the small town of Acepetagua about the cart trail to Huixtla we received the unexpected good news that there was now a new route over which trucks passed carrying coffee from the mountains down to the railroad. I was elated at the thought of being on a road again, but surprisingly it didn't make much of an impression on Helen. We followed the road through banana plantations, and then high into the mountains, where coffee bushes clung to the hillsides and waterfalls thundered to the valleys below. Trees poked through the mist like green lace on white absorbent cotton. Higher and higher the road twisted. It began to rain. Desperate to reach Huixtla, I drove recklessly, skidding around slick clay curves and bouncing over loose boulders. It rained steadily for an hour, and finally we began to descend only to find that the brakes, filled with mud from the swamps, wouldn't hold on the steep grades. Braking with the lowest gear, we slid down the narrow road, keeping the jeep as close as possible to the side of the mountain. By nightfall we were back in the lowlands again and learned with relief that there had been only light showers there. We also learned, however, that we had made a thirty-mile loop that had brought us but five miles closer to Huixtla, still eleven miles away. We made camp on a gravel bar in the middle of a river and the next morning continued over a good cart trail to Huixtla. As we drove that last twenty-five miles to Tapachula, through some of Mexico's richest coffee land, we felt the same elation that we had known four years earlier. After eleven days and 240 miles, and nearly fifty gallons of gas, we arrived that night, the tenth of March, in Tapachula.

The night life of the city, with its neon lights, juke boxes, and speeding automobiles, seemed almost unreal to us after the bright stars, humming insects, and creaking oxcarts. Blissfully we rolled along the smooth pavement looking for a hotel. Leaving Helen in the jeep in front of the Gran Hotel Internacional, I threaded my way through the lobby, where a group of fastidiously dressed men stood idly fanning themselves. No doubt I looked like a Steinbeck character. After one disdainful look the desk clerk said there were no vacancies. I was annoyed. While the men in the lobby whispered "*loco americano*," I explained to the clerk in my halting Spanish where we had come from, and after an uneasy glance at the guests in the dining room he reluctantly assigned us a room—with the pointed suggestion that we bring our bags around the back way.

With La Tortuga safely in the courtyard parking area, we were grateful for the darkness as we unloaded huge bundles of dirty clothes, cameras, suitcases, typewriter, and almost everything movable preparatory to working on the jeep the next morning. "Make Dinah heel," I warned Helen. "I was afraid to tell the clerk we had a dog too." Discreetly we climbed the service stairs to our back room.

The next morning I left Helen trying to persuade the laundress to take our heaps of dirty clothes while I took La Tortuga to the Willys agency. Agency is a rather misleading term for the open shed on one side of a fenced dirt rectangle where I supervised the removal, cleaning, and lubrication of La Tortuga's mud-filled wheels. While I hopped around keeping track of the parts being scattered all over the ground, the *maestro,* or head mechanic, sat in one corner and straw-bossed the activities of two men and three small boys. One by one I added my own tools to their inadequate supply when they used pliers and chisels instead of wrenches. Promptly at two o'clock they all dropped everything right where it was and knocked off for the afternoon siesta.

I took stock of the damage that La Tortuga had incurred in the last eleven days. Although Helen and I would regain the ten pounds we had each lost, La Tortuga would never be the same again. Her sides, back, and bottom were pocked with dents from rocks and stumps, paint was missing in long gouges where branches had dragged, and both gas racks were bent from the steep sides of ravines. In addition, while we forded a river, some twenty gallons of water had entered the hull through a punctured rubber seal. We had spare seals, but the dents and scratches were honored battle scars and we left them as they were.

Shortly after the men returned to work a green jeep drove into the shed. Too engrossed in making certain that all of La Tortuga's pieces went back where they belonged, I didn't pay much attention to it until one of the workers tapped me on the shoulder and said, "A countryman of yours."

Then I noticed the California license plate and, what surprised me even more, the University of California seal on the side. A tall young fellow with sandy hair and a crew cut and wearing a T shirt and khaki pants unlimbered himself from behind the wheel. With a big smile he said:

"So this is what had everyone so excited all the way from Arriaga to Tapachula. I'm Ed Markell."

"I'm very happy to know you," I said, looking again at the UCLA insignia. "If you had said you were Dr. Livingston I couldn't be more surprised. What brings you to Tapachula?"

"Well, I am a doctor," he laughed. "I'm doing research on tropical diseases for the university medical school. When I came through on the train, every time it stopped someone would tell me that two crazy Americans were trying to drive a strange apparatus through the jungles. I thought they were kidding me. I should have known it would be a couple of Californians."

"It wasn't easy," I said. "How about having dinner with us tonight? I'd like you to meet my wife." He seemed surprised that the other "crazy American" was a woman.

As it turned out, Dr. Markell was staying at the same hotel, and that night the three of us sat around a table having a regular school reunion. When Ed brought us up to date on the recent architectural developments at UCLA, I couldn't resist saying, "We consider ourselves almost alumni of the medical school too—we learned to drive there."

"You did what? I've heard of law schools being accused of teaching ambulance chasing," he laughed, "but this is the first time I've heard that a med school taught driving."

"Well, this was sort of a pre-med course. We used the excavations for the building to practice our jungle maneuvers."

"And," Helen added, "it was a very valuable course."

That was the first comment she had made all evening. A little later she asked to be excused. It wasn't like her, and I was concerned.

"It's nothing, my stomach's a little upset. I'll be all right in the morning."

"Where you've been, it's little wonder," Ed said. "I have some pills upstairs that should give you some relief. I'll be leaving in the morning, but if you don't feel better in a day or so you'd better see a doctor. Best of luck, Bruins."

The next day I left Helen resting in the room while I went back to finish the work on La Tortuga. That afternoon I received a telephone call from the hotel:

"Your wife is sick. Come quickly and bring a doctor."

Leaving everything, I called the doctor recommended by the hotel and rushed back to Helen. It was a hot, sticky afternoon, but she lay shivering in bed. The doctor took her temperature, and as well as I could, in Spanish, I answered his questions. When he left, I followed him into the hall.

"Your wife has a high fever," he said. "I think it's typhoid."

Stunned, I returned to the room. For the first time I realized that Helen's listlessness and lack of enthusiasm the past few days had been due to something more than fatigue.

86

But how could it be typhoid? We had boiled all our water, and we both had had all the inoculations. I told the doctor that when he called the next morning.

"My diagnosis is typhoid," he said. "It may be that the inoculations will prevent the symptoms from being so severe, but in any event it will be some time before you can travel again."

Each afternoon of the days that followed rain flooded the streets. Constantly I sat by Helen's bedside watching her temperature rise, recede a bit, and then climb still higher. I kept the covers on her when she tossed in fever, filled the hot water bottle when she shook with chills, and listened to her talk of home, of swamps, insects and flowers. How grateful I was that we had reached Tapachula when we did.

Each day the doctor came, prescribed more medicine, but each day Helen's temperature climbed higher. At 104 degrees it leveled off. She lay still, pale under her dark tan; several days passed before her fever broke. With relief I heard her ask for food, and when she made a few feeble puns, I knew she was going to be all right.

While Helen was gaining her strength back, I finished the jeep and stocked it with supplies, including two hundred feet of quarter-inch steel cable for the winch. When we left Tapachula, Helen was still weak, but anxious to be under way. We both knew that if the rains were early farther south, too, we were due for trouble.

Chapter Four

Wɪᴛʜ new mental pictures of the jeep's contents strewn about a customs inspector's office, Helen and I approached the Guatemalan border. We had a few nervous moments while officials eyed with suspicion the many bulges and hollows of La Tortuga's contours, but then, apparently believing that no self-respecting smuggler would travel in such an outlandish contraption, they stamped our passports without so much as a look inside.

The cool mountain highlands were a blessed relief from the humid heat of Tapachula. Dense forest that admitted little light covered the hillsides, wild orchids clustered to the bare lower branches of trees, and as we climbed still higher there was the paradox of evergreens and banana palms side by side. In the blue distance ridge upon ridge was differentiated by haze; in the valleys far below us tall trees projected from a mass of green, their slender trunks and leafy tops looking like tiny frayed toothpicks. As the afternoon mist settled, everything was bathed in an ethereal glow; delicate ferns and large leaf plants, a yard across, quivered gently under the droplets of moisture. In the mottled sky overhead the sun tried vainly to force its way through, edging each scudding cloud with gold. How good the cold rushing streams felt when we stopped briefly to bathe, and then hurried on.

And what a pleasure it was to snuggle in our sleeping bags in the chill night air.

Neat little villages, their streets cobbled, lined the dirt highway. Every dwelling was brightened with flowers, the sharp petals and delicate stamen of poinsettia, lazy undulant circles of bougainvillaea, and the riotous color of hibiscus. Extremely steep grades wound in hairpin turns, requiring all the turtle power the engine could muster. In spite of the fact that the low-octane Mexican gas made the motor sound as if there were a panful of marbles somewhere inside, we had filled all our tanks. Gas would be forty cents a gallon henceforth instead of the thirteen cents we had been paying.

Along the coil-spring road to Chichicastenango, Indians on their way to market looked like a string of multicolored beads. Each one carried a burden that would put even a burro to shame. It was Saturday afternoon, and although we saw them twenty-five miles from Chichicastenango, their seemingly slow trot brought them there in ample time to set up shop for the Sunday-morning market.

The next morning the plaza at Chichicastenango was swarming with Indians, their handiwork and livestock crowded under the shade of purple jacaranda trees. Unglazed earthenware pots were piled like cannon balls, laquered chests were stacked high, and there were pigs on leashes, chickens in baskets, the ever present dogs searching hungrily for a scrap of food, and the red combs and wrinkled necks of turkeys bobbing in tempo to the walk of little boys who carried them under their arms.

Near the church steps Indian women sat surrounded by baskets of pink and yellow rose petals. The colors of the flowers paled beside the women's scarlet embroidered blouses and headdresses. Obscuring the whitewashed façade of the church, smoke billowed up from fires on the semi-circular steps. Kneeling Indians prayed in a monotone of dialect, swinging censers tirelessly, the heavy-scented smoke of burning incense swirling around their dark faces. Their red turbans sooty, their black embroidered jackets and short black pants dusty, they moved up on their knees, pausing on each step. Inside the church they kissed the feet of an image of Christ dressed in the feathered ceremonial garb of the

Indians. They sprinkled rose petals on the floor and backed away to continue their prayers in front of a stone altar on a hill above the town.

The rains that had started prematurely in Tapachula had not followed us into Guatemala, but Helen and I both knew that we could not tarry. We worked out a rigid schedule, one which allowed little time for sight-seeing, and decided to travel as many hours each day as Helen's weakened condition would permit, and as fast as the combination of the jeep's low power, the sharp curves, chuckholes, and washboard road allowed. In Guatemala City we stopped only long enough to procure a visa for El Salvador, and then speeded on to the border, constantly shifting gears and steering around slides and boulders on the ill-kept road.

After having crossed two Mexican borders and two Guatemalan borders with only a few minutes' delay and with no inspection, we were full of confidence when we braked to a stop in front of the Salvadorean customs house. Before us was the longest stretch of paved road we had seen for almost a month and we were anxious to see how La Tortuga would perform at a speed better than twenty miles per hour. But the officials had other ideas. Perhaps it was just that it was close to siesta time and a hot sweltering afternoon, but our statement that everything was in compartments made no difference. Besides, the chief of customs was tired and it was all of thirty feet from his desk to the jeep. So we spent the next few hours carrying our things in to him. When everything was in order the chief of customs wanted to send one of his boys along with us to make sure we didn't sell anything, but he couldn't get any volunteers when, at our encouragement, Dinah made a very convincing show of her teeth. As it turned out, it might have been better if someone *had* gone with us—we might not have been stopped by police every few miles on our way to the capital.

El Salvador is the smallest, but most densely populated country in Central America, and one of the two countries in all of Latin America that has its portion of the Pan American Highway paved. Principally a coffee country, almost all of its wealth is in the hands of a few large producers, and it is said that there are more Cadillacs in its capital than in Beverly Hills. El Salvador has had a relatively peaceful revolutionary history in comparison with its neighbors, probably because of the government's policy of keeping taxes just low enough so that it is cheaper to pay them than to buy guns.

On our first visit we had entered on tourist cards, similar to those of tourist-wise Mexico. Apparently the El Salvadoreans had found that too simple a solution. They had reverted to the more bureaucratic and complicated visa system. I noticed, too, that the *chimbimbo*, our American dime, was still in circulation. I had been considerably confused on the first trip when I was handed a dime in change. The next time I bought something worth ten cents, I handed the clerk two nickels, but he wouldn't accept them. Later I learned that our dime was their official twenty-five-cent piece; their own contained too much silver and had disappeared from the market.

In San Salvador, the capital, Helen and I checked into the Hotel Internacional—there is always a Hotel Internacional —for a bath before making the rounds of the Honduran, Nicaraguan, and Costa Rican consulates for visas. We hired a cab for the morning. It turned out to be for the day. Previously our meetings with the consulates had been painless; it had never taken more than a few minutes to obtain our visas. It came as a shock, therefore, when an owlish-looking gentleman at the Honduran consulate peered over his glasses and said that there would be a ten-day wait.

"But," I protested, "we can't wait that long. Ten days could make the difference in being able to reach Costa Rica before the rains begin. We'll be in your country only a few hours. As much as we would like to, we can't even take time to stop in your lovely capital."

With that glowing reference to Tegucigalpa he warmed up. "Under those circumstances," he said, "I can issue a transit visa immediately—if you first have a visa for the next country on your route, Nicaragua."

I saw a strange gleam in his eyes when I said, "Fine, we'll

92

be back with the visas in a half hour." We learned the reason for that gleam when we arrived at the Nicaraguan consulate. There would be a *two-week* delay for visas to Nicaragua. It seemed that Somoza, Nicaragua's dictator—or pacifier, as he preferred to be called—had just dodged a bullet. He was personally approving all visas. The fact that there were more than a thousand miles of unpatrolled border where anyone with evil intentions could slip across with ease didn't matter. Anyone entering by the one patrolled highway was under suspicion. After an hour of explanation, persuasion, cajolery, and flattery we had gotten nowhere. There would still be a two-week wait.

We were desperate. In the trees outside of town thumb-sized beetles were praying for rain. According to local superstition, this particular type of insect begins to sing about

two months before the rainy season, and had already been praying, so we were told, for about six weeks. We had to be in Costa Rica before those prayers were answered.

Again we explained to the consul how critical timing was. The consul agreed to cable for permission, but added that it would still take at least seven days. Another hour passed while we went through the whole story again. Tired of arguing, the consul finally said, "I'll give you a visa under one condition—*if* you can get a personal recommendation from the American Ambassador."

To us this condition seemed tantamount to bringing back the Golden Fleece. Except for one unofficial and embarrassing contact in Nicaragua four years earlier, our experience with the American diplomatic service consisted of calling for our mail. Not quite encouraged by the Nicaraguan consul's compromise, we walked glumly out to the still waiting taxi and directed him to proceed with all haste to the American Embassy. We were met there by a very courteous secretary who listened sympathetically to our tale of woe and then informed us that the American Ambassador was in the United States. I could hear the thunder and lightning already. It was not at all difficult to picture La Tortuga engulfed in a sea of mud in the Guanacaste area of northern Costa Rica.

Just then a tall, slender, impeccably dressed Hollywood version of a young diplomat came down the stairs in time to catch the last act of the melodrama. He introduced himself as D. Chadwick Braggiotti, chargé d'affaires in the Ambassador's absence. In many subsequent encounters with the U. S. Foreign Service we never met a man who grasped a problem more quickly or with greater understanding than Mr. Braggiotti. Even though he was already late for a state function he took time right there to call the Nicaraguan consul and to instruct his assistant to draft a letter. He asked us to come back and see him later that afternoon.

By 4:00 P.M. we had all our visas, and also our permit to leave El Salvador, an item which normally would have taken two days to acquire. At the American Embassy later that same afternoon we were ushered into Mr. Braggiotti's office. A conversation followed that was to be of great consequence to us. He asked if we would do him a favor. Anything, I thought.

"You two are following closely behind Vice-President Nixon's good-will tour of the Latin-American nations," he explained. "One of the purposes of that tour was to promote interest in the Pan American Highway, and I believe that news of what you are doing to get through the unfinished portions could do a great deal to help that cause. I would like to introduce you to our United States Information Service officer, have a few pictures taken, and get some background material on your trip. If you have no objections."

After the interview with the USIS officer we were given a letter of introduction to other USIS officers along our route.

The next morning the insects' prayers were still unanswered as we left San Salvador for the Honduran border, 112 miles away. We arrived there in a few hours, but it took another few hours to get through customs. The officials were tired there too.

Honduras is the only country in Central America where the Pan American Highway does not go directly to the capital. There was a fine paved cutoff to Tegucigalpa, but we passed it by with reluctance. Now every day counted in our race against the rains. We were anxious to cross the ninety-five miles of Honduran cactus and sage and enter Nicaragua before nightfall.

In Managua, Nicaragua's capital, we ran into another snag—Somoza also had to approve exit permits. We were told at the immigration office that the only way to avoid the delay was to see Somoza ourselves. We weren't eager to climb the hill to his imposing palace, especially in such a tanklike vehicle as La Tortuga; however, without her we felt we didn't have a snowball's chance in hell of seeing him. On top of a prominence overlooking the city of Managua and Lake Managua his palace was a combination Forest Lawn and Fort Knox. Since the attempt on Somoza's life the guard had been doubled, and it was with considerable difficulty that we reached the gate. Accompanied by a platoon of twitching soldiers bearing submachine guns, we were escorted to the Captain of the Guard, who told us that His Excellency was out of town. We asked to see his secretary, and, after three offices and three subsecretaries, finally we were led into a lobby-sized room with overstuffed leather chairs. After waiting only a few minutes we were introduced to a stocky, well-set gentleman in a white linen suit. Quietly he asked our business and made a telephone call. We were advised to pick up our exit visas at the immigration office within the hour.

Managua had been an experience on the first trip too. Though we had had no difficulty procuring an exit permit, we had had trouble enough in other respects. Mostly money, or rather the lack of it. Arriving in Managua with just enough for a hotel or a meal, we chose the meal, and then picked up our mail. We were expecting an income tax refund. But apparently my slide rule had slipped; instead of a check there was a bill. Taking up residence in the park on the shores of Lake Managua, we were pondering what to do when an angel appeared in the form of a little round man who approached us with the air of a street peddler selling pornographic post cards. He was not, however, a peddler; he was a buyer. Did we have any nylons, women's underclothes, cameras, tools? He would buy anything. We had only one thing we could sell, but in a dictator-run country where anything more lethal than a water pistol was under government control we were a little hesitant to mention the .22 rifle we had smuggled across four countries. However, since it wasn't digestible in its present form, we decided to transform it into cash, and our little round friend was sworn to secrecy. He said he would call at our hotel that night. "Where are you staying?" he asked. When I told him that we were staying right there on the shores of the lake, he grew very impatient. Finally we convinced him, and although he could not understand Americans not staying in the best hotel, or at least some hotel, he told us of a park high above the city where we could camp in relative comfort. "It's cooler, there's running water and no mosquitoes."

With that Elysium in mind we followed his directions, given in Spanish, to a road leading out of town. We found the two lights, the guard, the high fence, just as he had described. With superb nonchalance we told the astonished sentry that we would like to make camp there for the night. With somewhat less composure he made a telephone call from inside his post, and then opened the gates. "Pick any place you like," he said.

We spent a heavenly night, sleeping among hibiscus and roses. The next morning the gardener asked if we would like to bathe. What hospitable park commissioners, I thought. After a refreshing bath in a trellis-shielded shower dotted with blue morning glories we heated the last of our coffee and, with a piece of Dinah's biscuit, had a breakfast fit for a dog. As I was rolling up the sleeping bags I saw a very impressive building away off on a hill. I asked the gardener what public building it was. "Oh," he said, "it's not public. That's the residence of the American Ambassador. You've been sleeping in his garden." We left an anonymous thank-you note with the sentry.

Baffled, we rode back to town, hoping that our black-marketeering friend was not also playing a joke on us with respect to buying the gun. When the transaction was completed, he asked us how we enjoyed the park. At my stormy reply he said defensively, "But, señor, you did not understand. I said go past the lighted gate, not through it. The park was just beyond." Our Spanish has improved much since then.

Our trouble over visas and exit permits this time was caused in part by the rather strained relations between Somoza and Costa Rica's President Figueres. Somoza blamed Figueres for the attempt on his life, and Figueres blamed Somoza for aiding the revolution that had been so recently foiled in Costa Rica. They were still on speaking terms, but the speaking was restricted to name calling. Tension was mounting between the two countries and there were reputed to be guerrillas in the mountains near the border. Our state of mind was not improved by a meeting with an Inter-American Geodetic surveyor.

"Don't stop for anything," he warned. "If you have a flat tire ride it on the rim."

With that comforting advice we left Managua, planning to cross the border that same day. But we overestimated the quality of the roads. True to the tradition of making it as difficult as possible to cross frontiers, the roads on either side of the borders in Latin-American countries are rarely maintained. We made camp near the shores of Lake Nicaragua, the only place in the world where there are fresh water sharks. But it wasn't sharks we were concerned about that night.

It was already dark when we finished supper and were ready to crawl in the jeep. Helen was the first to notice several bright lights moving very erratically across an open field several hundred yards away. They weren't coming from the road, so I knew they couldn't be automobiles, and besides, they were sweeping the country as if they were searching for something. It was with a decidedly squeamish feeling that we watched the lights get closer and closer; since we were only a few miles from the border, it wasn't difficult to imagine some overzealous patriot shooting and asking questions later. But there was nothing to do but stand our ground and hope they wouldn't discover us. We were overly optimistic. A stray beam glanced across the reflectors on the side of the jeep and they lit up like Roman candles. Simultaneously all the lights concentrated on us as if we were Sonja Henie at the ice show. Helen dove for the wings, and I took a bow.

"Good evening, gentlemen," I quavered. "We're friends. *Turistas norteamericanos.*"

There was a stony silence. Staring blindly into the lights, I tried to make out if they were in uniform, but all I could tell was that there were six men on horseback, all armed like comic book gangsters. The silence continued, and I was beginning to think they were all either unfriendly or mute. Eventually one of them asked me in Spanish:

"Where do you come from?"

"Alaska," I answered. There was another pause, and then in perfect English he said, "Well, what the hell are you doing here?"

The lights blinked off and in a wink I was enjoying a cigarette with six sportsmen from Managua who were deer hunting. Hence the sweeping lights. Not a very sporting way to hunt, but I was in no mood to question their ethics.

The next morning we crossed the border into Costa Rica. At the wooden frontier post there were graphic examples of the activity of the preceding few weeks—not a pane of glass was intact and every square foot of the walls sported a bullet hole. We waited four hours for the captain of the small detachment of soldiers to return from hunting down guerrillas before we were permitted to pass.

The Guanacaste region of northern Costa Rica is wild country, a coastal plateau of canyons, rocks, and scattered dense vegetation. Devoted principally to cattle raising, it had a Wild West atmosphere in other ways too. As we drove along the narrow dirt track, every man put his hand on a concealed gun as we approached. It was the memory of the dry-weather trail in this area that had caused us to rush across four countries to reach it before the rains came. Although the first fourteen miles were still very poor, the rest of the eighty miles we had worried about was an excellent gravel road, thanks to the U. S. Bureau of Public Roads.

In San José, the capital, we asked a policeman for directions to the Pension Internacional, the new hotel run by our old friends the Ramos family. Being a very obliging fellow, he offered to take us there. Zipping behind our first motorcycle escort, without regard for traffic, we felt we had at long last discovered the answer to our city driving problem. Until we found ourselves in front of a big square building that said *policia* instead of *pension*. There followed a cross-examination of very leading questions that intimated that harmless La Tortuga might be a Trojan horse with Somoza hidden somewhere inside. Fortunately they permitted me to use the telephone before we were placed incommunicado and in a few minutes an indignant Señor Ramos was down to vouch for us.

San José, Costa Rica, was both an end and a beginning for us. Up to this point we had had past experience to draw on, but henceforth everything would be one great big question mark. We knew that no one had ever reached Panama in a wheeled vehicle under its own power, and that there was not so much as a foot trail over the mountains. The customary procedure for the Pan American traveler was to put his vehicle on a ship at the Pacific port of Puntarenas and disembark in the Canal Zone, Panama. We felt we had a new route mapped out. From San José we intended to travel south to San Isidro del General, where the Pan American Highway ended, and from there over a winding mountain trail down to Dominical on the Pacific coast. The practicability of our theory depended on several things which only an on-the-spot investigation could tell us. That there were beaches we knew from maps and charts, but what the jeep would do in water other than a calm bay was still in doubt. At best, our plans would mean traveling two hundred miles along an almost uninhabited coast from Dominical to Pedregal in Panama, the first seaport where we could again reach a road. Our maps also showed that the beach was broken by river mouths and rock outcroppings which would have to be skirted by sea, and we were depending upon the availability of protected coves from which to land and take off. We estimated conservatively that the trip would take two weeks and, allowing for the worst possible conditions, would consume seventy gallons of fuel.

One of the first things on the agenda in San José was to get as much firsthand information on coastal conditions as possible, and Mr. Lee Hunsaker, the USIS officer, was of great help in arranging appointments for us with everyone who knew anything at all about the area. With Mr. Honiball of United Fruit Company, Mr. Paris of Union Oil, and Mr. Harshberger of the U. S. Bureau of Public Roads we studied maps and aerial photographs, but most of the available material was on the interior. Little was known of the coast line between Dominical and Pedregal. We were advised to look up Tommy Brower, an American who ran a small hotel at Dominical and who was supposed to know more about that part of the Pacific coast than anyone else. But when we left San José we still had nothing more concrete than an untried amphibian and a theory.

With scurrying around seeking information, procuring provisions, servicing the jeep, and searching for extra fuel containers the few days we spent in San José, Costa Rica, were busy ones. There was also the matter of a visa to Panama. At the consulate a white-haired gentleman cheerfully asked the necessary questions, but when he came to the one about mode of transport he automatically wrote down, "By air." I informed him we weren't going by plane. Before I could clarify that statement he scratched it out and wrote "By ship." Again I hastily corrected him.

"Well, how *are* you going?" he queried.

At my reply, "By amphibious jeep," he scratched out the whole question and just signed his name.

Mr. Hunsaker and his vivacious wife Jane took us under their wing during our stay in San José. Their gentle hospitality was a refreshing interlude after life in La Tortuga. Mr. Hunsaker arranged an interview for us with Costa Rica's President Figueres, a cultured MIT graduate who asked keen questions about our plans for getting into Panama, but who was just as dubious as the others as to La Tortuga's ability to get us there. As far as the President was concerned, La Tortuga's crew consisted of just captain and first mate.

We discreetly avoided any mention of our mascot because of a quarantine law which she was dodging. Dinah usually accompanied us to the Hunsakers' home and was very fond of their young daughter, Shelly. On one occasion, however, upon the arrival of the President's limousine Dinah was relegated to the kitchen. Dinah hated to miss out on a party, but Shelly, excusing herself periodically, kept her well supplied with hors d'oeuvres.

It was Palm Sunday, 1955, when we left San José for San Isidro over the hogback highway that skims along the top of the Talamanca range. A good portion of the distance was at elevations of between nine thousand and eleven thousand feet, and on clear days one is supposed to be able to see both the Atlantic and the Pacific oceans. The mist obscured everything that day, however, and by the time we had covered the seventy miles to San Isidro, rain was beating on the top of the jeep. We decided to accept Mr. Harshberger's invitation to stop at the Bureau of Public Roads encampment and spend a dry night before continuing to Dominical. If the hull had sprung as many leaks as the roof, we wouldn't get very far toward Panama.

Noon the next day found us at Dominical, a tiny group of ramshackle wooden buildings and an equally ramshackle hotel owned by Tommy Brower. We had some difficulty distinguishing which among the natives at the bar was Mr. Brower, but when we did we plagued him with questions about the coast line, only to learn that he knew little more about it than the people in San José. He did tell us, however, of a place three miles south along the beach where the surf was not so bad. It was obvious that we could never go through the breakers in front of the town. They towered twenty feet at the crest. We had heard their roar long before we had seen them.

Threading our way between trees and skirting patches of rock at the water's edge, we drove the three miles to the end of the beach and set up camp in a cluster of coconut palms. The beach was blocked by a shale cliff that jutted a half mile into the sea. Behind us was a dense impenetrable forest. There was no way around the cliff except through the breakers.

The rest of that afternoon we spent preparing La Tortuga for her maiden voyage. We repacked her with heavy things low down in the hull for stability and arranged our food into a daily menu. Topside, in a waterproof bag, I stowed the emergency gear: first aid kit, knife, a canteen of fresh water, three days' supply of food, insect repellent, mosquito netting, and extra socks. I inflated the one-man rubber life raft and put it on top, and tightened the lashings on the twenty-gallon drum of gas topside, which, with a five-gallon can inside and our regular supply, gave us the required seventy gallons. Underneath the jeep I inspected each of the rubber seals and checked for holes in the hull. The life preservers we kept handy inside.

Tommy Brower had told us that low tide should be about 6:00 P.M., and that it would be one hour later each day. When the jeep was ready, we strolled along the water's edge. The beach was hard, but there were hundreds of boulders awash in the ebbing tide. The rocks would complicate things when we took off but, being able to choose a path, we thought we could avoid them. However, on landing we would have no choice, and we decided it would be advisable to land at high tide, when there would be plenty of water to get us over the rocks to the sandy beach beyond. Mr.

Brower had also told us that the sea would be calmest in the morning and to limit our travel to those hours. Consequently we planned our first day on leaving at low tide at seven the next morning and making twenty miles to Mala Point, landing at high tide around 1:00 P.M.

That night coconuts mingled with the rain that pelted the top of the jeep as we lay on our bunks listening to the constant thrash of the waves onshore. It was not the quiet lapping of wavelets I had described to Helen in answer to her vivid word picture of combers thundering on a rocky coast. In Alaska, nine thousand miles away, I had tried to reassure her, saying we would surely be able to find a secluded cove from which to take off into the sea. In quieting her fears I had oversimplified the whole thing to the point where I believed it myself. We would merely drive along the beach until we came to a rock outcropping, then take to the sea in a calm bay that would be conveniently close, continue in the water to another stretch of beach, and so on until we reached a road in Panama. Lying there that night, neither of us speaking, we both knew that my theory was not very realistic. So certain had I been, however, that we had never even tested the jeep in surf.

At seven the next morning we were waiting at the edge of the water knowing no more about taking a jeep or even a boat through the surf than what the engraved brass plate on the dashboard instructed: "Approach at full throttle and steer course at right angles to the waves." In a very short time I learned that I wasn't the only one addicted to oversimplification. The engineer who wrote those instructions should have tried it himself.

Somewhere I had read that there is a rhythm to ocean waves, that a big one is followed by several smaller ones in a definite cycle. Sitting tensely in the jeep, we studied the supposed rhythm, but they all looked big. With the windows and hatches tightly closed the heat from the radiator poured into the cab, turning it into an oven. When what seemed like the biggest wave had passed, we eased into the sea, four-wheel drive engaged, propeller spinning. As we went deeper the wheels lost power; the jeep wavered slightly, yawed a bit, and we were afloat. Quickly I shifted the wheels into neutral, pressed the throttle to the floor, and steered directly for the line of breakers. The first comber was already spent when it hit us, but La Tortuga shuddered from the force and foam covered the windshield. Ignoring my instinct to step on the brakes, I kept the throttle floored and headed straight into the wall of water that rushed at us like a bull at the Plaza de Toros. The breaker curled its crest into a white froth as the jeep plunged into it. La Tortuga reared like a horse, Helen grabbed for the dash, Dinah was thrown to the back, and I held grimly to the wheel. I flinched as the full force of the ten-foot-high comber crashed against the windshield, and we were slammed into the trough that followed. The next one crashed down on us, swallowing us. And then another. Then, past the breaker line, we were rising and falling smoothly on the long ground swells.

It was several minutes before we recovered enough to notice that we were listing heavily to starboard. Shifting Dinah and everything movable inside, we tried to trim ship, but it wasn't enough. Already a half mile from shore, we would have to turn back and move the drum of fuel topside.

With the hatches again tightly closed and the jeep running at full throttle we headed for the same place from which we had taken off. Once inside the breaker line, there was no turning back. The first swell swept under the jeep; with the water traveling in the same direction as we were, the rudder had almost no control. Closer to shore the next wave lifted the stern, the bow pointed down, and we surfboarded toward the beach, fighting the wheel as the jeep yawed from side to side. With absolutely no rudder control we rushed along at what seemed terrific speed, tipped crazily on the crest of the comber, white water thrashing on either side. I felt the wheels touch bottom, I shifted into gear, and we rolled up on the sand.

By the time we had relocated the heavy fuel drum the tide was halfway in. There were only three hours left before high water. We decided to shorten our run to Uvita Point, some ten miles away. The surf was considerably worse when we took off the second time.

Once safely outside the breaker line and clear of the rocky point, we plotted our course for Uvita Point and tried to enjoy the novel experience of driving an automobile on the Pacific Ocean. At first, when the giant swells rolled toward the jeep, towering over us like mountains around a valley, we whipped the rudder around and tried to meet them head on. We soon realized that they only swept harmlessly beneath us, lifting us gently and then lowering us into the trough again. If we could ignore the feeling of insecurity, the knowledge that only a thin piece of steel and a few rubber seals kept out the fathoms of water below us, it was not much different than driving a jeep along the highway. The controls were the same, but the response was sluggish. The motor was making as much noise as if we were moving at thirty miles per hour, but instead of road shock there was a gentle rocking motion. The rumble of the propeller replaced the tire hum, waves slapped in the fender wells, and instead of a thirty-mile-per-hour wind there was only the three-mile-per-hour gurgle of the wake.

Our navigational aides were simple. We had a clock to check the tides, binoculars to check the shore, a hydrographic chart surveyed by the U.S.S. *Ranger* in 1885, and a compass which we had no intention of needing.

Our theory had already undergone several changes. We could see stretches of beach, but they were short ones, and the time saved in driving along them was not worth the risk of an unnecessary landing. Our revised plans were to stay at sea until nearly high tide, landing south of any outcropping of rock. Then, while waiting for the next low tide, we could drive along the beach to the next obstacle.

We followed the coast line about two miles out, avoiding masses of drifting seaweed. With the binoculars we scanned the shore line, trying to identify the landmarks and check them off on the chart.

It was almost high tide when we made out the turbulence that marked Uvita Point, a long sand spit that projected into the sea. The water looked calmest just south of a high headland that dropped into the sea about two miles nearer to us. Steering at right angles to the waves, we headed in that direction. When we had gone back at Dominical, there had been no indication of the height of the waves from the seaward side. It was the same as we approached the beach at Uvita.

With the accelerator floored we entered the breaker line. There was the same surge toward shore as the first unborn breaker passed under us, and then the same thrust from the stern. The bow nosed down. Again we surfboarded out of control. Standing almost on her nose, La Tortuga rushed forward, caught on the crest with the trough twenty feet

below. I felt as if we were in the front car of a roller coaster at the top of the first drop. Terrified, thinking we were going stern over bow, I let up on the gas, hoping the comber would slip under us and we would straighten out. Instead, with no propeller wash past the rudder, we lost the last bit of control. La Tortuga spun broadside to the waves, heeled over on her side. The engine sputtered and died. For an eternity we hung there while wave after wave slammed against the bottom of the hull, wondering why the jeep didn't go over, praying it wouldn't and knowing it should. The whole portside was completely submerged, water streamed in through the seals around the doors. Dinah and Helen scrambled for something to hang on to and tried to keep out of my way as I frantically worked the throttle and ground on the starter.

Miraculous is a word much overused, one that is often

applied to many things with common-sense explanations. But for us that day at Uvita Point it is the only word that explains the sudden lull in the waves, the way the jeep wallowed right side up, and the starting of the gasoline-flooded engine. On the deserted shore we climbed limply from the hatch and stared back at the surf. It was every bit as high as in front of the hotel at Dominical.

The rest of that afternoon we sat under the palms that edged the shore, our mouths dry, our hearts pounding. Red crabs played at our feet, the beach was strewn with coconuts, a few of which helped to quench our thirst. That landing caused a complete reversal of our by now thoroughly shaken theory. We were determined never to land at high tide again. Perhaps if we landed at low tide the surf would be less severe. This opposite approach, however, imposed other problems. During that week low tide came early in the morning and after dark at night. It would be necessary to start as soon as it was light enough to see and to plan on the very short runs we could make in the few hours before the morning low tide.

At 5:30 A.M. the next day we headed for Mala Point, some ten miles away, planning to land there shortly after low tide at 8:00 A.M. Staying as close to shore as possible, we scanned the beach and the water, straining to make out details in the early morning light. Through the muting haze we could see several rock islands ahead. The chart located these islands about two miles out and showed a string of smaller rock pinnacles on either side, but it indicated a clear channel between them and the cliffs onshore. We debated whether to go out around the string, which would mean an additional five miles. We decided to trust the chart and head for the channel rather than land two hours after low tide.

Thrusting from the blue water to heights varying from a few feet to 116 feet, the string of rocks formed an arc from shore like a funnel, with the channel at the far end its neck. We cut the throttle and watched the birds nesting on the massive bare crowns of the rocks and the white froth blending with their chalky bases where the sea had left rings of salt. There was no indication that the chart was in error until we were almost to the channel. In the trough between swells we saw jagged fingers of stone break through the surface of the water. We were too close to turn around. Reverse gear had little effect. In slow motion we drifted toward the rocks. To give the rudder more control I floored the throttle. Almost blindly I picked a space between the fingers. Like an ant between the teeth of a saw we crawled through on the crest of a swell. Dumbly I gripped the wheel long after we were clear. How long, I wondered, would Lady Luck ride as supercargo?

Landing at low tide gave us the same chill as before, but we reached the beach safely about 8:30 A.M. With the next low tide coming after dark that night, we couldn't put to sea until the following morning. To the south we could see a long stretch of beach that curved to join the flat horizon of blue and brown. Behind the beige strip of beach were salty marshes and mangrove swamps. The chart showed fifteen miles of shore line broken by only a few river mouths. Keeping on the hard sand near the water's edge, we drove as fast as twenty miles per hour until we came to the first river mouth. It was a wide shallow delta of brown water, choppy from the meeting of the current and ocean swells. Following the shore line to the narrowest part, about a half mile across, we eased down the slick bank unaware that one of the side radiator exhaust hatches was ajar. There was no

direction to the waves, they slapped on all sides as we
churned erratically toward the other side. Near midstream
an extra-large wave splashed through the crack in the hatch
that was ajar, flooding the engine with salt water. With the
jeep drifting helplessly, the hood open to any stray wave, I
worked nervously on deck, drying the spark plugs and distributor. I signaled Helen to press the starter button. The
motor would not respond. She threw me another dry towel,
and I wiped everything again. With relief I heard the engine
cough and take hold. I secured the hood and quickly
climbed over the windshield and through the open top hatch
into the cab.

By the time we were across the tide was in, and the beach
was too narrow to drive on. With her front wheels awash,
we parked La Tortuga among the debris of bleached driftwood and took protection from the sun in the only shade,
under the rear overhang of the jeep. There was no sound
but the thrash of the sea; we wondered what else it held in
store.

When the tide receded, we continued along the beach, getting stuck in the black mud of river mouths and in the soft
uncertain sand of the shore. For one stretch of several miles
a six-foot wall of sand kept us driving partly in the water. At
high tide the wall would be covered. When the wheels fell
into a soft patch of sand and I winched out to a buried log,
I thought of what would happen if the tide caught us between that wall and the sea. At dusk we reached the widest
river mouth and made camp, planning to cross in the morning.

That night a fisherman approached our camp, the first
person we had seen since leaving Dominical. A young fellow,
he reminded me of Tomás in southern Mexico. Curiously,

and hesitantly, he asked where we had come from. Squatting on the black sand in the white moonlight, he described the coast line ahead. He could not understand how we had gotten so far, but he said that what lay ahead was worse. He suggested that we go back. But going back was out of the question.

Since that time I have often wondered what would have happened if we had not met that fisherman. I have cursed him for what happened and blessed him for saving us from what might have happened, but always I have wondered. If he had not come to talk to us that night, the next morning we would have continued as we had been, feeling the same sickening chill when we entered the surf, the same numbing fear when we landed. Maybe we would have reached Panama as planned, maybe we would have turned turtle on some desolate beach, or maybe we would not have been so lucky at steering a course through a maze of rocks. I wonder.

The fisherman returned the next morning as we were picking a spot to cross the river mouth. He asked to see our chart. Running a calloused finger over it, he said:

"Up this river fifteen kilometers there is a United Fruit Company plantation. When I worked there five years ago, there was a road to a little town called Piedras Blancas, where the Rio Esquinas flows down to the Golfo Dulce." He traced a course that would cut off a hundred miles of sea and beach travel around the Peninsula de Osa.

I don't know why I believed him. Officials of the United Fruit Company in San José had said there were no roads. The fisherman swore he had seen one. We should not have taken the chance, but we were both too unnerved by what had happened and too afraid of what might lay ahead. We were ready to grasp at any straw, no matter how slim. We reasoned that just as there was a forgotten trail in southern Mexico there could be a forgotten trail in southern Costa Rica. We changed our plans again and headed down the steep bank into the river and upstream toward the banana plantation.

The incoming tide pushed La Tortuga up the sluggish brown river. The sound of the sea grew fainter; we felt almost as if we had been reprieved. Keeping close to the deep-cut bank, we steered clear of the flotsam that drifted by. On either side mangrove trees sat like giant spiders on their

spindly roots, and in their branches black-faced monkeys played. Overhead brilliant-plumaged parrots filled the sky with color and the air with their raucous cries. As the river curved back on itself, we watched for the merging tributaries the fisherman had described. A few stilted grass and cane huts spotted the gray shore with yellow, and below them on the muddy banks of the dark river were long dug-out canoes.

After five miles or so the water appeared fresh, and we

thought of a bath, the first in fresh water in almost a week. Dinah reluctantly parted with her pan, and Helen crawled out on the bow to dip water from the river. Just from the way she scrubbed I could see how relieved she was; I felt the same way. When she had finished, Helen took the wheel and I took my place on the hood. I was still covered with soap when a sharp jolt nearly threw me over the side as the jeep came to a squishy halt. We had gone aground.

"Some navigator," I jibed. Scrutinizing each log and shadow on the bank for the alligators the fisherman had warned of, I jumped in and pushed off. As we continued up the river, the dark green jungle banks gave way to the yellow green of banana palms. Approaching the plantation, we heard the foreign sound of another motor. A small launch with a surrey-like shade of palm fronds drew alongside with four astonished plantation workers aboard. After they had asked the three questions, one of them tossed me a can of beer from an insulated box under one seat of the boat. All this and cold beer too! The one dismaying factor was that none of the men knew anything about a road to Piedras Blancas. But they said there might well be one and suggested that we ask at plantation headquarters.

The tide was full when we reached Puerto Cortés, an outpost on the edge of the plantation. It looked like an easy ascent up the riverbank to firm ground, and with all wheels driving and the propeller engaged we hit the bank. The jeep buried its wheels in soft gumbo clay that had the consistency of wet cement. With confidence I secured one end of our new steel cable to a big palm tree and engaged the winch. The cable tightened, the jeep moved a little deeper into the mud, and with a twang like a guitar string the cable snapped. I tried to back up, but we were stuck fast. Doubling the cable, I tried again. The jeep moved forward a bit, and then a loud clatter came from the winch housing. Something inside had sheared, and I had no spare parts for the winch.

With the tide at its highest and the winch out of commission, there was no way to get out by ourselves. A plantation dump truck tried to pull us, but it just sat and spun its duals. One of the men put in a call to Palmar Sur, plantation headquarters a few miles away, and in a half hour what must have been the granddaddy of all tractors rumbled into view. As easily as a pair of tweezers picks up an insect the long crane on the front of the tractor picked up La Tortuga and set her on the firm bank. I'm afraid that we rather disrupted the work at the plantation that afternoon. By the time we were clear, scores of natives had come from the fields to watch.

On either side of the gravel road to Palmar Sur were forests of banana palms. Hiding among their shiny drooping leaves, stems of green fruit hung pendulously, accented by the deep red of their heart-shaped buds. Tractor-pulled low-bed trailers carried the burlap-wrapped fruit to the sheds where they were washed, sprayed, and covered with clear plastic bags before being shipped immediately to the U.S. markets.

We had been advised to see Mr. George Newell, the general superintendent at Palmar Sur. Covered with river mud, unshaven, I hesitated even to walk up the flower-lined path to his home. With an expression something like shock Mr. Newell greeted me at the door. I tried to make my story as brief as possible, and then asked about the road.

"Yes," he said, "there is a road, but it goes only twelve miles. And even if you could get to Piedras Blancas, the Rio Esquinas, which you plan to navigate, is just a rapid-filled rocky stream. Good for fishing, but that's all."

It was late afternoon when we received that disheartening information, and Mr. Newell suggested that we put up at the Palmar Sur guesthouse, have a good dinner, and talk about it later.

Palmar Sur was an amazing example of what good organization could do. The United Fruit Company had turned a jungle wilderness into a model community of neat houses, parks, and gardens, where roses and shower of gold bloomed prolifically. In the stilt-elevated guesthouse overlooking the golf course Helen and I bathed under a strong hot shower, refreshed with a cool one, and made repeated trips to the refrigerator for ice water. Later that evening, looking more presentable but no more cheerful, we sat in the Newells' living room. Over cool drinks Mr. and Mrs. Newell listened sympathetically to the story of the trip, but their only suggestion was a flatcar on the United Fruit Company railroad to Corredores, some fifty miles away.

"From there," Mr. Newell said, "a bull-dozed trail leads over the mountains to Volcán, Panama, where you can again catch the Pan American Highway. We'll be happy to make arrangements for a flatcar to take you to Corredores."

I thought of southern Mexico and what we had done to avoid taking the train. "Thank you, but we can't do that," I said. "In the morning we'll go back down the river and continue along the coast."

"Why don't you think about it? Tomorrow's a holiday, Good Friday, and, according to tradition, nothing moves in Costa Rica. Even the banana company shuts down. We couldn't load you on a flatcar until Saturday anyway—Good Friday is the one day in the year the trains don't run. Take it easy—the Pacific will wait for you. Think it over."

I *was* thinking. A whole stream of thoughts. That was

pretty big talk about going back to the beach. With a useless winch what would I do if we got stuck in the sand again and the tide rolled in? Good Friday. The only day in the year that trains don't run. It would mean a compromise which we were not willing to make in southern Mexico for even a few yards, but we would still be traveling under our own power.

"Mr. Newell," I asked, "would it be possible to drive over the railroad bed to Corredores? If it's only fifty miles I'm sure we could do it in one day."

Mr. Newell thought a moment. "I'm sorry, but the company would never give permission. Besides, the tracks are unballasted. They're on a fill, narrow-gauge, with a drop off of eight to ten feet and more on either side. Your jeep would be pounded to pieces."

"After what the jeep has been through, I'm sure it could take it, and we promise to be off the tracks before the trains start running again."

Still not convinced, nevertheless, Mr. Newell made a telephone call. When he hung up the receiver he said, "The head office will not give permission. But, since there will be no traffic tomorrow, they will not prohibit you from trying —provided you're off the tracks by midnight." He brought out a map of the railroad. "In the morning I'll go with you and put you on the right track. For the first fifteen of the fifty miles you will have a dirt road, so that leaves only thirty-five miles on the railroad bed. Now I think you had better get a good night's sleep."

The next morning we checked over the jeep, drained the sea water from the differentials, and left Palmar Sur along the dirt road that paralleled the tracks. The Costa Rican police garrison, for some unknown reason, insisted on sending a soldier along with us. Poor Humberto, he was about to have the roughest duty he would ever see.

We made a strange caravan that Good Friday morning, with the Newells leading the way in their car through the plantation camp. In one of the open fields the natives were hanging an effigy of Judas Iscariot. Inside the jeep was a huge picnic lunch packed by Mrs. Newell, and our gallon thermos jug was filled with ice. Full of hope, we followed to the end of the road, where a flat area made easy access to the tracks. The Newells were still waving as we bounced off toward Corredores, thirty-five miles away.

Mr. Newell had been right about its being a rough road-bed, but I had no doubt as to La Tortuga's ability to take it for a mere thirty-five miles. With the ties sitting on top of a fill, set twelve to eighteen inches apart, and with no gravel ballast between, the jeep bounced along like a marble on a washboard. The jeep's tread was too wide to fit between the rails of the narrow-gauge track, so we rode with the left wheels between and the right ones rubbing against the outside of the rail. To make things worse, the jeep's wheelbase was of such a length that both front and rear wheels were between the ties at the same time. At very low speeds we dropped between each pair of ties; at high speeds we skimmed over the top of them, but with no steering control. We found ten miles per hour a fair compromise, and the springs and shock absorbers took most of the shock. However, dozens of switches and spur lines prevented us from maintaining that speed, and time was consumed in getting over each one. There were unguarded trestles over chasms with rocky streams below where we crept along with only a few inches of tire riding the end of the ties. Each time we were forced to stop there was the agonizingly bumpy period of getting up to speed again. The inside of the jeep became a shambles as the contents of the cabinets showered to the floor. Cameras, typewriter, large chest of film, everything almost floated with the constant jolting. After a few miles of this the drum of gas topside cut its lashing and we jettisoned it beside the tracks. I had the steering wheel to cling to, but Helen, Humberto, and Dinah just floated along with everything else, hitting their heads on the ceiling and being slammed against the sides.

When we stopped for switches the wheels lodged between the ties, the hull clanged against the rails, and it was only with low-range, four-wheel drive and Helen and Humberto pushing that we could rock free. At one spot we slipped sideward and hung over the edge of the fill. Just the left wheels caught on the rail kept us from sliding to the bottom. An inch at a time I maneuvered for over an hour, following Helen's frantic signals, before we were back on the tracks.

By two o'clock in the afternoon we had covered but ten of the thirty-five miles when all four shock absorbers failed. They had become so hot that all the oil had boiled away. After that there was no speed at which we could stay on the tracks; on every tie the jeep was flung to the side, once coming down diagonally across the rails. Getting back consumed more of our dwindling time. Unable to continue with all four wheels bouncing on the ties, we maneuvered the two left wheels up on the rail so that at least half the jeep rode smoothly. With the upper part of my body hanging from the open door I drove looking down at the wheels and steered blindly, listening to Helen's directions.

As long as the track was straight or there were only left curves, I could keep the wheels on the rail, but at spurs, switches, or right curves the jeep slid off. The clutch began to slip a little, and a queer click came from the transmission. At dusk we were still moving ahead slowly, the headlights boring twin holes in the mist that crept down from the mountains. The moisture made the rails slippery and we slid off more and more often. We had covered another ten miles when the right front tire blew out—the constant rubbing against the rail had worn completely through the sidewall. The right rear tire was through two cords and the left rear had a big piece torn from it. They could never last the remaining fifteen miles to Corredores.

With one spare, the other three tires barely holding air, the clutch slipping, something amiss in the transmission, and with no shock absorbers, we had but four hours until midnight, when the trains would start to run again. I knew we could expect another blowout at any time, and when that happened it would be impossible to get off the tracks. I thought of reversing the tires, but I knew I was kidding myself. It had taken all day to come twenty miles. Allowing at least an hour to switch wheels, how could I hope to go that last fifteen miles in the dark, and in less than three hours? At the first wide spot we turned around and limped back a half mile to a plantation camp, where we called Mr. Newell. Humberto slept that night in the camp while Helen and I lay sleepless in the jeep. A little after twelve the first train rushed by.

The next morning we left Humberto with battered La Tortuga beside the tracks, and Helen, Dinah, and I climbed aboard another train for Palmar Sur. The conductor said no dogs, so the three of us rode in the baggage car. Technically we were out of bounds there too. A sign on the wall read, "Only those accompanying the sick and the dead are allowed in the baggage car." But as we sat dejectedly back to back on a packing crate we felt that we met that requirement well enough.

In Palmar Sur, Mr. Newell met us as we walked sadly up the walk. "I'm sorry, Frank. I thought sure you'd make it. Come on in and make yourselves at home."

That night we didn't stay in the guesthouse—the Newells invited us to stay with them, and did everything they could to ease the sting. I still couldn't accept the thought of a flatcar, but orders had come from the head office that under no circumstances could we continue on the ties. With the jeep full of holes, she would sink in a minute even if we could get her back to the sea. We had but two alternatives—leave her where she was or build a ramp and take her to Corredores by rail. I asked Mr. Newell to make arrangements for a flatcar.

The next day, Easter Sunday, we rode with Mr. Newell in a rail auto to where the jeep sat. The efficient United Fruit Company railroad had already built a ramp of old ties, and a flatcar was waiting. But poor tired Tortuga just couldn't make it up the steep incline without help. With the whole crew pushing, she finally groaned onto the car and was lashed securely in place with her own broken winch cable.

The train that hooked on to the flatcar later that day took us only a few miles, to Coto Junction, where we spent the night. Of all the places we camped on the whole trip I think the most depressing was on that flatcar. Another train picked us up the next morning and carried us to Corredores. I adjusted the clutch and broke out our supply of tire-repair material. Avoiding the use of the noisy second gear, we headed for Volcán, Panama.

The mountain trail over which we drove had been bull-dozed and forgotten by the Army engineers during World

War II. Maintained in places by a colony of Italian immigrants, nothing more than a narrow dirt path in others, the trail clawed along the sides of the mountains, dropped into dense forested valleys and over unbridged streams. Less than seventy-five miles from Corrédores to Volcán, it took two days to get there. It was another two days over the part-gravel, part-concrete Pan American Highway to Panama City.

Chapter Five

BARELY in the Canal Zone, we were just beginning to enjoy the feel of smooth concrete beneath the wheels when we heard the wail of a siren, and a big unsmiling Zone cop pulled us over to the curb.

"Ah, civilization," Helen commented. "I wonder who they think we're hiding this time?"

The policeman parked his motorcycle ahead of La Tortuga, walked over, and leaned against the door. His stern look changed to a sheepish grin. "That was a mean trick," he said, "but when I saw this thing going by I just had to get a good look at it."

Helen and I both let out a whoosh of breath. "Look all you want, Officer." He asked a few questions, and then I asked one. "Do you know where we can get a good hamburger and a chocolate malt?" We had been looking forward to that bit of Americana for a long time.

With that welcome to the Septic Strip and a warning that Dinah really should be in quarantine, we continued over the bridge across the Panama Canal to Panama City, about the quickest transformation it is possible to make from the United States to Latin America. At the Ford agency we unloaded La Tortuga, and with the back of a taxi crammed with her contents we went to the hotel recommended by Señor Ramos in San José. It might have been a fine hotel when it was built fifty years ago, but since that time nothing obvious had been done in the way of maintenance or cleaning. But it did fit our pocketbook, an important factor since it had taken quite a beating from the flatcar charges and would be even flatter before the jeep was in condition again.

At the desk a buxom woman, whose reddish hair was uniformly gray halfway from the roots, looked apprehensively at Dinah, then in all directions about the lobby, under tables, and behind the wastebasket. There was nothing big enough for her to hide behind, so I reassured her:

"Don't worry about our dog. She's as gentle as a puppy."

"It's not your dog I'm worried about. It's my cat."

"We always keep Dinah on a leash. We won't let her hurt your cat."

"But you don't understand. I'm afraid my cat will hurt your dog."

I could not imagine even the most anti-dog cat going out of its way to attack one-hundred-pound Dinah, but we found out that this was no ordinary cat. The next day as we were taking Dinah for a walk we saw it—a battle-scarred, gray-striped tom with ragged ears and a super superiority complex. He clearly believed that he was a direct descendant of Leo the Lion. Lying on the hotel desk, he surveyed his domain with an expression that defied man or beast to usurp his place. Even Dinah was impressed and backed away. But that was not enough. Carefully the cat stretched, flexed his muscles, and unsheathed his claws, all with premeditated and leisurely assurance. With a yowl that would make a Zulu cringe, he leaped. The three of us stood frozen. The quick-thinking manager made an off-the-fence, one-handed catch and grabbed him by the tail. For the balance of our stay there we took no chances. Helen scouted ahead to make sure that the cat was not around, then Dinah and I sneaked out.

Our room was a long narrow cell on the third floor, and from the balcony window—we always asked for a balcony room so Dinah could sun herself while we saw the town on foot—was a view of the old cathedral. Near the waterfront on a point of land jutting into the bay, the hotel was in one of the oldest sections of Panama, an area of odd-shaped blocks with wooden and tin-fronted buildings. Overhanging balconies seemed to provide the residents of the town with their main source of recreation, watching the activities of the street. A few blocks from the hotel was the palace of the President of Panama, a white stone building where tame egrets strutted around a fountain in the mother-of-pearl mosaic foyer. Crossroads of the world with the Panama Canal, the city had an international air: shops with names like Sun of India, Bazar Hindustani, Tahiti, and French Bazaar lined the main Avenida Central, displaying luxuries from almost any country one can name. One thing, however, was the same as in all Latin-American streets, the snail's pace of the pedestrians.

When we called at the USIS office in Panama City we found that Mr. Casler and Mr. Rambo were expecting us. Mr. Hunsaker had written to them from San José. They asked what our plans were from Panama. On a large wall map I traced our proposed route. Between Panama and Colombia there is nothing but mountains and the impenetrable Darien jungle. Someday the Pan American Highway will run through there, but at that time not even a survey had been made. As in Costa Rica, we planned to bypass this last break in the highway by sea.

"So far," I said, "this is still only a theory and, as I learned

126

in Costa Rica, my theories don't work out too well. In the Pacific the eighteen-foot tide and the heavy surf caused most of our difficulty. That's the main reason we have chosen the Caribbean with its foot-and-a-half tide to reach Colombia. Also it is the shortest route, some two hundred and fifty nautical miles. At Turbo, Colombia, there is a connecting road to the Pan American Highway. This time we plan to see the coast line first by plane. If there are protected coves not more than twenty miles apart, with luck we should be able to make it."

Mr. Casler shook his head. "That part of the Caribbean is some of the worst water in the world. It's thick with coral reefs, the San Blas Indians are reputed to prohibit white men from spending a night on their islands, and storms come without warning. How about your jeep? How seaworthy is it?"

"Well, right now it's not seaworthy at all, after the beating it took on the railroad. But I can make it seaworthy again. I'm looking for a place where I can work on it. I have my own tools, and what spare parts I don't have are standard jeep parts. I can get them at the Willys agency."

"Let me call a friend of mine," Mr. Casler said. "He might be able to help." He lifted the phone and asked for Albrook Air Force Base, public relations officer. "I have a couple of people in my office who are traveling the Pan American Highway the hard way—in an amphibious jeep. They are planning to take to the Caribbean in it to get to Colombia."

I could hear the "You're kidding" across the room.

"No, it's the truth, but their jeep took an awful beating in Costa Rica. They have all their own stuff to do the job, but they need someplace to work on it. How about sticking them away in some corner of the vehicle maintenance shop on the base? Fine, let me know when you've found out."

Mr. Casler put down the phone. "He's going to call me back." Continuing, he said, "One of our jobs here is to disseminate information on Latin-American affairs, and the Pan American Highway could use a little publicity. Would you mind giving an interview to the English-language press?"

Later that day we learned that permission had been granted to work on La Tortuga at the Air Force base, the first of many wonderful things that the armed forces did for us during our stay in Panama.

The next day held several surprises. The first occurred in the afternoon when we were trying to sneak Dinah into the hotel past the sleeping cat. Waiting in the lobby was an old friend.

"I almost dropped the paper when I picked it up this morning and saw you two staring from the front page. How about moving in with me while you're in Panama?"

It was Lee Slick, with whom I had worked in Alaska. An electrical engineer, a bachelor, and a jolly fellow with a keen sense of humor, he was now working for the Panama Canal Company. We thanked him for his generous offer, but declined.

"We'll be in Panama for quite a while," I said, "and two extra people and a dog would be more than a crowd in a small apartment."

"That's all right," Lee grinned, "I like dogs. I'll be down to move you in at six o'clock Monday morning."

And that was that.

The second surprise came when we went up to our room. I saw a torn scrap of paper lying on the floor in the dark

128

hall. I don't even know why I picked it up. On it was scrawled, "snider admerl 5 auto," and a telephone number. The Negro maid was nearby, and I asked her if she knew anything about it.

"Wha, yes suh," she said in her lilting Jamaican English. "Ah left thot note fo ya. Ah'm the ony one what speaks English heah, so Ah tuk tha message."

"Thank you, but who was it?" I inquired.

"Oh, Ah don know, suh, but it wuz a 'mercan gennul-man."

When I called the number, I heard, "Commandant's office. Captain Green speaking."

I was sure there was some mistake, but I gave my name and said that I had received a note with that telephone number.

"Oh yes, Mr. Schreider, I'm glad you called. I have been trying to reach you all day. The commandant has invited you and Mrs. Schreider to a little party this afternoon. If you can make it, a car will pick you up at 5:00 P.M."

It was four-thirty then. The helpful maid dug up an ancient iron, and, using a wobbly round table for an ironing board, Helen frantically pressed her one party dress and my wrinkled suit. We were ready when a gray Pontiac with the two stars of a rear admiral stopped in front of the hotel. My shirt already sticking to my back, fresh collar wilting, my suit feeling like a fur parka in the 95 per cent relative humidity, I was uncomfortably set for a very formal evening. I was in for a surprise.

As the car pulled into the circle drive of a royal-palm-ringed home in the Canal Zone, the sound of marimbas came from the open windows. At the door we were met by a tanned, vigorous Naval officer wearing white trousers and a white short-sleeved sport shirt with shoulder bars.

"You must be Helen and Frank," he smiled. "I'm Admiral Miles. Come in and take off that coat. We don't stand on formality here."

That was our introduction to Rear Admiral Milton E. Miles, Commandant of the 15th Naval District, Canal Zone, Republic of Panama, an officer and a gentleman by much more than an act of Congress. We were led into a spacious living room, where a cocktail party was in progress in honor of the officers of a Colombian destroyer. On the veranda the ship's band was playing, flanked by the yellow, blue, and red Colombian flag, Old Glory, and another flag which I looked at twice before I believed it—a navy-blue, long, triangular pennant with three question marks, three exclamation points, and three asterisks, ???!!!***. At a convenient moment I asked Admiral Miles about it, but his eyes just twinkled, and all he would say was, "Oh, that's my what-the-hell pennant."

At seven o'clock the party broke up, but the admiral's aide asked us to stay. It was a starry night, and the fragrance of cape jasmine filled the air. While the other guests were departing, we looked at reminders of the admiral's China tours of duty: subtle Chinese scrolls, tiny jade wine cups, ivory and crystal figures, and some signed netsukes. On the desk in the study was a miniature of a lovely lady, Mrs. Miles, who at the time was touring South America. After everyone had gone, Admiral Miles brought out a thick bundle of hydrographic charts.

"I read in the paper this morning that you plan to navigate an amphibious jeep through the Caribbean to Colombia. I feel it is my duty to warn you that this is a very

dangerous and unpredictable stretch of water." He spread
the charts on the floor and pointed out the hazards. From
the book of Sailing Directions he read to us of the winds,
currents, and stormy seasons. "After seeing these charts
what do you think?"

"Well," I admitted, "it doesn't look very encouraging."

"I suggest that you think about it tonight. Would you
care to go to church with me at the Navy chapel tomorrow
morning?"

After Sunday services the next morning Admiral Miles invited us to his home, where he again brought out the charts.
"What have you decided?"

"Helen and I talked about it until late last night. We can't
turn back now. We have to give it a try."

He was very serious. "Officially I must advise you against
this. But if you are determined to do it, I can't stop you."
He smiled. "And so we want to help you all we can. Now
let's go over these charts again."

In the weeks that followed, while Helen caught up on
long-overdue letters, I worked every day on the jeep. Its condition was even worse than I had imagined. In addition to

new shock absorbers and three tires and tubes I installed a new clutch and three new rubber seals in the bottom of the hull. I overhauled the winch, transmission, carburetor and generator, and ground the valves. It took a welder a full day to repair the holes in the battered hull. For added security I bought and installed a 15-horsepower outboard motor for emergency power in case of failure of the main engine. The overhang, which had bothered me when we built the cab, provided a perfect mount for the outboard motor. By cutting a hole in the bottom of the overhang and inserting the stem of the motor through it, we had access to all controls from inside the jeep. With a piece of old inner tube I sealed around the motor stem so that water could not enter.

At the end of three weeks La Tortuga was ready for her post-overhaul shakedown, and Admiral Miles was on hand to witness it. As we tested her in a bay near the entrance to the Canal, we were enthusiastic about her lively performance. Unloaded, she had almost a foot of freeboard, though admittedly her stern still drooped. We circled the bay and returned to the beach. Though I knew the admiral was a man of few words, I thought he would make at least some comment. Instead he just shook his head and walked away.

We had arrived in the Canal Zone via the Pan American Highway along the Pacific side, and would leave via the Caribbean. This presented no problem since there is a fine concrete road across the Isthmus, some fifty miles. But it was suggested that since La Tortuga had been through everything else she really should go through the Canal too. We thought it was a fine idea. Accordingly, Captain Green put in a call to his friend, Captain Abe Lincoln, the Balboa port captain.

"Hello, Abe," he said. "I've got a jeep here that wants

to go through the Canal." . . . "No, I'm not pulling your leg." . . . "Okay, I'll send them right over."

Captain Green turned to us. "Captain Lincoln said that he wants to see any jeep that can go through the Canal. So go over and introduce him to La Tortuga."

Captain Lincoln, a stocky, genial Naval officer wearing a civilian white linen suit, was waiting for us when we drove into the parking lot of the port captain's office. After one look at La Tortuga he laughed. "When do you want to make the transit?"

Although we wanted to make a complete transit of the Panama Canal from the Pacific to the Caribbean, there were two factors which made this impossible in the opinion of the Canal authorities. One was the low speed of La Tortuga, which would tie up traffic. The other was the terrific turbulence that results when water floods the locks to raise ships from sea level on the Pacific side to the eighty-five-foot elevation of Gatun Lake, near the Caribbean, the highest part of the Canal. However, in going from Gatun Lake toward the Pacific there was no such turbulence. Consequently it was decided that we would make only a partial transit, and in the opposite direction from which we were heading.

But it was all in fun and, tongue in cheek, the Canal authorities gave us the full treatment. Like a regular ship, La Tortuga was admeasured for her Panama Canal tonnage certificate and charged at the official rate of seventy-two cents per ton. After paying her tolls of $1.44 we received our ship's papers and were introduced to our Canal pilot, Captain R. G. Rennie. Old-timers jested that this was the first time any ship was admeasured on dry land and then drove to the port captain's office to pick up her pilot. Before we were permitted to continue, however, since our craft was not quite up to standard, we were required to sign a release from indemnity. It solemnly declared La Tortuga's more obvious deficiencies: there were projections on the sides, there was no Plimsoll mark, chocks and bits were inadequate, vessel was probably overloaded and had excessive drag (the understatement of the year), and the first mate had no Coast Guard certificate.

With Captain Rennie we drove to a steep bank near the entrance to the Gaillard Cut, where we slid into the water of the Canal. At 2:38 P.M., on May 11, 1955, with her flag flying, the M.S. *La Tortuga* steamed into the Pedro Miguel Locks, dwarfed by the tanker *Cristobal*. For lack of a bridge Captain Rennie sat on top.

Since this was a historic crossing—the first commercial transit of an amphibious jeep—the Canal authorities had declared open house, and children were let out of school to witness the performance. For us $1.44 was a cheap price to pay for the experience of going through a project that cost almost 400 million dollars. We had already learned one thing in searching for a place to enter and leave the Canal. Contrary to our belief, it did not run east and west, but ran closer to north and south.

Just before the end of the locks Captain Rennie gave the command, "Back full," and we stopped at the huge chain and waited while the four-hundred-ton gates swung shut, and enough water to supply a city the size of Boston for one day roared out by gravity through eighteen-foot culverts. Feeling like a minnow in the ocean, we dropped with the water thirty-one feet in less than ten minutes to the level of Miraflores Lake. The heavy gates swung open, the chain clanked down, and the jeep chugged into the lake and around to the landing of the Pedro Miguel Boat Club. There Brigadier General J. S. Seybold, Governor of the Canal Zone, headed a welcoming committee. There was considerable merriment when Governor Seybold, after taking a look at the size of La Tortuga, said that we must have been overcharged, and offered to refund our tolls. Later that day we were made honorary members of two yacht clubs. But the thing that caused endless jokes was our Wrong-Way Corrigan act in going toward the Pacific. "If they don't even know which way the Caribbean is, how do they hope to navigate two hundred and fifty miles of it?"

The last part of that comment, the reference to navigating the Caribbean, was something that Helen and I were thinking about in a more serious vein. Still shaken by the experience in Costa Rica, we knew that charts alone provided no indication of actual conditions. An aerial survey seemed the only answer. In a low-flying airplane we checked the coast line, marking on the charts what appeared to be possible places to go ashore for the night or in case of a storm. Jagged rocks and cliffs broke the dense jungle that grew to the sea, but worse was the barrier of ugly brown coral reef that lined the shore. The water, emerald green, speckled with silver, mottled with reef, and snowy with foam, was dotted for a hundred miles with the islands of the San Blas Indians. The plane swooped low over several of the islands, and there was a pandemonium of activity as the Indians ran from their thatched huts, their red headdresses like bright confetti on the white sand.

From the flight it was obvious that we could count on no beach driving. The entire operation would have to be by sea, but, as bad as the coast line was, there appeared to be places where we could thread our way through the reefs to get to shore. In order to reduce our draft as much as possible we shipped home everything we could do without, extra clothes, portable radio and, sadly, most of our library. And everything we would not need for the next three weeks, including our two suitcases, we sent ahead to Bogotá, Colombia. Costa Rica had shown that our gas consumption at sea was greater than I had anticipated, but despite this, because of the great need to reduce our load, we decided not to carry any extra fuel in addition to the regular forty-six gallons and the six gallons in the outboard motor tank. For the rest of the estimated hundred gallons that we would need, we would have to rely on the small boats that plied the coast to trade with the Indians.

After five weeks in the Canal Zone we were ready to leave. Lee Slick, our host, true gentleman that he is, said he was sorry to see us go. Our last Sunday we again attended church services in the base chapel, where Chaplain Cyril Best gave us a copy of the small Armed Forces Prayer Book. The chaplain, in his usual quiet way, smiled and said, "I've marked the Navy hymn. There might come a time when you would like to refer to it."

Before we left, Admiral Miles requested that we give a copy of our day-by-day itinerary to Captain Thorn, commanding officer of Coco Solo Naval Air Station, near Colón, on the Caribbean side of the Isthmus. "Since this next part of your journey is to be entirely by sea," the admiral said, "we want to know where you plan to be at all times. The communications officer here will loan you a small two-way radio. In case of emergency or change of plans you can communicate with the practice patrol flights in the area. You can return the radio to the Naval mission when you reach Bogotá, Colombia."

At Coco Solo we went over our route with Commander

Beebe, who was in charge in Captain Thorn's absence. With the pilots we were checked out on the radio, a handie-talkie with a range of about six miles. The Navy's identification was, appropriately, "Angel," while we answered to "Turtle."

On Wednesday morning, May 18, the M.S. *La Tortuga* was ready for what we conservatively believed to be a three-week journey. She was provisioned with a month's supply of Army C rations, a case of canned dog food for Dinah and, as peace offering to the Indians, a good supply of soap and cigarettes. Before she set sail there was a steady stream of Navy personnel to inspect her. Along with more dire predictions, there were warnings about the *chocosanos* that were due at any time. Everyone wished us well, and there were even one or two who thought we might make it. One of the last visitors was Commander Bookhammer, who pressed into Helen's hand a small square box. With a wink and a big grin he said, "Every ship should have an extra compass."

At María Chiquita, the end of a dirt road ten miles northeast of Colón, Admiral Miles and several of his officers and their families waved from the shore as we drove into the Caribbean and kept going.

Chapter Six

THE sea was a gray undulating sheet under the overcast sky. There was a light wind, and the jeep rolled with the ground swells. It was several minutes before I got the feel of the controls again. I felt the same thrill, almost of wonderment, at the thought that a half hour before La Tortuga was weaving in and out of traffic, and now she was waterborne. Except for two things there was really little difference between her and the big ships we saw far out to sea heading for the Canal. She was a little smaller, somewhat slower, and she was not following any shipping lanes. The waters we were navigating were given a wide berth by all but a few small boats that traded with the natives along the coast, and even they kept well out from the shore. Although the tide was negligible and the surf of no consequence in most places, the water ahead was a maze of reefs that could tear the bottom from La Tortuga. But in spite of this we skirted the coast line as closely as possible, ready to head for shore at the first sign of a storm, constantly alert for any change in the color of water or the froth of foam that might indicate the presence of shoals. Not trusting the charts, absurdly cautious with the memory of Costa Rica still fresh, we steered a circuitous course around anything that broke the monotonous gray color of the ocean, even to going several miles out of our way to avoid what turned out to be merely floating vegetable debris.

While the motor ticked off a reassuring even drone, Helen sat on top marking the points and promontories on the chart. Eight nautical miles away lay our first stop, Portobelo, a forgotten town that was once the most important commercial center on the Atlantic coast. At the wheel I wondered how Columbus felt more than four hundred and fifty years earlier when he had cruised along this same coast line, studying the same frothing sea against the same rocks and the same dark green wall of jungle. On his fourth voyage to the New World, still searching for a non-existent strait to the Indies, his four battered caravels had taken refuge in the harbor for which we were headed. Without charts he must have stumbled on it by accident—even knowing where it was, we had trouble finding it.

It was Columbus, in 1502, who had named Portobelo, Portuguese for beautiful port. Later, when gold and silver started flowing from the mines of the Incas to the Spanish galleons, and then to the coffers of King Philip II of Spain, Portobelo became the terminus of the narrow trail across the Isthmus over which burros and slaves transshipped the treasures of the Pacific to the Atlantic. Once each year Portobelo had roused itself from its tropical lethargy, merchants set up shop in the alleys, and cocoa, jewels, and wool from Peru were bartered for rice, corn, hogs, and cattle from Cartagena, which in turn were exchanged for goods from Spain, and the galleons left for Europe loaded with as much as 100 million dollars in treasure.

It was difficult to imagine the harbor filled with galleons as La Tortuga churned the shallow muddy bottom looking for a place to get to shore. On either side ruins of old stone forts commanded the entrance, forts which the Spanish had thought were impregnable until pirates Parker and Morgan came along. Jutting into the bay was a crude wooden dock where some two dozen Negroes pointed in awe as we circled and pulled alongside. Helen jumped from the jeep to the dock and asked if there was a canoe landing. A young boy, his black naked body shiny from the gently falling rain, loped excitedly a few hundred feet to where a shingle slope

ran up onshore. There were exclamations as La Tortuga surged from the sea and bumped over the stone walk, the first vehicle to enter Portobelo.

With two or three hundred inhabitants, practically the whole population, hooting and skipping behind us as if we were the Pied Piper, we drove among tumbled ruins, over stone bridges, and under stone arches to the remains of the King's Treasury, nothing but a few columns supporting the sky.

In its heyday Portobelo had had four sections, Triana,

Merced, Guinea, and the Shambles. Now the whole village was a shambles. The jungle had reclaimed everything: the growth was as luxuriant inside the walls as in the encroaching forest behind them. Attacked by pirates and plague, rendered valueless when the Incan treasures dwindled, what was left of the town became the heritage of the slaves who built it, the ancestors of the people who followed us. The alcalde, chief of the town, a slender graying Negro in white shirt and pants, welcomed us with a smile, and offered us food and a place to sleep. Thanking him, we asked to spend the night among the ruins of Fort Geronimo, at one end of the village. Except for what was left of three forts, the Treasury, and a church, Portobelo was a tin-roofed, wooden-fronted jumble of dilapidated hovels. The old gold trail was overgrown, but still visible. The walled slave mart was now the cemetery, and in the crumbling niches of the fort rusted cannon lay where they had fallen when fire destroyed their wooden mounts. When we parked the jeep by a watchtower in a corner of the old fort that overlooked the town, a vulture flapped into a nearby palm tree. With its wrinkled neck and bald head it looked as if it might have been there when William Parker had burned and sacked Portobelo in 1601. Dropping back to the buttress, the vulture looked on greedily while we prepared lunch. Its predecessors had feasted well when Henry Morgan had taken the town in 1668, killing and torturing almost all the inhabitants. It was an unhealthy place then—those the pirates left the fever got until the whole coast became known as the Graveyard of Spaniards. And of at least one famous Englishman. At the bottom of the serene bay lay a leaden casket with the remains of Sir Francis Drake, who had died of dysentery while on a raiding expedition.

In the one remaining church the alcalde showed us the image that is reputed to have saved the town from a pestilence that ravaged the entire coast. In a glass case stood the Black Christ. Carved from dark brown wood, it was a life-size figure with sorrowful eyes turned skyward and forehead bloody under a crown of thorns. Though there are several stories as to the origin of the image, this is the one related to us by the alcalde:

"In 1658 a ship carrying the Black Christ—a gift from Spain to a church in Cartagena—put in at Portobelo for water and supplies. Each time it tried to leave the harbor it was turned back by storms. After five attempts the captain ordered the statue thrown overboard believing that it preferred to stay in Portobelo. The people of the town rescued it and placed it here. Shortly thereafter a cholera epidemic devastated the coast; only Portobelo was spared."

The next morning, after going over the chart with a fisherman, we headed for Isla Grande, eleven miles away. (All distances in this stretch are in nautical miles.) The water was like a sheet of glass, a mirror reflecting the rocky coast and the broken overcast of the sky. In trying the outboard motor we found its gasoline consumption disappointing. With a top speed of only two knots it consumed over three gallons of fuel an hour as compared to the regular engine's five knots with the same consumption. Nevertheless, it was comforting to have, and it would serve for the purpose intended, that of emergency power.

At about half throttle we cruised at three knots, Helen at the wheel, and Dinah asleep on the bunk, while I sat on the bow watching for shallows and rocks. Several miles out the sea broke hoary white over Salmedina Reef, and to our right waves lashed the jagged coast. Ahead the sky was blue,

142

but behind us the horizon was grayed by a dark mass of clouds. Three hours after leaving Portobelo we sighted Isla Grande, a small hilly island with palms lining the silver sand spit of its eastern end. Progressively the water changed color from a Prussian blue to a deep green, and closer to shore it was emerald broken by splotches of mottled brown coral. Grateful there were no breakers, we cut the throttle and drifted in with just enough power to maintain steerageway. From the cab I couldn't see the reefs below, so Helen stood on the bow and directed me. Without experience in judging the depth of the transparent water, we had a few frightening moments when the wheels bumped and the jeep tilted on the high points of coral. Then near the white sand I engaged the gears and stepped on the gas. With the front wheels at the water's edge we bogged down, but deflating the tires gave us sufficient traction to climb onto our first island camp.

The beach had been deserted when we approached, but by the time we were on solid ground it was swarming with excited children, their eyes and white teeth like beacons in their smiling black faces. Little girls filled Helen's arms with fragrant bundles of tropical flowers, ginger, hibiscus, frangi-pangi, and flor de india. Little boys twirled coconuts by their stems and offered them to me. Following the children came the adults and the alcalde of the island, another smiling friendly Negro who bid us welcome. More than caring where we had come from, they were just fascinated by our being there. They inspected the jeep from every angle, but soon the little boys lost interest in La Tortuga when they discovered that Dinah was an eager retriever of coconut husks. We've always doubted her pedigree—although it says German shepherd, I'm sure there must be a little water spaniel mixed in there somewhere.

By the time the formalities were over it was three o'clock. Hungry when we arrived two hours before, by that time we were starved. The simple statement that Helen would like to bathe was enough to clear the beach, and after a refreshing swim in the crystal-clear water near the shore we set up camp under a low-hanging palm tree. Washing down the C rations with coconut milk, we sat on the sand and looked in the direction from which we had come. The air was still, the sea calm, but there was a purple hue in the sky.

The rest of that afternoon we received a steady stream of visitors as the children returned with more flowers until La Tortuga was so bedecked she *could* have qualified for the Tournament of Roses as the service station attendant in Pasadena had thought. Returning from their small farms on the mainland a mile or so across the channel, men came to inspect the jeep, bringing us calabashes filled with mangoes, pineapples, bananas, and avocados. At their invitation we went to the village a half mile away. Led by a flock of children, we followed along a winding path through tall coconut palms, vine-covered trees, ferns, and large-leafed plants. At the village beach *cayucas*, or wooden dugout canoes, were pulled up on the sand, some filled with fruit, coconuts, fish, or lobsters. Built on stilts, the houses were of palm frond and cane, with bamboo ladders leading to the doorless entries. Underneath the huts were tied giant sea turtles, three feet across, while nearby were the shells of those that had gone before.

Back at camp we had a supper of avocados, limes, and coconuts. Alone for the first time, we watched the sun set through a fan of palms. Feeling we had stumbled on a paradise, we weren't anxious to leave, but with the *chocosanos* expected within a month, I set the alarm for an early depar-

144

LEFT—Helicopter view of La Tortuga en route from Panama to Colombia. (United States Navy photo)

ABOVE—Aerial view of our camp on the sandspit of Isla Grande in the Caribbean. (United States Navy photo) BELOW—Helen "keeps house" on Isla Grande.

ABOVE—The islanders enjoy salt water soap too. Isla Grande. BELOW—Helen and friends on Isla Grande.

ABOVE—Children scatter as La Tortuga comes ashore at Playa Chiquita, Panama, never having seen an automobile before. BELOW—La Tortuga at sea among the islands of the San Blas Indians off the coast of Panama. Picture taken from Padre Kolb's boat.

LEFT—Helen and Frank make a friendship pact with San Blas chieftain Ikwaniktipippi on the island of Ailigandi. BELOW—Interior of San Blas Indian hut on Ailigandi.

ABOVE—Aerial view of La Tortuga surrounded by San Blas Indians on the island of Ustuppo. (United States Navy photo) BELOW—Squeezing sugar cane on Ustuppo.

ABOVE—River scene on the mainland of Panama where San Blas Indian women get fresh water, wash their clothes, and bathe. BELOW—San Blas child takes good care of her little brother.

ABOVE—Helen tries on San Blas
finery. RIGHT—San Blas woman
makes a new blouse while her pet
marmoset sleeps in her hair.

ABOVE—Customs formalities at Turbo, Colombia. BELOW—Campsite in parklike Colombia near the Colombian-Ecuadorian frontier.

In Colombia, Helen does the wash while Frank brings the log up to date inside La Tortuga.

ABOVE — Snow-peaked Cayambe straddles the equator in Ecuador. LEFT—Contrast in Quito. BELOW — Ecuadorian Indian woman tends her flock at the base of Mount Illiniza, south of Quito.

LEFT—Wild llamas give us a disdainful stare on the *altiplanos* of Peru. BELOW—Child of the Peruvian *altiplanos* sits near a South American-style cache and temporary shelter.

TOP—Child of Pisac, Peru, near Cuzco. BOTTOM—Lima, Peru. **C stands**
for cat.

TOP — Indian chieftain in Pisac shows Helen his silver-tipped staff of office. CENTER—Peruvian Indians inspecting us in town of Pisac. LEFT—This twelve-cornered stone hewn by Incan stonemasons in Cuzco, Peru, stands undisturbed after centuries.

Indian of Pisac, Peru, near Cuzco.

Old man of the Peruvian Andes.

LEFT — The Spanish Church of Santo Domingo in Cuzco, Peru, was destroyed by earthquake, but the Incan Temple of the Sun on which the church was built was unharmed.

ABOVE—The Incan fortress of Sacsahuamán on the plateau above the city of Cuzco, Peru. RIGHT—Dining-car service on the train to Machu Picchu, Peru.

ture. As in Costa Rica, we had been advised to travel only during the morning hours.

Between scratching sand flea bites—there was a thorn on the rose—and listening to the thunder and the wail of the wind, we didn't sleep too well that night. Early the next morning we looked through the window screens to see the same children peering from the undergrowth. As soon as they saw we were awake they came running to the jeep, their arms again filled with flowers. While I was checking over La Tortuga, the alcalde came carrying two green bamboo poles about fifteen feet long. He had heard me ask one of the young men if there was any bamboo around big enough to be used for poling over reefs and for determining the depth of the water. He had gone to the mainland that morning and cut them for us. We were to find those poles the most valuable navigational instruments we had.

"I know you planned to leave this morning," he said, "but until the change in the moon the sea will be rough."

"When will that be?" I asked.

The alcalde shrugged. "Perhaps two days."

The sky was still threatening toward Colón, but ahead it was clear so we decided to go on. Waving good-by, we poled over the hedge of reef and headed into mid-channel between the island and the mainland. Nearing the end of the island, some two miles from the sand spit where we had camped, the jeep began to plunge its bow into the waves. With the sea covering the winch and steaming from the muffler, I closed all the hatches and started the bilge pump. Thinking it was just a rough turbulent area, we continued. We were heading for a rocky point about a mile away where the waves leaped high in the air like a reverse cataract. But beyond that point we would be in the lee of the mainland for a time, and if the weather didn't clear we planned to take shelter in a cove on the other side. Once we were clear of the lee of Isla Grande, however, the wind swept unimpeded from the sea and the waves smashed against the port bow of the jeep, covering the windshield. La Tortuga was rolling heavily, and I headed her slightly into the wind, counting on tacking around the point. But the wind was too strong for her low power and square lines, and I quickly learned she had still another limitation. That was the first time it had been necessary to run the jeep at full throttle with all the hatches closed. The temperature gauge was climbing to the danger point. I knew we would never clear the point before the engine boiled.

It was blowing harder all the time. Though I knew we couldn't go on I hesitated to turn around. Broadside to the waves, the jeep heeled over in the troughs, yawed frighteningly, and then, with the wind pushing against her flat square stern, she fairly flew back to the island. We were barely ashore when the whole village flocked to us again. The alcalde warned against starting out when Hellsgate, the point we had been heading for, was frothing. That was the last time I ignored the advice of the natives. When a practice patrol flight flew over that afternoon, I warmed up the radio.

"Hello, Angel, this is Turtle. We've had a change of plans. We're staying put on Isla Grande until the local weather prophets say it's okay to leave."

Not too disturbed at the prospect of spending another day or two on our island paradise, we set up a more permanent camp in preparation for the storm the alcalde said would accompany the change of the moon. Among the odd assortment of gear which we had accumulated was a large nylon tarpaulin, blue on one side and yellow on the other. A couple of pieces of driftwood for support turned the tarp into a fine shelter from the sun and an excellent rain catcher for drinking water. With the emerald sea lapping against the white sand beach not far from our feet we settled back in our "lanai" to wait, rather looking forward to the life of beachcombers.

Like everyone else who had read *Robinson Crusoe* or *Swiss Family Robinson*, I had had romantic dreams of being on a tropical island, and Isla Grande was as perfect a spot as one could ask for. With our paratrooper stove set in a windbreak of sand, a bleached log to sit on, and a pile of coconuts to quench our thirst, we relaxed in the shade of the tarp, overwhelmed by a feeling of laziness. Except for the quick measured movements of sandpipers, the jetlike plunge of pelicans after fish, and the darting of crabs the whole atmosphere was one of indolence. The *cayucas* moved slowly over the waves, propelled with ease by black muscular arms; the beat of drums from the village across the channel had an unhurried quality; and it was even difficult to breathe rapidly when the sea took such long regular breaths. With a couple of books to read, a palm-edged beach to stroll, crystal water to swim in, and plenty of food we lived an idyllic existence for a few days.

Sometimes we visited the village, but mostly the village visited us. From early morning our camp became a mecca for all the children. Life on a desert island that was not deserted had its complications—it became necessary to set the alarm to go off before dawn. Then, back in the jeep, we dozed until we heard the conch shell blowing, a long mournful sound like the bleating of a calf, notifying the islanders that a turtle had been caught in the traps offshore. But no matter how early that was, the children were waiting for us to stir.

Always polite and considerate, they never came from the bushes until we climbed from the jeep, but from that moment they were with us until sunset.

While everyone in the village paid a visit to our camp sometime during the day there was one group of children who were our constant companions. With no prompting by us two little girls took it upon themselves to keep us supplied with flowers, clean the jeep, and help Helen when she washed clothes. And there were three little boys who followed me about and kept us supplied with coconuts, shinnying like monkeys up the slender palm trunks. The boys, all between five and seven, wore no clothes at all, but the little girls, about the same age, wore simple cotton dresses and tied their kinky hair with bits of white cloth.

While they enjoyed playing with Dinah, or watching us prepare meals and sharing the crackers and jam from our C rations, the big event of the day for the kids was wash time, be it dishes, clothes, or ourselves. The first time they saw us scrubbing in the sea their mouths opened in astonishment. Soap of any kind was scarce, but our special Navy soap that lathered in salt water was nothing short of magical to them. Offered a bar, they passed it around and worked their woolly heads into foam, covering their bodies until they looked like little snowmen. Then, with a froglike leap, they disappeared below the surface of the water, splashed about, and came up all smiles, asking for more. It was fortunate that we had a good supply.

About the only time we had any privacy was during the afternoon rain, when the children ran to the shelter of the village. The seascape became a striped varicolored scarf with the deep gray of the sky, the faint outline of the dark green mainland, the purple horizon of the sea, the white of the

148

waves lashing the reefs, and the emerald near the beach. And when the rain came it was like a waterfall. In fifteen minutes we filled both five-gallon cans, the gallon thermos jug, and all the pots and pans, with enough left over for a luxurious rain water bath and shampoo. Then with a piping-hot cup of coffee we crawled into the jeep to read and enjoy the solitude.

It was for moments like this that we had so carefully selected our library, and now, ironically, most of the books were back in California. But the few we had allotted ourselves, *Lives of Famous French Painters, Story of Philosophy*, the *Iliad*, and *Captain Horatio Hornblower*, provided sufficient diversion for these brief interludes.

Although each day the sky darkened and was filled with thunder and lightning, and the waves rolled into billowy whitecaps, the alcalde told us the real storm was yet to come. One afternoon a fishing boat took refuge in the cove near our camp, and the captain hailed us in English to come aboard. Helen and I swam out to his craft and reached for the ladder. That was when Captain Parker of the *Sea Horse* welcomed us with his gloomy prophecy, which he repeated even more emphatically after a closer inspection of La Tortuga.

"I don't wish you any bad luck, kids," he said, "but you'll never make it. No, sir, I've got ten to one bet you won't make it."

At those odds we should have taken a little of that bet, but after being turned back by Hellsgate we weren't too sure ourselves. Instead we comforted ourselves with the thought that he was just an opinionated old goat who had run his own boat aground on the reefs and prided himself on the fact that in forty years in Panama he hadn't learned a word of Spanish.

After that our island paradise took on a new aspect in spite of the daily encouragement by the alcalde:

"Tomorrow will be better, and when it's calm one can go to sea in the shell of an egg."

But tomorrow was always just as bad. We became restless, our sedentary life as beachcombers grew intolerable, so anxious were we to be under way. With the men of the village and those who stopped to chat we studied the charts, and they warned of the dangers ahead:

"Go out around Punta Manzanilla; don't put in at Cuanga; be careful opposite Escribanos; and circle the reefs near Porvenir."

They told us of their friend who had disappeared among the islands of the San Blas Indians. They cautioned us never to stop on an inhabited island—the opposite of what we had been advised in the Canal Zone. Also that we must never stay on any island more than one night. At the mention of Tiger Island, a possible stopping place, their eyes opened wide and as one they said, "No, no, the Indians of Tiger are very bad."

We had been on Isla Grande almost a week when the long-awaited storm came. The children playing in the sand near the jeep sang out, "*Ya viene, ya viene* [Here it comes, here it comes]," and ran. In a moment a gust of wind ripped the tarp from the poles and the heavy swells from the sea crested with white. The palms bent over, their fronds clacking and glaring in the lightning that cracked from the blackened sky, and thunder rolled like a chorus of bass drums. I resecured the tarp and dropped several large coconuts in the center to hold it down and form a basin for catching the

150

rain that blotted out everything but the small sphere around us, and we climbed dripping into the jeep.

All that day and the next the storm raged with but brief periods of quiet, when the air hung still and heavy with unfulfilled fury. With each new outburst it became more difficult to read, and we found ourselves just sitting in the jeep watching the tumultuous sea. La Tortuga began to shrink until I could see her as the alcalde's eggshell.

On the eve of the seventh day on Isla Grande the alcalde came to us and said that the next day we could travel. That evening, while the sun burst like an orange ball through the purple sky, the villagers came to say good-by, bringing fresh flowers and fruit. Except for cigarettes and soap they had always refused anything in payment. I asked them if there was any favor we could do them. One of the younger men said quietly:

"You are friends here. Perhaps someday one of us will come to your land and you can welcome him as we have you."

At dawn we were up and preparing to leave. The sky was clear from horizon to horizon, the palms were reflected in the still water, and what had for a week been the surging mass of Hellsgate was a tranquil passage around the point. With both sides of the channel spotted with the white of the villagers' clothes we eased over the reefs into deeper water and headed once more for Colombia, 225 miles away.

Our schedule had included a short run that day to Nombre de Dios, another forgotten Spanish town, which had preceded Portobelo as a port for the Spanish galleons, but since the alcalde had predicted fair weather we continued past it toward Playa Chiquita, on the mainland twenty-one miles from Isla Grande, and, according to the villagers, a good place to put in.

La Tortuga was performing beautifully, rolling a bit with the smooth swells, but otherwise very stable. Keeping in mind the instructions of the people on Isla Grande, we steered well away from the coast, watching through binoculars the waves splashing against the rocks. About an hour past the entrance to Nombre de Dios we heard a drone in the sky coming from the direction of Colón. Through the binoculars we could see the dragonfly shape of a helicopter. Helen took the wheel and I got out the handie-talkie and heard:

"Hello, Turtle, this is Angel. Where are you?"

I recognized the voice of Chief Karls, one of the Coco Solo pilots. We must have looked mighty small—even with the bright yellow side of the tarp spread over the top of the jeep he couldn't see us.

"Make a 45 to starboard," I instructed. "We're about a mile off your starboard bow."

The helicopter changed course and headed our way. Directly over us it hovered, the blast from the rotors bringing a mist of sea water into the air. Holding the receiver tightly to my ear, I heard Chief Karls again:

"Stand by for a drop." The side hatch on the copter opened and, like catching fish in a barrel, a paper bag on a string was lowered right into the hatch of La Tortuga. Inside was a copy of *Time* magazine with a story about our Panama Canal transit, and written in the margin was "Good Luck," signed "Mrs. Karls."

Chief Karls's voice chuckled from the receiver. "Look on the back cover."

Turning it over, Helen gurgled—a Cunard steamship-line advertisement read, "Getting there is half the fun!"

We told Chief Karls about our change of plans, signed off, and watched the dragonfly whirl back toward Coco Solo. Those brief contacts with civilization were reassuring even though we knew that in a storm they wouldn't be out, and even if they were La Tortuga would be more difficult to find in a rough sea than the proverbial needle in the haystack.

As the alcalde had predicted, the weather was good all day and we made the twenty-one miles to Playa Chiquita in six hours, an average speed of three and a half knots. As we neared the sheltered cove by the village, a handful of Negroes waved frantically for us to drop anchor. Having been told on Isla Grande that there was a sand bottom, we kept going. When we rolled up on the beach, they scattered and ran, and it was several minutes before they recovered enough to come back and see who we were.

That night another torrential rain fell, and the next morning the sky was dull and gray with a steady drizzle, but what little wind there was was from the land. The villagers said no storm that day so we left early to reach Porvenir, twenty-five miles away. It was a longer run than we had wanted, but we were trying to make up for the time lost on Isla Grande.

Up to that time we had had no difficulty conversing with the Spanish-speaking inhabitants of the coast, but from Porvenir for more than a hundred miles we would be in San Blas Indian territory, where the Indians' own dialect, Cuna, was spoken. From what we had been told in Panama City, we would have to use signs or, if we were lucky, we might find one of the men who had been to the Canal Zone to work and knew a few words of English. With more than four centuries of isolationism the San Blas Indians had acquired a hostile reputation for acts that were natural results of atrocities by the conquistadores in the fifteen hundreds, and the French Huguenots in the seventeen hundreds. The last outbreak came in 1923, when the Indians revolted against the Panamanians for unjust treatment and abuse, and massacred some two hundred officials, as well as their consorts and progeny. After a treaty was signed, the Indians were given the right to self-government with no intrusion beyond Porvenir, the island of the Panamanian administrator. Our route would take us among the more than three hundred islands of the San Blas group.

The rain that had fallen since early morning stopped about noon, and as the wind from the land shifted the long swells turned into short choppy waves that slapped the blunt bow of the jeep and splashed back over the muffler and windshield. With the change in the sea the jeep pitched more violently, rocking and yawing until Dinah, usually content to sleep on the bunk, stuck her nose out the window for some fresh air. Helen scrambled through the medical supplies for Dramamine and we each took a tablet while we were still able to swallow. Although La Tortuga spent a good portion of the time with her bow submerged, when I engaged the power-operated bilge pump little water was ejected from the outlet beside my seat. With each hour we gained more confidence in our amphibious apartment.

After eight hours we were still several miles from Point San Blas, where we would change course for Porvenir. Though we were still pumping periodically and apparently taking on no water, La Tortuga seemed more sluggish than usual, and seemed to be settling deeper in the sea. It was not until water seeped through the floor boards that I real-

154

ized that we were slowly sinking. No wonder that no water had been coming from the bilge outlet. It was clogged. There was no place within miles where we could get through the reefs to shore.

There was too much water in the bilge to locate the leak, but I knew it must be a small one or we would have sunk long before. We were in no immediate danger, but the sea was increasing. I unfastened an inspection plate in the floor board in front of the right seat and inserted the hand bilge pump. For the next two hours Helen and I alternated pumping. When we rounded Point San Blas, there was only a small stream of oily water flowing from the hose of the hand bilge pump.

In keeping with beachcomber tradition, I had not shaved since leaving Coco Solo nine days before, and Helen had been chiding me with the Burma Shave slogan, "If Crusoe'd kept his chin more tidy he might have had a lady Friday." Still a half hour from Porvenir, she started again.

"If you want to keep your lady Friday, you'd better shave. Besides, you want to be presentable when you meet the officials on Porvenir. They could refuse us permission to continue."

I wasn't too concerned about losing my lady Friday—there wasn't anyplace she could go—but the thought of the officials persuaded me. "Okay," I grumbled, "but it will spoil a wonderful passage of time sequence for our movies. Are you sure you understand how to approach the channel to Porvenir? The last time I tried to clean up aboard ship you nearly threw me in the river."

There were two entrances to Porvenir: one, with no reefs, for strangers, and the other, about five miles shorter, for those who knew their way. The latter was a narrow meandering channel lined with coral to the surface on either side. We planned on taking the longer way. We studied the chart together, and Helen assured me that she knew which island to sight on and at which point to turn. Sadly I began scraping away with salt water soap and Dinah's pan full of ocean. I was just half shaved when Helen let out a dismayed wail. "Frank, we're in the wrong channel."

We weren't in the wrong channel. We weren't in any channel at all. We were in the middle of a bed of coral. I climbed out on the bow with the bamboo pole and pushed off, searching for the entrance to the channel. When a short bull-necked native paddled near in a *cayuca*, I hailed him in Spanish:

"Where's the channel to Porvenir?"

He looked at me blankly so I tried it in English, but still no response. I made motions with my hands, but he paddled away, leaving us to figure it out for ourselves. After running up on the coral three times we found a patch of clear water and headed cautiously toward Porvenir, a half mile away. When we reached the deeper water near the dock three uniformed men signaled us to drop anchor, but the beach was clear and I had to get ashore to fix the leak and the bilge pump. Dragging a harvest of seaweed, I steered La Tortuga up onshore to where the three men had increased to a dozen, most of them armed. Leading the group was a short, mustached, swarthy-skinned fellow in a soiled white suit. One look at them and I knew that Helen needn't have been concerned about my being unshaven.

Expecting at least a civil greeting, I introduced myself, told them our destination, and asked permission to spend the night. They acted as if they hadn't heard me. The fellow in the white suit drew himself up to his full five feet three, and with an air as if he were pounding his chest he said, "I am the secretary to the administrator. *I* am in charge here in his absence."

I groaned inwardly. We had had experience enough with petty officials who were given a bit of authority.

"Excuse me, Excellente," I said. "With *your* kind permission we would like to spend the night and continue through the San Blas Islands tomorrow morning."

"There are no accommodations here."

"We aren't expecting any; we have our own." I opened the door of the jeep so he could see the bunks inside. Then I produced a letter of introduction that had been given to us by the Governor of Colón.

"Perhaps this will explain our presence."

Before White Suit could read the letter a uniformed man with a Sam Browne belt and a .45 pistol stepped forward. "You have to have *my* permission too. I am the Captain of the Police."

White Suit finished reading the letter and with a sneer handed it to the captain, who looked at the signature and carelessly stuffed the letter in his pocket. Whereas before they had treated us as intruders, after reading the letter they made us feel like spies, which is probably what they thought we were. Every boat that entered the San Blas territory was required to stop at Porvenir for clearance. Isolated as they were, it was an ideal situation for a bit of collusion.

"You can stay there," White Suit condescended, indicating the far end of the island.

Porvenir was a narrow strip of sand and coral with a half dozen wooden frame buildings and a hundred or so coconut palms. Our host could not have chosen a spot farther away from his activities unless it was in the middle of the palm grove, and then he couldn't have kept an eye on us.

By the time we were situated the sun was low in the sky. The trip from Playa Chiquita had taken ten hours, and except for a few crackers we had eaten nothing all day—we hadn't wanted anything. But with the ground solid beneath our feet once more, our appetites returned, and we fixed a C-ration dinner of canned spaghetti and meat balls. We were still taking Aralen and vitamin tablets, although the latter had cracked from the heat. As we were putting things away we saw black *cayucas* skimming under sails tinted pink by the sun, moving over the green water from the dozens of islands that surround Porvenir.

In a few minutes we were hemmed in by a horde of chattering Indians, their dialect sounding all the stranger in their excitement. I felt I was watching a spinning color wheel as they milled about us. The women touched Helen's clothes and her hair and pointed, giggling, at her red lips and white clown's nose—a triangle of zinc oxide. Helen was just as fascinated by their make-up, a black line carefully drawn down the bridge of their noses. Under their headdresses, a rectangle of red and yellow cloth, their black hair was cropped in long bangs. Heavy gold rings dangled from their noses and rested on their upper lips; four-inch discs of hammered gold hung from their ears. Around their necks were strings of brilliant beads and silver coins, and their arms and ankles were bound with bands of tiny orange and scarlet beads so tightly that the flesh swelled around the edges. Knee-length skirts were wrapped around their waists. With an exquisite color sense they had appliquéd orange, purple, fuchsia, yellow, and blue bits of cloth over backgrounds of scarlet to make primitively symmetrical patterns on their loose blouses.

158

Inside La Tortuga, Dinah growled at the commotion. The jeep was getting its inspection from the men. Looking drab beside their technicolor women, the short thick-necked, barefoot men wore felt hats and nondescript pants. Their saving bit of individuality was their necklaces of barracuda teeth. They kept a good distance from the jeep until Helen took Dinah out, opened the doors wide, and with a gesture invited them to look. Screwing up their courage, they touched the tires, twirled the propeller, and peered inside, clapping their hands gleefully.

About eight that night the end of the island cleared sufficiently so that we could go to bed. The next morning I inspected the hull for the leak, but there appeared to be no holes. The spring hanger bolts were tight, and the rubber seals were intact. I finally located the trouble in the waxed flax packing around the propeller shaft. A few turns of the packing-gland nut fixed the leak, but it took a little longer to remove the wad of Dinah's hair that had clogged the bilge-pump screen. She had been shedding steadily for two months, and despite the daily brushing a good portion of her coat had sifted through the cracks in the floor boards into the bilge. While I had the floor boards open I made a general checkup and greased the fittings on the pump and propeller shaft, and added oil to the transmissions.

While I was working on La Tortuga, the Captain of the Police warmed up a bit. I soon found out why. He wanted American cigarettes. After he had mooched almost a pack, one at a time, I gave him some I had saved for just such a character, a mildewed package from a box of C rations dated 1944.

Our feeling of uneasiness about Porvenir increased. There was an atmosphere of tension as if the island were a prison and the men were just waiting out their sentences. We were anxious to leave, but each time I asked White Suit for clearance he found some reason to stall. It was the same when I requested the return of the governor's letter, which was addressed to whom it may concern, and which we had been instructed to carry with us all along the coast.

White Suit was a nervous Peter Lorreish character who sneaked around the island and in and out of buildings checking up on everyone. But he stayed well away from the jeep—in fact whenever I looked for him he was nowhere around. How anyone could hide on an island that small was a mystery, but he managed to do it. That afternoon I tracked him down and cornered him in his office. Again I asked for the letter.

"It's Saturday," he replied sullenly. "My office is closed. You'll have to wait until Monday."

He left me standing with my mouth open, and Helen and I resigned ourselves to an uncomfortable wait.

The next day a trading boat bound for Colón steered into the channel, and we were able to buy enough gas to fill our tanks. Because of rough seas we had used almost twice as much fuel as I had anticipated; it had taken thirty-six gallons to travel the sixty-five nautical miles from Coco Solo. In the twenty-three hours of actual travel time we had averaged almost three knots.

When the trading boat was cleared with no delay, even though it was Sunday, I knew that White Suit was just being difficult. It was already late afternoon; we had lost two beautiful traveling days. It looked as if he would go on stalling forever, so I tried a bluff. When I threatened to radio Colón, he promised to have everything taken care of the next morning. I was glad that he didn't know that our handie-talkie wouldn't transmit much farther than I could shout.

Monday dawned bright and clear. White Suit came through with the necessary clearance and returned the governor's letter—slightly the worse for wear, crumpled, and with a cigarette burn through it. With no regrets we left Porvenir.

The twenty-seven-mile run to our next stop, the island of Nargana, was all in the protected water between the mainland and a string of islands. After easing through the reefs and around the protruding mast of a sunken ship we relaxed and enjoyed the panorama of tropical beauty we were passing. Since receiving our ship's papers and the Canal transit we had become quite nautical, at least insofar as the M.S. *La Tortuga* was concerned. With Helen on the top deck keeping the log and Dinah asleep on the bunk aft, I was at the helm, sitting on the edge of the top hatch and steering in a rather unorthodox manner for a ship's captain—with my feet.

At our regular three knots we cruised past island after exquisite island, emeralds set in silver sand against a backdrop of turquoise water. Gradually we learned to read the depth of the sea by the color, and where it changed to the ugly brown of reef we steered well around the area. But sometimes, where the coral lay five or six feet below the surface, we cut the throttle and drifted over it, watching the variegated shapes and colors through the clear water, the orange-and-black tiger fish, the waving spines of purple sea urchins, and the rainbow of old shells catching the rays of the sun.

Sharp smacking sounds and silver flashes on the water signaled the presence of tarpon, but either they weren't hungry or they didn't fancy the war-surplus red-feathered spoon

I trolled a couple of hundred feet behind the jeep. Giving up my attempts at fishing, I contented myself with watching the antics of a school of porpoises that cavorted around La Tortuga. Half as long as our dinghy-sized amphibian, they arched through the water, performing the acrobatics effort-

lessly, their shiny gray-black bodies making loops in the air in a long line that made the sea serpent stories of old mariners seem real. For several hours they literally swam circles around us, until, tiring of such a slow companion, they left in search of more exciting sport.

Closer to Nargana a few sailing *cayucas* scudded across the green water, heeling over in the light breeze while their Indian navigators balanced precariously on the gunwales to keep them upright. Twenty to thirty feet long, they were carved of a single log; with no keel, centerboard, or leeboard they looked difficult to handle, yet the Indians had been known to make trips to Colón in them.

We had been looking forward to landing on Nargana, our first Indian island stop. But instead of brilliant blouses the women wore shapeless cotton Mother Hubbards, and in place of a gesturing island chief we were met by a white-frocked young priest with a crew cut, riding a red motor scooter with a black-and-tan dachshund sitting on the back. Dinah and Mopsy the Dachsy took a liking to each other right away and it was the same with us and Padre Kolb, who had spent twelve years among the San Blas Indians since leaving Pasadena, California.

"You're just in time for supper," he said.

A special dispensation was made on the spot, and that evening Helen, Dinah, and I joined Padre Kolb, three other priests, and Mopsy in the dining room, where we were served a well-balanced dinner by a kindly German nun. We learned that the Catholic mission wasn't responsible for the drab attire of the native women. That was brought about by a missionary who had spent ten years on Nargana prior to the rebellion in 1923.

After dessert of German-style white cake Padre Kolb brought out some of his special brew, an adaptation of the natives' drink of fermented sugar cane juice and ground corn. "Strictly a scientific experiment"—he winked—"to test the effects of the beverage."

I'm certain it couldn't have been the one thimble-sized glass that I had of the sweetish-sour clear yellow liquid, but, whatever the cause, that night I dreamed that La Tortuga, Dinah, and I were being chased over a storm-tossed sea by an elephant-sized dachshund and a monstrous amphibious motor scooter driven by a San Blas Indian woman speaking German. Wearing a barrel-hoop nose ring and a red Mother Hubbard, Helen laughed at me from a saddle on the back of a porpoise that kept getting in the way of my flight. I woke up when the porpoise turned and opened its mouth and swallowed the lot of us like Jonah and the whale.

The next morning I helped Padre Kolb repair the wiring on his boat and he took us for a spin around the island, showing us how to get through the channel and on the course for Ratón Cay. The weather looked threatening, and when Padre Kolb told us that a boat was due that afternoon with some gasoline for the mission which we could buy instead, we decided to wait another day. I was beginning to be concerned about the problem of fuel. Beyond Nargana the trading boats called only at very irregular intervals, at Ailigandi, forty miles ahead and at Obaldía, near the Colombian border, over a hundred miles away. Unless we could make definite arrangements at Nargana for gas to be left at Obaldía, there was a good chance we might be delayed, and the natives predicted the *chocosanos* would be early. When the boat did not arrive that day, Padre Kolb graciously sold us twelve gallons of his own supply and offered to speak to the captain of the *Rio Indio*, which would be making a run to Obaldía that month. With our tanks again topped off, in calm weather we could just make Obaldía on the fifty-two gallons.

Wednesday morning the sun was shining brightly, and we headed for Ratón Cay, twenty-one miles away. One of the difficulties we had experienced in navigating by sight was identifying the many islands since not all of the hundreds of bits of sand and palm showed on the charts. It was the same that morning. Ahead of us the sky was clear, and scattered against the blue horizon dozens of islands seemed to float just above the surface of the water. For the first few hours after we left Nargana the sea was calm, but dark clouds were forming in the mountains to our right, where lightning

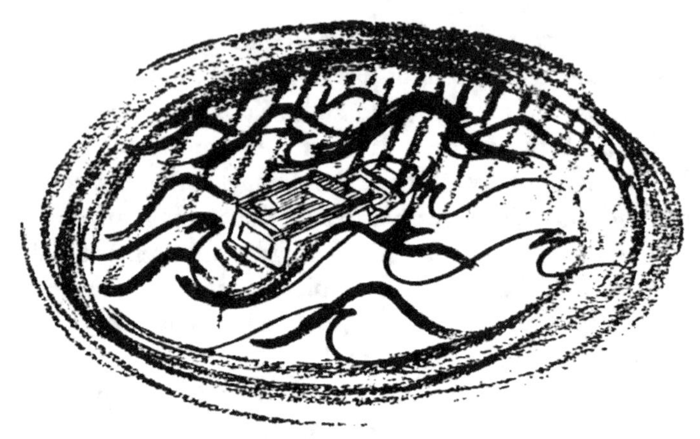

flashed like a waving white sheet. We weren't too concerned since the storm that had threatened the previous day had been a false alarm: a glorious afternoon had been followed by a fiery sunset. Reassured by the light breeze coming from the azure sky ahead, we continued even though the waves became choppy, buffeting the bow of the jeep and leaving a white cake of salt on the steaming muffler. With the front hatch closed and the windshield wipers swishing constantly, I reduced the speed of the engine to prevent its overheating and engaged the bilge pump. Since fixing the propeller shaft on Porvenir we had taken on no water, but with the waves breaking over the bow a little had seeped past the rubber gasket of the hatch. Five miles from Ratón Cay the waves slackened and our small flag drooped. A few minutes later it stiffened again as the wind shifted and blew directly from the mainland, where the dark mass of clouds had mushroomed into a canopy of black that filled the entire horizon. Ratón Cay was the closest place where we could get ashore, and with the wind whipping the crests of the whitecaps into spray, I floored the throttle hoping to make the island before the engine boiled or the dark shroud closed in. We were still more than a mile from Ratón Cay when the blackness dropped over us like a sack, cutting off the sight of land, the island, everything.

Somewhere to our left lay a scattered chain of reef called Spokeshave, to our right was the mainland fringed with coral, and in between was Ratón Cay, on either side of which was a wide breach of open water. I kicked myself for not having installed a spare compass—the one on the dash had been gyrating like a dervish since shortly after leaving Coco Solo. With only a general idea of the direction of the island, there was one chance in a thousand of hitting it before running straight out to sea or going aground on the reefs. The only thing to do was to sit tight—I pointed the bow into the storm and kept it there with just enough power to maintain steerageway while the wind rose to a gale that smothered even the sound of the exhaust.

As I gripped the wheel and struggled to keep the jeep from yawing and turning broadside to the waves I was doing some rapid mental calculating. We had come twenty miles in rough seas since Nargana. The gas gauge was hovering around the zero mark, but I figured that at the rate I was pushing the engine to keep control there was enough in the main tank for another hour. In a pinch the outboard motor might be good for another hour and a half. We had two and a half hours to ride out a storm that showed no sign of abating. To conserve the main engine fuel for a landing I switched to the outboard motor and sat on the bunk with the control arm clamped in my hand and tried to forget that I had said this was the one thing that could never happen.

Although very excitable in a *minor* emergency Helen was

extremely calm. On her lap was the little book Chaplain Best had given us. It was open to the Navy hymn:

> Eternal Father, strong to save,
> Whose arm hath bound the restless wave,
> Who bid'st the mighty ocean deep
> Its own appointed limits keep.

For more than an hour I kept La Tortuga pointed into the storm that shrieked over us. The jeep shuddered each time a wave crashed down, lurched as its bow plunged into a trough, and I wondered how that thin sheet of glass in front of us could keep out the force of tons of water. Except for the flashes of lightning that split the sky and glared from the white tassels of the waves everything was as black as night.

With the thunder came rain, lightly at first, but as the drops became larger it seemed that the wind let up a bit and the waves calmed. By the time the outboard motor tank went dry we were sitting under a deluge on a flat stippled sheet of gray water in the middle of a gray void, silent except for the rain that rattled like buckshot on the roof.

With the main engine just idling we drifted on the calm for another half hour when Helen spotted a single break on the horizon. Faintly outlined was an island. I groaned. "If only we had a compass. We could take a bearing before we're socked in again."

Helen sputtered. "We do have a compass. Remember?" She fumbled through the cabinets and came up with the small box Commander Bookhammer had given us in Coco Solo.

I had just enough time to take a reading before the island disappeared again. Blindly following a compass course, we

headed for it. Two hours and fifteen minutes from the time
we were blacked out we sighted Ratón Cay through the rain
and poled our way over the surrounding reefs to the beach.
It was too steep and narrow to get completely out of the
water so we left La Tortuga where we landed, with her bow
high between two coconut palms and her stern half submerged. For a few minutes we sat on the beach and just
enjoyed the feel of solid ground before investigating our
refuge.

I had always wanted to explore an uninhabited island.
The whole trip I had looked forward to landing on one, and
though we were soaked through by rain and salt spray, and
the conditions weren't exactly as I had pictured, I could
hardly wait to explore Ratón Cay. We pushed through the
heavy growth, enchanted by the exotic flowers, the pink
shells on the sand, and the fan-leafed plants that glistened,
newly washed by the rain. In the one deserted grass hut we
poked among the bits of pottery and straw mats, and then
on the way back to the jeep we picked wild bananas and
coconuts for supper. All the while we were alert for any sight
or sound that might indicate the presence of snakes. When
Dinah's hackles bristled, we froze and then laughed as she
backed cautiously away from the island's one inhabitant, a
lone cat. Later the moon sent streaks of silver through the
palms and a gentle breeze fresh showers of water from the
rain-soaked fronds. It was a tranquil starry night: the waves
bubbled on the beach and crabs scampered before them, and
occasionally we heard a coconut falling.

Inside La Tortuga we were preparing for bed. The steep
angle at which we had landed was uncomfortable, but that
night we could have slept standing up. Helen was about
to crawl onto her bunk when she saw flashes a few hundred

yards from shore. We made out the dim form of a *cayuca* with four or five Indians in it. Padre Kolb had warned us that the Indians regarded the islands as personal property and were suspicious of anyone stopping on an uninhabited island. Each island was a bank where money grew on trees. The coconuts were worth four cents apiece in trade.

"What do you suppose they're doing?" Helen asked nervously.

"Oh, they're probably hunting for lobsters on the reef." I wasn't as casual as I tried to make out. "Let's be quiet and maybe they won't discover us."

Helen sat there a few minutes more and then climbed over the seat to her bunk, but she wasn't very quiet about it. Her foot hit the horn button and the silence was blasted by a sound as foreign to the San Blas Islands as a conch shell on Broadway. The lights from the *cayuca* vanished.

"Well," I said disgustedly, "if they didn't know before that we're here, they do now."

I got out some cigarettes and soap to make peace and waited. A few minutes later I heard a noise near the jeep and switched on the headlights, but instead of an Indian vigilante committee it was the cat busily devouring the remains of Dinah's supper. Helen pointed to where we had seen the lights. The *cayuca* was shooting across the water toward the mainland, the Indians paddling as if all the demons in hell were after them.

The next morning we zigzagged back over the low-lying reefs to the safe Prussian blue of deep water and headed for Ailigandi. For the next forty miles the charts were useless: in place of soundings there was an empty blank space, and even the shape of the coast line was indefinite, traced from a Spanish map dated 1817. But it was that lack of knowledge that made it more exciting, for perhaps in that area might lie the undiscovered location of the legendary Swan's Nest, the secret harbor Sir Francis Drake had concealed by training trees to grow over the entrance.

Profiting by the experience of the previous day, we stayed close to shore, ready to dash in should the warning black clouds swell over the mountains again. Around noon the wind freshened. We were navigating between two parallel shoals of brown coral, and I gave the jeep full throttle to get to the end or a low spot where we could get through to shore. But even faster than the day before the clouds closed in and the waves started thrashing. With Helen probing with the bamboo pole on the bow, we found an opening and steered for a bit of white sand beach. When she shouted "Stop," I wasn't ready. Before I could throw the jeep into reverse, Helen lunged against the pole trying to stop the jeep before it ran up on a sharp point of reef. But two and a half tons doesn't stop easily. The pole was flipped from her hands and she was thrown sprawling to the edge of the jeep, which was tilting up on the reef. Cutting the engine, I climbed through the hatch, pulled Helen back, and then jumped in after the pole, but it was gone, carried away by the wave that had concealed the reef until we were on it.

What we had thought was a channel was a blind alley with no way open to shore and no room to turn around. For a half hour I stood with the remaining pole on the bobbing bow of the jeep trying to keep it from being battered against the reef while Helen ran the engine in full reverse until the rain fell and the waves calmed. We were poling backward into deeper water when an Indian paddled by in a *cayuca* and offered to lead us to Ailigandi. For the next four miles he sat in the jeep, piloting us with assurance over shallows where to me it looked as if even his canoe would go aground and avoiding places that seemed safe to me but where he said were sharp points of coral. In his *cayuca* tied to the back of the jeep his frightened wife wailed loudly, and it wasn't until we were almost there that we could persuade her to join us in La Tortuga.

For the next three days the weather varied from overcast skies to torrential rains as we waited impatiently on Ailigandi for the sea to calm. During that time we enjoyed the hospitality of Dr. and Mrs. Iglesias, leaders of the only Protestant mission in the islands. Dr. Iglesias was a San Blas Indian, educated in the United States by the same missionary who had so diluted the customs on Nargana. Ailigandi, however, had suffered no such drastic change, the women still wore their exquisitely bizarre costumes, their nose rings and heavy ear pendants, but it did seem incongruous to hear them sing "Onward Christian Soldiers" in Cuna dialect.

The second day on the island the *Rio Indio* arrived with a drum of gasoline for us. Paying for the whole drum, I filled our tanks with twenty gallons and requested the captain to leave the rest at Obaldía. The remaining thirty-five gallons in the drum would be enough to get us to Turbo.

On Ailigandi, as on Porvenir and Nargana, we were subjected to an intense scrutiny by the Indians. More than just looking, they seemed consumed by a desire to touch and feel everything, especially La Tortuga. As for Dinah, they were both terrified and awed by her. They had never seen a dog as large as she, and whenever she came near them they whispered "*Achu, achu.*" I refrained from saying "*Gesundheit*" when I learned that *achu* was a legendary carnivore that probably dates from the fighting dogs of the conquistadores.

Perhaps because they pitied her lack of a nose ring, the women of Ailigandi took a special liking to Helen. They ignored me completely, but wherever Helen went they nodded to her vigorously, saying, "*Nuete an ai* [Good friend]." One evening an old woman reached through the crowd surrounding the jeep and dragged Helen by the arm into her hut, the other women of the island streaming after them. Her abductress was a medicine woman, a wrinkled weathered crone with a stubby black pipe stuck between brown teeth and a nose ring that sagged from a stretched loop of flesh halfway to her chin. I pushed through the crowd, past a dozen hammocks, to a corner where the light from the cooking fire sent flickering shadows on the cane walls and danced from the nose rings and ear pendants of the women. Helen called my name and I broke through to where she was standing, half expecting to find her being fitted for that mark of San Blas beauty. Instead the old woman was showing her the carved wooden dolls with which she cured the sick. As she pulled each one from an overflowing box she pointed to the markings on it, the location indicating where the patient it had cured had been ailing. The more marks, the more cures and the more valued the doll. As she took out the last one she held it contemplatively a moment and then impulsively gave it to Helen, exclaiming, "*Nuete an ai!*" It was a new doll, an image of a man with a long sharp nose. Carved of balsa, about ten inches long, it had cured only a few people but, according to the old lady, it had a great future and she wanted Helen to have it. There was a murmur of approval from the other women and one of them put a string of beads around Helen's neck, motioning her to sniff them. Made of brown seeds, they emitted an exotically spicy aroma, but still another woman made a contemptuous gesture, took off her own beads, and gave them to Helen, inviting her to test their infinitely better fragrance.

When we had arrived on Ailigandi, there was a rumor that a canoeload of Indians had been attacked by a sea monster. The night it happened five men were hunting turtle eggs near Ratón Cay when the monster had come up from the

depths of the sea to the beach. Barely escaping with their lives, they had paddled all night to reach their island of Ustuppo, where they told the chief what had happened. The chief called a general assembly and the men repeated their story, how a monstrous shape had crawled from the water, roaring horribly, with people in its mouth, and with eyes flashing like lightning. One of the elders, a man much respected for his knowledge of tribal lore, stood up and described the legendary giant sea turtle which their ancestors said would one day come to devour the people. "The sea monster has come," he proclaimed.

Each time we heard the story it was embellished a bit

more, and it wasn't until the day before we left Ailigandi that we learned that La Tortuga had assumed a new role— first a scout car from a flying saucer, then a rose parade float, a tank, and now the sea monster of San Blas. Oledebiligini, high chief of all the San Blas Indians, explained what had happened when he paid us a call from Ustuppo. He was a short stocky man wearing a shapeless felt hat and loose pink shirt. There was a keen intelligent look about him as he spoke to Dr. Iglesias, who translated:

"My people were afraid when the five men told them what they had seen, but when a messenger said there was a strange machine on Ailigandi, that it swam in the water and walked on land, and that there were people inside, I knew that you were the sea monster. Now they are no longer afraid; they want to see and touch your Yauk Temar so that they will enjoy a full life in heaven. They will not work, the men will not go to their farms on the mainland, the women will not go to the river for water for fear that you will pass while they are gone. I have come personally to invite you to make Ustuppo your home for as long as you wish to stay."

I was both awed by the invitation and a bit confused as to what the connection was between our visit and heaven, but I thanked him and promised to stop there. When word spread that we were going to Ustuppo, there was a protest from nearby Achituppo. "Why should the people of Ailigandi and Ustuppo have more in heaven than the people of Achituppo?" their chief asked. I couldn't answer that question so I asked Dr. Iglesias.

"My people," he explained understandingly, "believe that what they experience in this life they will experience in the afterlife, so they try to see and do everything they would like to see and do in heaven."

Apparently the thought of owning an amphibious jeep was very appealing because after that we received many invitations, and it became almost mandatory that we stop at all the islands along the way, if only for a moment, so that the people could touch our Yauk Temar. I'm afraid there's going to be an awful traffic jam in Indian heaven with more amphibious jeeps running around than Ford turned out during the war. And I suppose that now, instead of placing a tiny *cayuca* on the chest of a dead man to carry his soul to the hereafter, there will be a miniature La Tortuga.

That evening we were invited to a birthday party, a rather recent innovation since the San Blas people were not accustomed to keeping track of age. Helen and I stooped under the low eaves of the hut where the festivities were taking place and entered the dim interior, lit by a single smoking lantern. At the far end hammocks hung, and on the rafters, the San Blas clothes closets, were neatly folded skirts and blouses.

Standing around a long low table were a score or more of elaborately decorated Indians. We had been briefed by Dr. Iglesias on the formalities to be observed, but we were happy to see so many people. If we made a mistake it would probably go unnoticed. But such is not San Blas custom. We were the guests of honor and everyone else stood around, watching carefully to make sure that we enjoyed ourselves.

We had little difficulty with what to them is ice cream, rice boiled in coconut oil, but we saved until last the thin brown liquid in the small cups by our plates.

"Do you think it's real *chicha?*" Helen whispered from the side of her mouth.

"I don't know, but we don't want to offend them," I answered. (*Chicha* is a masticated corn drink. It's not that we're squeamish but, being an independent sort, we prefer to chew our own corn.) "Bottoms up, and make believe you like it," I whispered in return.

With forced smiles we raised the cups to our lips. It had a strange sweet smell that somehow seemed familiar. At the first taste our strained expressions turned to ones of pleasure. Instead of *chicha* it was cocoa made with water and a large amount of sugar. And that concluded the party, except for the parting ritual. It hardly seemed right to repay the hospitality of our hostess by spitting on her floor, but dutifully we took a mouthful of water from a small blue bowl, rinsed our mouths, and spit over our left shoulders in the prescribed manner.

The next morning the chief of Ailigandi summoned us to his hut. Dr. Iglesias went along to interpret, explaining that the chief was about to make a friendship pact. Seating us on a carved wooden bench, the chief stood a few feet in front of us holding a bowl containing two white eggs. With great ceremony he began to chant, bending at the waist and moving forward and backward rhythmically:

"I wish you a safe journey, and a long and happy marriage. I will think of you when we are apart and hope that you will think of me."

With each phrase he leaned over and handed me the bowl of eggs, but as I reached for it he pulled it back, walked away, and chanted anew. When he finished his salutation he handed me the bowl, saying, "We are now lifelong friends."

Then it was my turn. The old chief sat next to Helen on the bench while I repeated the ceremony with the same bowl:

"Thank you for your hospitality and may you continue

in good health. May we return someday to renew our friendship."

When I finished he nodded stoically, took the bowl, and
handed me the eggs one at a time. During the entire ritual
he had ignored Helen—friendship pacts were made only between men—but as a consolation prize he gave her a beautiful avocado. Later we ate the avocado, but the eggs were
beyond that stage.

When the performance was over, the chief climbed into
the jeep, and as if La Tortuga were a royal coach he waved
and nodded to his subjects as we drove slowly across the
block-sized island to the *cayuca* beach. Awkwardly he
jumped out amid cheers from the people, and we edged into
the water toward Ustuppo.

It was a short run to Oledebiligini's island and we made
good time, considering that we stopped at Achituppo on the
way so that the people could touch the jeep and assure
themselves of its possession in heaven. The bottom around
the island was too soft to get ashore, so they all waded out
to us, rubbing and stroking La Tortuga.

From the sea, a few hundred yards off Ustuppo, the brown
huts seemed so close together that there would be hardly
enough space for the jeep. The people were there en masse
to greet us: men were busily picking rocks from the shallow
water of the channel, and Oledebiligini was waving from
the shore. The beach was steep and we approached rapidly,
the wheels and propeller churning the water to a muddy
froth. In the soft sand near the water's edge our progress
stopped and the men crowded around, then scattered like
autumn leaves before the wind as the wheels took hold and
La Tortuga lurched up onto the solid sand and coral of the
island. Following slowly behind Oledebiligini, we drove

178

through the narrow paths between the huts, winding in and out with the whole populace around us. The men were excited, but the women were terrified. Even though they had been told that the sea monster had not yet come, screaming mothers dragged their children into their huts, grandmothers shuddered with fright, clutching one another and hiding in doorways, but still peeping out inquisitively. In an open space in front of the main council hut the inspection began, shyly at first, and then with more vigor when they saw we really weren't going to eat them.

Inside the huge council hut, a cane and thatch structure more than a hundred feet long, the islanders crowded to hear their chief welcome us, their faces illuminated by the striped pattern of sunlight that filtered through the bamboo slat walls. Sitting on high benches, the men chewed on their pipes, the smoke curling up through openings in the roof. The women stood around the walls and the children hung from the bamboo eaves or peered from between the legs of their elders. In the center of the council Oledebiligini reclined in the hammock from which all official business was conducted. One of the men who had been in the Canal Zone translated as he spoke loudly so that all could hear:

"I regret that I cannot speak your language, but this man shall be at your disposal. If you wish anything, just ask. You are among friends."

And we were. We were free to come and go when and where we desired, and always we were met by friendly smiling faces. It was difficult to believe that these were the people who had garnered such an evil reputation over the years. It was still true that on many of the islands a stranger was not allowed to spend the night, but apparently that rule didn't apply to me since I had brought my own wife. Besides, we had a magical machine that swam on the sea and walked on the land, and a fascinating dog that understood Cuna. We had taught Dinah to put out her paw in response to "*Ak an ai*," and she never forgave us for it. After one day in which she obliged at least half the islanders she retired to the jeep with a case of politician's cramp. She would come out only when it was time to eat.

A few feet above the level of the sea Ustuppo was a flat table of coral and hard-packed sand. It was one of the largest of the San Blas Islands, about the size of six city blocks, where almost two thousand Indians lived in crowded bamboo and grass huts. Like the other inhabited islands we had passed, it was less than a mile from the mainland and the mouth of a river. With no fresh water on the island and with nothing growing except a few palms, the people preferred to live crushed together where they were safe from the spirits of the trees, rocks, and animals that haunted the mainland at night.

The only clear space on the island was in front of the main council hut, and it was there that we parked La Tortuga for our two-day stay. The children flocked around bringing their pets, a baby foot-long alligator on a string, and a black-and-white marmoset that clung to the long hair of its little mistress and screamed loudly when she plucked it loose for us to hold. And there was a green parrot that learned to say Dinah's name, much to her disgust. Although the chief loudly and sternly ordered the kids to keep a fair distance from the jeep while we prepared our C-ration meals, they always moved in close when he wasn't around. But they really scattered when the island master-at-arms ran from the council hut brandishing his wand of authority. Seldom spanked by their families, they had great respect for the three-foot length of thorny vine that was used freely about once a week at a general assembly when the kids were given the appropriate number of whacks for their misdeeds as reported by their parents.

The second day Helen went with two of the women to the river, paddling several miles upstream through a tunnel of dark green foliage, where lizards darted on the leaves and blue crabs played on the banks. Leaving the canoe, they waded still farther upstream to a deep pool where they bathed, and then, picking mangoes, pineapples, and avocados on the way, they returned to the island in a canoe so laden with gourds of fresh water that there was less than an inch of freeboard. Although Helen was constantly afraid that the canoe would tip over she told me that all the women could talk about was how they would fear to go to sea in La Tortuga.

While Helen was gone, I watched the men spear fish and bring the corn, rice, plantains, and bananas from their farms. Near the huts women squeezed sugar cane between two springy logs or sat sewing the appliquéd blouses that took as long as ten weeks to make. In the evening the people brought us fruit and little stools to sit on. Carved of a single piece of wood, they were as comfortable and functional as any Eames chair.

When we were ready to leave, one of the women presented Helen with a richly appliquéd blouse of red, orange, purple, and green pieces of cloth, insisting she put it on. Helen was most obliging, and with a borrowed wrap-around skirt, which she had difficulty keeping on, and a red headdress all she lacked was a nose ring. I thought a nose ring might be an ideal thing by which to assert my masculine prerogative, but when I suggested to Helen that the costume be completed she didn't take kindly to the idea.

When Helen's attire was complete, the women stood back and walked around her, chattering and nodding their approval. One of them made a comment to which the others replied with a loud titter.

"What did they say?" Helen asked the interpreter.

He smiled. "They said your eyes may be blue, but your skin is darker than theirs."

And they were right. In the three weeks since leaving Colón, Helen was burned a deep bronze by the sun.

Mulatuppo, our next stop, was almost at the end of the San Blas chain, and was supposed to be the island where Balboa married a chieftain's daughter, but if his in-laws were as unpleasant as the Mulatuppoans of today it was no wonder he left. Perhaps they had a different concept of heaven, or maybe it was because their chief was old and sick, but, whatever the reason, they were a belligerent and restless lot. After being the center of a torchlight parade all night and the object of angry mutterings we took off early in the morning. The threatening sky looked more inviting than the cloudy faces of the Indians.

The seas from Mulatuppo were as rough as any we had been in, but daily we acquired more confidence in La Tortuga's ability to weather them. When earlier in the trip we would have dashed for shore, we now consumed increasing amounts of Dramamine and pushed on. With storm clouds mounting we covered the forty miles to Obaldía near the Colombian border in two long runs, where with relief we found our gas waiting for us. Obaldía, out of San Blas territory and the last Panamanian port, was a sleepy little Negro town of a few hundred inhabitants. The one white resident, the storekeeper who had our gas, also had a radio over which he and the rest of the town had had word of our coming from a Panamanian news broadcast, but the information was slightly incorrect. We were described as German nationals and millionaires. We thought it rather amusing until they warned us that revolutionary trouble was again brewing in Colombia, and that some places were decidedly unhealthy for anyone, let alone two people reputed to be wealthy. To add a little more spice to the situation, guerrillas were being supplied with arms by gun-runners operating in the waters between Obaldía and Turbo. And to top it all a fisherman predicted a *chocosano* within the week.

With about eighty miles to go to Turbo we spent a full day at Obaldía checking and servicing the jeep. It had been performing perfectly, but we had been taking on a lot of water and I wanted to make certain it was from the heavy seas and not from a leak in the hull. Finding nothing wrong, I went over the bolts and seals to be sure, and then with our tanks filled we left for Punta Goleta, a long twenty-four miles away.

Bahía de Goleta: ". . . heavy swells with crests which break in nearly six fathoms have been observed. In heavy weather the swells pile up and may be dangerous." So say the Sailing Directions, published by the U. S. Navy Department, Hydrographic Office. But at the time we approached for a landing we didn't have a copy. A bit green after eight hours of pitching and rolling, I had only one thought—to get to shore as quickly as possible. There was no sign of reef and there appeared to be no surf, but I had forgotten that from the seaward side surf wasn't always apparent. I remembered very quickly as the bow pointed down and La Tortuga became the front of the roller coaster again. On the shore a Negro family was waving madly at us to stay out, but by that time it was too late and the jeep surfboarded toward the beach yawing and swaying.

When we climbed out, Helen looked green too. "I thought there wasn't supposed to be any surf on the Caribbean side."

I had nothing to say. I was getting used to my theories being shattered.

The next morning we headed out through the breakers again toward the first mouth of the Rio Atrato. An hour after we left, a three-layer bank of clouds with a long tail started forming to the south, from whence came the *chocosanos*, but rather than risk another landing we kept going. Around noon the water calmed and I moved in closer to shore, which was some of the most desolate I had ever seen. There was a narrow beach littered with debris from countless storms, a wall of bleached driftwood and dead brush pushed by the waves to the edge of the jungle lowlands beyond. There were no towns or habitations of any kind from there to Turbo, and it came as a shock when we passed a high rock island and saw a nondescript boat nestling against a cliff on one side. About fifty feet long, its gray hull was uncared for; there was no flag or indentifying mark. It appeared to be waiting for something or someone, and through the binoculars I saw six men studying us. There was a sudden belch of black diesel fumes from its stack and it swung our way.

"Run up the American flag," I told Helen, "and get out the radio. Maybe we can bluff them as we did White Suit." But either they didn't know what it was or they were aware that our handie-talkie had no range for they kept coming. Flooring the accelerator, I pointed La Tortuga for the shore; we couldn't outrun them on water, but on the beach we could leave them far behind. Without a thought to the surf we hit the beach with all four wheels churning, the propeller still engaged, and a stream of water shooting from the bilge

184

outlet. It was like running a *slalom* weaving between fallen trees and around debris until four miles later we were stopped by the muddy banks of the Rio Atrato. Because of a bend in the shore line we couldn't see the boat. With the jeep concealed behind a pile of brush we waited, and several hours later we saw a trail of black smoke heading across the Gulf of Darien.

With a sigh of relief Helen commented, "Storms, reefs, and gunrunners. Believe me, I'll never go to sea in a ship that doesn't have wheels."

That night the *chocosano* hit. Were we glad to be onshore! The tail of the triple-decker dark cloud rose even higher as the wind shifted from north to south, lightning split the sky with jagged red fingers, pronged spears, and sheets that turned the horizon into a wavering white line in the blackness. Increasing steadily, the wind swished in gusts, whipping the waves to froth and sending them rolling up on the beach through the debris and washing the sand from beneath the wheels of the jeep. Already back as far as we could go against the woven dense jungle growth behind us, we worked quickly to build a barricade of driftwood in front of the jeep, but before we were finished the tires were buried six inches deep.

The main storm center lasted almost an hour, but all night lightning stabbed and thunder rumbled incessantly. The torrent of rain that came with the first gust of wind continued until almost morning. When the sun rose, another cloud was forming, and we decided to wait another day. For breakfast we halved the usual ration. The month's supply of food was almost gone even though Helen had been eating very little the past few days.

Our campsite was not the most desirable. Right at the mouth of the river the water was thick with brown mud.

Trees and islands of floating vegetation drifted down from the jungle interior forming a green delta in the center. Sand fleas invaded the jeep as if the screens were not there. Thriving on insect repellent, they apparently considered it a delightful hors d'oeuvre before their main course. And we couldn't relieve the itching by bathing in the sea. Ugly brown sharks circled endlessly in the river mouth, coming so close to shore that they squirmed on the muddy bottom, their eight-foot-long bodies half exposed in the murky water.

Later in the day we sighted a distant Navy patrol plane, identifiable through the binoculars, but we were unable to make contact. The rest of the afternoon we watched almost spellbound as the black fins of the sharks swung back and forth, sometimes exposing their gray bellies, sometimes thrashing furiously when two of them fought over a fish. That night it stormed again, a repetition of the previous one, but the following morning was clear, and after retracing our way a half mile along the beach we started on the next-to-the-last lap.

Less than thirty miles away across the Gulf of Darien lay Turbo, but it was thirty miles of mudbanks and strong currents from the Rio Atrato. Our plans were to edge along the shore to the narrowest part of the gulf, and then to cross the ten-mile stretch of open water as quickly as possible, coming ashore on the spit of land where the chart showed the customs house to be located.

All along the shore a mud shelf extended into the gulf, and we proceeded slowly. If we went aground, I wanted to be able to push off from the bow with the pole and not from the water, as I had done in Costa Rica. There was a sharp line of demarcation between the blue of the Caribbean and the opaque brown water of the Rio Atrato. Heading directly across the fan of current that spread from the mouth of the river, we dodged scattered masses of bobbing vegetation that were being carried out to sea. It wasn't until we were halfway across that we saw we were being carried with them. Pushing the engine to its full six knots, I headed closer to shore, tacking back and forth across the current, keeping just beyond the shelf of mud, until we reached a short black sand beach near Bahía Candelaria. There was the current of two more branches of the Rio Atrato to buck, but through the binoculars we could see Turbo's customs house ten miles away. When a patrol plane found us that afternoon, I notified the pilot that with good weather we would land at Turbo the next day.

We were too excited to eat much that evening, so we didn't mind saving the last of the C rations, a can of beans, for breakfast. And with the rain and the sand fleas we didn't sleep too well either.

Day broke with a beautiful orange sunrise and a calm sea. At 7:00 A.M. we took off through gentle surf and pointed La Tortuga toward Turbo. Tacking at full throttle in the currents, letting the engine cool off in between, we reached the halfway point. The customs house grew larger, a few specks on shore became people, we could make out the shingle beach, the logs that cluttered it, and the uniforms of the customs officials. Twenty minutes before we hit the beach at Turbo, just thirty days from the time we left Coco Solo, a Navy patrol plane zoomed low. To our surprise, from the receiver came the voice of Admiral Miles.

"Glad to see you made it. Are you both all right?"

We assured him that we were. The plane circled twice, dipped its wings, and headed back toward Panama. As we watched it disappear, I signed off.

"So long, Angel—and thanks."

Chapter Seven

APPROACHING the beach rapidly, we headed for the group of people who had congregated onshore. The hard-packed gravel offered no resistance, and when the wheels took hold the jeep surged right for them. I stepped hard on the brakes. Even though wet they should have slowed us a little, but nothing happened. There was a flurry of flailing arms as white shirts and khaki uniforms scattered like tenpins until we came to an abrupt halt against a piece of driftwood. Feeling that the first vehicle to reach South America under its own power could have gotten off to a better start, I hastily apologized to the customs official for nearly running him down. But if a Martian had landed on the beach he couldn't have been more confused. He muttered something in Spanish about a car navigating the Gulf of Darien or a boat driving up to the customs house and then asked for our papers. He stamped the passports and tourist cards, ignored Dinah's health certificate, and lingered an especially long time over the certificate of title for the jeep.

"Is it a car or a boat?" he asked.

"It's both," I replied.

There was a whispered conversation between the customs official and his crony. One said to let us go, and the other one said he wasn't sure. I didn't know what it was all about, but I had learned many borders ago not to complicate matters by opening my mouth. Ten minutes of head shaking and creased brows were climaxed by much shoulder shrugging, after which they returned our documents and waved us on.

"Well, that was easy," Helen commented cheerfully as we climbed back in the jeep. It wasn't until we tried to leave Colombia that we learned it had been much too easy.

From what we could see, Turbo was nothing more than a customs house, a few wooden shacks, and an airstrip on the edge of the jungle. Parking the jeep in the shade of one of the shacks, we relaxed a bit. For the first time in a month I felt no tension, the ground felt good beneath my feet, firm and solid, and I could look at the choppy water without apprehension. My only regret was that I couldn't see Captain Parker's face when he paid off his bets in Panama.

The customs official had pointed out the road to Medellín, Colombia's second city, but, although it was only 240 miles away, we would have to procure supplies and service the jeep before continuing. With tools, grease, and oil that I had brought from Panama I was prepared to do the job on the spot. But a half hour later when I had removed one of the front wheels I found something for which I wasn't prepared. The brake linings had all but disappeared, ground away by sand and salt water. I was pondering the problem of where to procure new linings when a very foreign sound broke the Turbo silence—a soft Texas drawl. It seemed that the Lone Star State had emissaries everywhere.

Tall and lanky, the speaker even looked like a Texan. Dressed in faded khakis, he was about fifty, with thinning gray hair and a neatly trimmed mustache, but his eyes had a youthful merry twinkle. "Howdy," he said. "I'm Louis Coulson. Aren't you the folks that plane was looking for the other day? Radioed it was hunting a missing craft of your description."

"I didn't know we were lost," I replied. Then I remembered the distant speck in the sky and our failure to make radio contact.

Coulson walked around the jeep. "You were mighty lucky to get across the gulf in that," he said.

"We've been mighty lucky all along. We'll be even luckier if we get to Medellín." I showed him what was left of the brakes. "Is this all there is to Turbo?"

"Oh no," he said. "The rest of it is across a shallow bay, but you won't find any brake linings there. There isn't even a road into the town. You have to get there by dugout canoe." He thought a moment. "Say, I've got a friend who can fix you up. He's head of the road commission camp a few miles from here, and you won't need brakes to get there either. The road's flat."

"That's great," I said. "I don't suppose there's anyplace we can send a telegram around here, is there? We would like to let our family know we made it."

"Sure thing. I've got a friend in the telegraph office. Say, a friend of mine has a dugout. Why not let me show you Turbo—what there is of it?"

I thanked him, and laughed. "You've sure got lots of friends around here, Mr. Coulson."

"Yes sir, after twenty-two years in Colombia I sure do." He chuckled. "That's the only way you can do business here."

"Mr. Coulson"—Helen hesitated, "you don't happen to have a doctor friend too, do you?"

"Why, as a matter of fact, I have. What's your trouble?"

190

"I don't know, but I'd like to have him take a look at my mouth."

Helen hadn't said anything to me about her mouth hurting but she hadn't been eating much. When I saw the roof of her mouth I knew why. It was covered with red ulcerated sores.

Hurriedly I put the wheel back on. I had finished before I realized that I had left out the universal joint that was essential for four-wheel drive, but Coulson assured me I wouldn't be needing it before reaching the road camp at Sunga, thirty miles away. At Mr. Coulson's suggestion, we left Dinah to watch the jeep.

The small port of Turbo lay across a narrow arm of water from the spit of land where we had come ashore. Maneuvering the outboard-powered dugout between the stumps and logs that filled the bay, Coulson shouted over the noise of the motor, "Turbo used to be a busy place. But that was hundreds of years ago, before the Rio Atrato filled the bay with mud. In those days it was a stopping place for Spanish treasure ships." He slowed the engine and pointed at the dark opaque water. "There's still a chest of gold down there."

From the open bay we skimmed through a narrow channel where the water was a mirror and double-ended trees lined the sides until the wake from the boat sent the reflections rippling away. At a crude wharf Coulson tied the canoe to a piling and we climbed a rough plank boardwalk that led to the town. On either side were more dugout canoes, some of them incongruously graced with shiny outboard motors. Near one of them stood an immense Negro. Tobacco juice stained a snarled beard that almost concealed a red flannel undershirt.

"That's Santa Claus," Coulson laughed. "Don't let his appearance fool you. He's one of the richest men in Turbo. Owns half these boats you see. Old miser—never spends a cent except for a plug of tobacco."

Turbo might have been a busy place at one time but there was no evidence of it that day. There was an air of quiet about the place, a stillness, as if the people were afraid even to speak for fear of using their last bit of energy. As we walked along the wooden sidewalks, past blue- and green-painted houses, the sun sent heat waves dancing upward from the metal roofs, and I found myself stifling yawns and moving slower and slower. The atmosphere was contagious.

Coulson, it turned out, actually lived in Medellín. He had flown to Turbo for a fishing trip—with a friend of his. He seemed to know everyone in town, and the doctor, whom we met in the street, greeted him like a lost brother. Younger than Coulson, with straight black hair and a big black mustache, he was also the local druggist. When we were introduced, a few people on the sidewalk pricked up their ears, a few more came running over, and by the time we arrived at the doctor's office we had quite a following. They all crowded in behind us to help him make his diagnosis. Quite conveniently the doctor's office was in his drugstore, behind the railing that served as a counter. Seating Helen on a chair, he asked her a few questions and then said something to another man, who disappeared into the back room. His aide returned with a spoon and meticulously wiped it off with his thumb before handing it to the doctor.

Helen opened her mouth; everyone leaned forward to look and emitted a sympathetic moan. Asking them quietly to move back so he could work, the doctor prodded Helen's mouth. There was another moan from the crowd when she gargled a protest, and a nod of complete agreement when he made his diagnosis: "A serious vitamin deficiency, early stages of scurvy." He reached for the shelf behind him and blew the dust off a box of pills. "Take four of these each day. In a couple of weeks you'll be all right." He smiled. "Since you're a friend of Don Luís, there will be no charge."

Back at the jeep again Mr. Coulson gave us directions for getting to Sunga and invited us to spend a few days with him in Medellín. I was beginning to see why he had so many friends.

The road from Turbo to Medellín was a new one, open only a short time after being under construction for almost thirty years. In fact, there was still some machinery along the way: one piece in particular, a huge shovel, was parked right across the road between a mass of jungle on one side and the gulf on the other. Five or six cars were waiting patiently, one of them since early morning. "This," I said jokingly, "looks like a job for Super-car," and without hesitation drove into the water to bypass the shovel. Less than ten feet from shore La Tortuga stuck—no four-wheel drive. And with the winch on the front we could not pull ourselves out backward. What a twist. After two hundred and fifty miles of ocean we were scuttled by a steam shovel. We dug and we pushed. The people in the cars waded out to push. We deflated the tires, but without four-wheel drive it was no use. And with the front wheels under water I would have needed an Aqua Lung to replace the universal joint. Two hours later a road commission truck arrived with a crew to move the shovel and the men hauled us out at the same time. Feeling rather sheepish, we continued to Sunga and arrived there late that afternoon.

Mr. Coulson had told us to ask for his friend, Dr. Solís.

I couldn't imagine a doctor being in charge of a road-construction camp, but this was Colombia. We learned that all professional people are called Doctor, whether they are lawyers, engineers, or medical men. Dr. Solís was an engineer, a most genial person. "Yes," he said, "I think we might have some jeep brake linings around here." He assigned a couple of his men to help me and invited us to stay with him.

Helen eyed enthusiastically two boiler-sized washtubs and a scrubboard which looked as modern as a Bendix after washing on the rocks in the rivers. The next morning Helen shocked the servant girls—that a guest of Dr. Solís should do the family wash. But what surprised them even more was that the man she was traveling with was her husband. In Latin America apparently that was rare. And when they learned how long we had been married they were incredulous. "Americans," they exclaimed, "married eight years! Aren't you ready for a divorce?" Even in remote Sunga, Hollywood had had its effect.

Sunga, a clearing in the jungle lowlands, was a large camp, and there were lots of pets—most of them for sale. If Helen had had her way, La Tortuga would have been a rolling menagerie with marmosets, baby alligators, and parrots. The snakes she would gladly have done without. There was one animal we hadn't seen before. Called a *guagua*, it was a large zebra-striped rodent about the size of a pig. Its owner assured us that if we didn't want it for a pet, it would make a delicious roast. To all I politely said that one big dog was all the pet we could handle, but Helen almost persuaded me to add one more member to our crew.

"It's only two dollars," she coaxed. "And what a wonderful playmate it would make for Dinah."

Admittedly it was cute, a furry spotted bundle purring

194

contentedly in Helen's arms, a month-old jaguar kitten. Already bigger than a house cat, in a year it would weigh a hundred and fifty pounds. Dinah was most interested but, remembering the cat in Panama, we decided that this one for sure would be more than she could handle.

By evening the differentials were drained, flushed, and refilled with lubricant, the wheel bearings were cleaned and repacked with grease, the motor oil changed, chassis lubricated, and the brakes completely reconditioned with new cylinders and new linings. When the mechanical work was done, I removed the outboard motor, padded it with life preservers, and lashed it securely to the rack on top of the jeep. We wanted to take good care of that motor; the money from its sale would go a long way toward finishing the trip.

In Turbo I had changed a few dollars for Colombian pesos, but after paying for the brake parts and tipping the mechanics we had only four pesos left, the equivalent of about ninety cents U.S., when we left Sunga. However,

Dabeiba, the next town, was less than a hundred miles away and we had enough gas to get there.

From Sunga the dirt road started to climb, gradually at first, through a green wonderland of tall ceiba trees overhung with creepers. Slender trunks stretched their necks for a glimpse of the sun and limbs spread their branches into a canopy to catch the maximum light. Green parrots darted between the trees and lacy ferns covered the ground. Often there were clearings, a lighter green swampland steaming in the heat or man-made clearings where bananas grew luxuriantly. In places the road tunneled through trees, and as it rose even higher the ground fell away on one side, and we drove along a shelf in the side of a cliff. Then at the crest of the foothills of the mighty Andes we stood on the road and filled our lungs with the first naturally cool air we had breathed in four months.

Dabeiba was a small town set on the top of a green dome-like hill. There was no bank. We tried to change money at the general store, but the clerk had never heard of a traveler's check, and the only thing he recognized about a twenty-dollar bill was the numbers. He admitted they looked impressive, but that they should be worth good Colombian pesos, never. We tried the hotel—five rooms and one bath—and the owner, a pleasant woman about fifty, fingered the currency approvingly and agreed to change it. It was late afternoon by that time and we decided to spend the night.

After supper the elderly mother of the innkeeper asked if we were Catholic. At our negative answer she replied "No importa," and invited us to see the town's principal church, a new one, in use although not quite finished. The Gothic style clashed with the reinforced concrete construction, but there in the glow of the stained-glass windows and the last rays of the setting sun we felt peace and gratitude at having safely crossed that two hundred and fifty miles of ocean.

The next morning I asked for the bill. Conferring with her mother a few moments, the innkeeper wrote something on a slip of paper and handed it to me. On it was written, "You owe us nothing. May God go with you." We were overwhelmed.

As we rolled over the hills toward Medellín, however, our money problem was still with us. But we still had four pesos, a little gas in the tank, and there were several towns ahead where there might be a bank. The department of Antioquia is noted for the unique masculine custom of carrying ornate fur-trimmed shoulder pouches. But despite the emphasis on these oversized wallets there was a shortage of money-changers. In each of the tiny hilltop towns we passed I again tried to convert dollars to pesos. Always there was the same interest in seeing what American currency looked like, but also the same unwillingness to change it. Keeping an anxious eye on the gas gauge, we reduced our speed to conserve fuel, but by noon we had to part with our last four pesos, which bought about five gallons, just enough to get us to Medellín.

As we climbed steadily into the highlands, the air was pleasantly cool. The road wound through rugged country, as green as a park and mostly uncultivated. Sparse herds of cattle grazed, but with nothing to eat since early morning by midafternoon I could see them only as steaks smothered in onions. We forgot about our hunger for a few minutes while crossing a seventy-year-old wooden suspension bridge that undulated and swayed several hundred feet above the Cauca River. But on the other side a bakery truck swishing by reminded us. I had a brilliant idea.

Stepping on the gas, I tried to catch the truck. I honked the horn. It speeded up. I honked insistently, but all the driver did was honk back and go faster. After several miles of hare and hounds he saw my frantic waving and pulled over. The driver was about thirty, slender and tall and with the heavy black mustache without which it seemed that all Colombian men would be undressed.

"Pardon me, señor," I said, "but would you be willing to trade a loaf of bread for some American cigarettes?"

"Ah, señor," he replied, "but I do not smoke."

My face dropped. He quickly added, "But if you are hungry I will give you bread." With that he started hauling loaves of bread and boxes of cookies from the back of the truck until we had more than we could eat in a week. He refused to accept the cigarettes.

"No, señor," he smiled. "I am happy to give it to you. Besides, Don Luís would want me to."

"Don Luís?" I questioned.

"Yes, señor, he is a good man, a friend of mine—in fact he is my boss, Don Luís Coulson, owner of the bakery."

Manna from Coulson! And when the driver learned that we were on our way to visit Don Luís he insisted that we follow him. He drove slowly in front of us for the next sixty miles, stopping at every village for *refrescos*. Trying to thank him was like trying to talk back to a radio. Becoming satiated after a snack at every town, we finally convinced him that we were not hungry any more. A good-natured happy fellow, he even led us directly to Coulson's door.

It was after nine o'clock when we arrived in Medellín. When we stopped to telephone Mr. Coulson's home, a young voice answered the telephone in Spanish. It was Coulson's youngest son, Jorge, who told us that Don Luís was expecting us, but was away for the evening. He asked us to come to the house and wait.

The Coulson home was a sprawling Spanish colonial overlooking the country club. Jorge met us at the door. A towheaded boy of ten, he assured us in Spanish that he spoke English. But in the few days we spent with the Coulsons we never heard him speak a word of it. He was a perfect host, mixed excellent cocktails, and kept us well entertained for a half hour until the door burst open and Don Luís flew in.

"Howdy. Change your clothes. You have just enough time to meet the new American Ambassador to Colombia. There's a reception for him at the country club."

"But all our clothes are in Bogotá," Helen said. "Frank has nothing but slacks and a sport shirt, and I have only a cotton dress."

"Well, wear your cotton dress. Dick, my oldest son, is about Frank's size. Let's see what he has." He reached into a closet and pulled out a dark blue flannel. "Here, put this on, and hurry."

We hurried, but when we arrived at the country club Ambassador and Mrs. Bonsal were just leaving. The Ambassador smiled as Don Luís introduced us. "Well, how do you do?" he said. "Admiral Miles wrote to me about you two. We'll be looking forward to seeing you in Bogotá."

Medellín was the industrial center of Colombia, a city nestled in a green valley where the saw-tooth roofs of modern textile factories encroached upon the surrounding hills. But in the center of the city wide avenues and trees festooned with Spanish moss and laden with orchids preserved its colonial heritage. The climate was springlike, warm days and cool evenings, but, at Mr. Coulson's suggestion, we purchased two *ruanas*, Colombian ponchos. In the mountains between Medellín and Bogotá these woolen rectangles would be our wraps by day and blankets by night. We had sent even our sleeping bags ahead from Panama. Before we left Medellín for Bogotá, three hundred and fifty miles away, Don Luís warned us against camping in the country, reminding us that there was still an active though unofficial civil war going on. In the midst of so much Colombian hospitality and kindness we had forgotten that, but news of recurring guerrilla activity in the mountains ahead was not reassuring.

"If you insist on camping," Don Luís said in parting, "stop at any coffee *finca* along the way and ask permission to camp on their land."

All that day we alternately froze and roasted as the dirt road took us high into the Andes and then quickly down into tropical valleys. It seemed that we never actually crossed a range of mountains, but just ran along the side, climbing to the ridge, shooting down to the valley and back again up the other side. Dark green patches of cultivated coffee land, where some of the best coffee in the world is grown, stood out vividly from the fallow pastures. It was slow going, the little engine whined and puffed up the steep grades, and at altitudes greater than five thousand feet the power fell off rapidly, so that we were in low gear much of the time. When dusk came, we decided to heed Don Luís's advice. At a sign that said Finca de Café we turned onto a narrow track, still muddy from the recent rain, and followed it for a quarter of a mile. At the end of it was an eight-foot wall with an iron-studded wooden gate. Raising the heavy brass knocker, I let it fall. Almost immediately we heard a

shuffle of footsteps, a sharp click, and from behind the
closed gate a muffled voice asked, "What do you want?"

"We are North Americans, tourists. We would like permission to camp on your property for the night."

"All Americans are rich," was the answer. "They do not
need to camp. I do not believe you."

The newspaper in Medellín had run a story about the trip;
I slipped a copy under the still closed gate. I heard two men
talking. One said that he thought it was all right, but the
other said that it was a trick, that we were guerrilla bandits,
that he was afraid. The fear of the *finca* guards was too real
to ignore. We spent that night parked in front of a police
guard station on the highway.

The next morning we continued over the roller coaster
road, bumping and jolting, along the sides of cliffs, through
lush valleys, and once in a while over a pass where the chill
wind whistled under our ponchos and tugged at our thin
clothing. Late in the afternoon we were winding down the
side of a long steep hill when the wheels hit a deep chuck-
hole and a metallic clunk came from the transmission. When
I tried to change gears, the shift lever was immovable. It
was jammed in high.

Coasting to the side of the road, I unbolted the plate in
the floor boards and removed the cover of the transmission
housing. It was a futile move since the design of a jeep transmission is such that no part can be adjusted or replaced without removing the whole unit, but I was anxious at least to
see what was wrong. I was too concerned to notice the jeep
that pulled alongside. We were accustomed to having people
stop, gawk a bit, and then go on without a word. But this
time the driver got out and approached us. About twenty-
five, slender, clean-shaven, and wearing a dark blue beret, he

bowed gallantly to Helen and then in Spanish addressed himself to me:

"Tomás Escovar at your service. May I be of some assistance?"

"Thanks," I said, "but I'm afraid not. We have transmission trouble."

"Well, you can't stay here. It's too dangerous. You can coast to my *finca* at the bottom of the hill and work on it there." And then he added, "*Aquí se matan rápido.*" In Spanish it sounded even more ominous than its English translation: "Here they kill quickly."

All day we had seen no more than a half dozen cars, and as we coasted behind Tomás I was convinced of two things: that the proverbial luck of the Irish—from my maternal grandmother—was riding with us, and that Colombians were mighty nice people.

The sun was low when we pushed La Tortuga under the overhanging eave of the big two-story house where Tomás lived alone except for an old servant woman. At supper he unnecessarily apologized for the fare, explaining that it was simple Colombian country style. But to us the hard biscuit-like *arepa*, crisply fried bacon *chicharón*, brown beans, and fresh milk were all treats. Especially the fresh milk. Afterward on the broad veranda we sat watching the sun slide behind the quiet rolling hills and listening to the stream bubbling over rocks a few yards away. The tranquil mood made my question seem almost ridiculous. I asked Tomás what he meant by "*Aquí se matan rápido.*" In answer he took from his pocket a small German pistol and spoke of a loaded rifle by his bedside. He whistled once, and almost immediately four dogs bounded toward him from the shadows.

"Without these," he said, "it would not be safe to stay alone in the country. Although the civil war ended three years ago, there are still guerrilla bandits."

A gentle, soft-spoken man, Tomás went on to discuss with a modest assurance the economic problems of his country, the lack of roads, the potentials, and untapped resources. After listening to him for a while I wasn't surprised to learn that the *finca* was merely a summer home. Tomás was an economist, a graduate of the National University in Bogotà.

Early the next morning I began work on the jeep. But not with enthusiasm. It was then that I began to think about resigning my membership in the "Do it yourself club" and applying for that more exclusive group, the "Let somebody else do it club."

Working on La Tortuga is especially difficult since, unlike conventional vehicles, it is completely enclosed on the bottom. Everything must be done in the cramped confines of the cab where the chief asset of the mechanic, besides the proper tools, is his ability to work standing on his head or contorted into a corkscrew. With the experience gained in overhauling the jeep initially I had become mildly proficient in this art. Before the trip was over I was a master at it.

I hadn't had time to give more than a superficial examination to the transmission before Tomás came by the previous day, but I had determined where the trouble lay. The bronze synchronizing rings that made shifting smoother between second and high gear were worn and had slipped out of alignment. Even if I had replacements for the rings, to install them meant removing either the motor or the transfer case. Either way it would be a three-day job with the best of facilities.

Not at all eager to begin, I sat in the jeep staring through the hole in the floor boards at the black oily interior of the transmission. If only the engineers who had designed these things, I thought, had tried to work on them. If only the synchronizers could be kept closer together, then they couldn't slip out of alignment. A spacer behind them would do it—if only I had a spacer. But even if I did I would still have to pull the transmission to install it. But a split spacer might be the answer—if I had one. What a lot of wishful "ifs." Then I had an idea. That old standby, bailing wire. If it worked we might be able to make it to Bogotá. If it didn't—well—nothing would be lost but a few hours.

Pawing through my collection of bolts and miscellaneous supplies, I came up with a roll of wire, but it was too thin. Tomás, however, contributed a piece of fence wire which was about the right thickness. Cutting it to length, I wrapped one turn around the shaft behind the synchronizing rings. When the nut on the shaft was tightened, the wire was clamped in place. I put the cover back on the transmission, started the motor, and shifted into low. As I let out the clutch I held my breath. I didn't have to hold it long. The jeep lurched forward and screamed a howling protest. In reverse it clashed and groaned. And then mysteriously the noise stopped. I tried the other gears. They worked smoothly. Shifting several times through all the gears, I drove around in front of the house. Everything functioned quietly. Thinking it best to be under way before La Tortuga changed her mind, we thanked Tomás and left for Bogotá. It was rugged driving over pitted roads in the shadow of mighty snow-capped ridges half hidden in the afternoon mist, but the transmission ran perfectly. Even in the torrid Magdalena Valley it didn't overheat, and when we reached the outskirts of Bogotá late that night it was working so well that we decided to leave well enough alone. In fact, our bailing-wire repair job lasted for more than five thousand miles, and when we did have trouble with the transmission it was from another cause.

Bogotá was cold. After spending a rather restless night in a gravel pit outside of town we were anxious to pick up the sleeping bags and clothes we had sent ahead from Panama. But first we needed a hotel. As usual, the one recommended was the most expensive, the Tequendama, a tall concrete and glass bit of contemporary architecture. It had been the same all along the way. In Panama it was the exclusive El Panamá, which even exiled Perón joked was too expensive for him. Ask anyone about a hotel, be it policeman, taxi driver, or bartender, if you are an American the only hotel for you is the most luxurious one. Reverting to our established practice of scouting for ourselves, we were soon comfortably located in a modest hotel a few blocks from the center of town.

The Hotel Claridge, with its mellow wood paneling and worn velvet drapes tied with gold tassels, had the dated dignity of a nineteenth-century carriage. The straw mattresses were not Beauty Rests and it was a long walk to the bath at the end of the hall, but the hotel was very clean and the four-dollar-a-day tariff included three good meals. After a hot bath we walked down to the dining room, where the white linen glowed in the yellowish light of undervoltaged bulbs. As we started to sit down, the maître d'hôtel scurried over to us. His black dress suit was frayed and his stiff shirt kept popping out, but he couldn't have been more solicitous:

"Surely you must be tired after your long trip. Wouldn't

you care to take dinner in your room? Of course there would be no extra charge," he added hurriedly.

"No, thank you," I said. "We feel fine."

"Oh, but you would be so much more comfortable in your room. I'll send the waiter up right away."

He seemed so genuinely anxious to please us that we didn't argue. When we climbed the flight of stairs again to our room, a waiter was already waiting.

After dinner we went to pick up our clothes. Bogotá, at an altitude of almost nine thousand feet, was cold even in the early afternoon and we wore our *ruanas* despite the looks of scorn we received from the somber-suited men and women on the streets. At the airport we called for our things. Everything had arrived except one suitcase, the one with my suit in it. By mistake it had been sent to Cartagena; it would be a week before it would arrive. The week's delay didn't bother us—we had planned to stay that long anyway—but I was beginning to believe that in formal Colombia a sport shirt was not the correct attire for a gentleman. My suspicions were confirmed that evening when the maître d'hôtel again insisted that we would enjoy our meal more in our room.

When we called at the American Embassy for our mail we saw Ambassador Bonsal again. It was Thursday afternoon. He warmly invited us to the Fourth of July party at his residence the following Monday. That was sufficient excuse to shop for a suit—a dark gray flannel, a product of Colombia's progressive textile industry that had become one of the most important in the country.

The next few days were a relaxing change from the helter-skelter pace we had been maintaining. Bogotá was the largest city we had seen since Mexico, a metropolis where the red tile roofs of colonial homes contrasted vividly with the newer buildings and residential areas that spread over the broad plateau. Near the center of town was a high hilly park with a funicular railway that climbed steeply to the top. As the small cage crawled slowly up the almost vertical incline, I thought of the joke about the appalled American passenger who, upon reaching the top and seeing the frayed cables, complained to the operator that they were unsafe, that they should be changed. The perplexed operator answered, "But, señor, we never change them until they break."

Sunday morning, indeed every morning we spent at our little hotel, we were awakened by the rustle of a newspaper being slid under the door and Dinah's lunge to intercept the potential intruder. Always failing in this, as if to make up for her shortcomings as a watchdog she brought the paper and with much tail wagging dropped it in our faces. A few minutes later there was a gentle knock and Fernando, the waiter who had seemingly adopted us, entered with two glasses of orange juice and two cups of steaming coffee. With a cheerful "*Buenos días*" he took our breakfast order. It didn't take long for us to become accustomed to the luxury of steak, eggs, toast, and coffee in our room.

On July 4 we drove along the broad avenues through town and then out to the exclusive Chapinero district, where the State Department maintains the Ambassador's residence. Normally we would have taken a cab rather than risk the hazards of city driving, but on this particular occasion we had been asked specifically to bring the jeep. Parking at the end of a long string of cars, we walked along the circular driveway through the beautifully landscaped grounds and joined the reception line in the foyer to shake the tired hands of Ambassador and Mrs. Bonsal.

"Why, hello. Where is La Tortuga?" he asked.

"She's parked several blocks from here," Helen answered.

"That's no place to moor such an extraordinary vessel. Why don't you sail her up to the door?"

Accordingly, while Cadillac limousines deposited their important guests at the entrance and then drove away in search of a parking place, I drove lumbering La Tortuga nonchalantly through the imposing iron-grill gate and, at the Ambassador's direction, parked her next to the portico.

In Bogotá we learned that there are two types of parties, standing-up parties and sitting-down parties. The Fourth of July celebration was a standing-up party where almost all of the fifteen hundred American residents of Bogotá milled about the wings of the elegant and tastefully appointed mansion. Almost always we were introduced as the "couple with the amphibious jeep." Helen, dressed in her green moiré taffeta, appeared hardly capable of pulling her weight at the end of a winch line or spelling me with a shovel. As she answered the usual queries she looked as if the closest she had been to the jungle was the potted palm in the foyer, and as if the most strenuous thing she had ever done was to fish the olive from a martini. A rotund lady with a sable stole draped in a carefully careless way questioned her:

"Of course, my deah, you're staying at the Tequendama. What an interesting trip you're making. I understand that you have just come from Panama. I just adore traveling too. Tell me, deah, how were the accommodations along the way?" Flipping her long cigarette holder, she continued without waiting for an answer. "This may be a bit personal, but how do you manage to have your laundry done? It's simply dreadful what these maids do to my clothes."

Helen sipped slowly from her martini before answering.

208

"I don't find it too much of a problem. I just beat them on the rocks, the way the Indians do."

There was a moment of silence. The woman drew back, and then broke into a fluttery laugh. "How perfectly delightful. What a sense of humor you have, my deah."

While in Medellín we had tried to sell the outboard motor, but with no success. We were advised to try in Bogotá, where we were in turn advised to see a certain party in Cali, the next large Colombian city on our route.

After a week of parties and night life in Bogotá the more normal routine of traveling again was almost a vacation. As we followed the Pan American Highway toward the Pacific, the road to Cali was more of the same tortuous mountain driving that we had experienced all the way from Turbo. Precipices fell off on either side, mist obscured the road, and the Colombian drivers were about as considerate as a subway crowd at rush hour.

Where the many ranges of the northern Andes divide Colombia into three and sometimes four parts, the roads are steep, narrow, and winding, shooting up and down from elevations of a few thousand feet to more than twelve thousand at the passes. At the higher elevations La Tortuga wheezed valiantly, but slowly, which was fortunate since on almost any curve we were likely to meet a truck or a bus on the wrong side of the road. Not always—sometimes they were in the middle. There were only two speeds recognized —wide open and standing still. Because of mechanical breakdowns the latter condition was a common one, and wherever the mishap occurred was where they stopped. But they were very thoughtful otherwise. Whenever anyone had difficulty, everyone who came along stopped to give advice, blocking traffic for miles.

Our entrance to Cali was along the main drive, a wide avenue with a fresh green park and flowing river on one side. On the other side an occasional old cathedral broke the monotony of the sharp angles of contemporary architecture. At a much lower altitude than Bogotá, Cali was hot, and cotton dresses and sport shirts were common on the streets. But when we took refuge in an air-conditioned restaurant we found formality still the order of the day. It was an inviting place, modeled after an old Spanish inn with polished dark paneling and blue porcelain china. From the grilled windows there was a fine view of the streets, but when we took a table near them a waiter politely but firmly pointed to a sign on the wall: GENTLEMEN ARE NOT PERMITTED IN THE DINING ROOM WITHOUT COAT AND TIE.

"But since you are travelers," he condescended, "we will make an exception. Please sit over here."

Feeling like poor relations, we ate our filet of corvina shielded from the more decorously attired patrons by an embossed leather screen. "When in Rome——" Helen remarked. "Yes, or pay the consequences," I finished.

After lunch we looked up our prospect for the outboard motor, but he had already purchased one. "It will bring a better price in Ecuador anyway," he consoled us. Our financial condition was not at that time critical, but the repairs, the purchase of the outboard motor, and other expenses in Panama had eliminated any surplus we might have had for emergencies.

We were ready to leave Cali when several trucks disgorged a troop of well-armed soldiers. Traffic was stopped for two hours while a full-scale military parade blocked the streets. First the cavalry, horses with their heads high, their riders carrying gilded wooden spears with banners waving, then the band, the infantry, the jeep squadron, the riot squad, each man with a tear-gas gun and a vest full of cannon-sized shells. Trailing behind came the volunteer militia, youngsters striding along energetically, and old men trying desperately to keep up with them, sweat pouring down their faces. I asked an onlooker what it was all about.

Proudly he said, "July 20 is Independence Day, and President Pinilla is coming to visit Cali."

"But today is the eighteenth. What was this parade for?"

"This is rehearsal," he said logically.

We returned to the jeep to find it in the midst of a throng looking like Gulliver teeming with Lilliputians. Shouldering our way through, I heard one discerning woman say to her husband, "Why, that looks like a boat."

"How ridiculous," he replied firmly. "It's just one of those late-model cars."

One little boy breathlessly asked, "Are you part of the circus?" The Royal Dunbar Circus was currently playing in Cali. Like the wide-eyed child in Mexico who asked, "Does it fly?" his enthusiasm dwindled at my "No." But the rest of the crowd was enthusiastic enough for poor Dinah, who had slunk back to the most secluded corner of the jeep amid catcalls and barks. La Tortuga was getting a complete inspection, including tire-kicking, hull-pounding, and window-peeking. Several of the men were trying to lift the jeep, and two more were opening the hood. Some of the more musically inclined had discovered that the gas cans along the side emitted a variety of tones when thumped and, in keeping with the festive spirit, were busily engaged in playing what sounded vaguely like the Colombian national anthem. Then someone discovered the propeller and there was a joyful shout. The news was out. It *was* a boat. Considering it unthinkable that a boat should have a hole in it, one helpful individual started plugging the bilge pump outlet. Later I discovered that others had had the same idea. When I overhauled the bilge pump I removed one marble, three wads of gum, innumerable bottle caps, a handkerchief, and one Colombian peso. Unfortunately we were out of the country by that time and couldn't spend the peso.

Helen and I stayed around awhile to answer all the questions about La Tortuga, but when the second show started and new faces asked the same questions we excused ourselves and headed south.

At Cali we had traveled almost a thousand miles from Turbo, a thousand miles of twisting, turning mountain roads, of towns set high on hilltops, and rugged green country that was for the most part uncultivated. But the remaining three hundred miles to the Colombian-Ecuadorian frontier passed through green pastures and yellow fields of waving grain, a rumpled patchwork quilt where hedges formed the boundaries between hilly farms. From the road along the ridge that overlooked the valleys it seemed that the almost perpendicular sides of the mountains were too steep for a man even to stand, let alone till the soil.

Amphibious jeeping presented another problem when we arrived at the border and tried to leave Colombia. It was Saturday morning and we hoped to clear customs and enter Ecuador before noon, when the offices closed. On the Colombian side a heavy chain was stretched across the road in front of a small cement building. A black-uniformed gentleman in a peaked cap that said "Aduana" examined our passports.

"These seem to be in order," he mused. "Let me see your car papers."

I handed him the California certificate of title. That wasn't enough.

"Where are the papers that they gave you when you entered the country?"

"What papers? They didn't give us anything at Turbo."

"Turbo!" he exclaimed incredulously. "Nobody enters at Turbo."

"Well, we did. Why do we need papers, anyway? Proof of ownership was all we ever needed before."

"You need something to guarantee that you won't sell your car in Colombia."

I looked at a big arch a few yards away. It said "Welcome to Ecuador." Patiently I explained that we were leaving Colombia, not entering, that we had no intention of selling the jeep. But that made no difference. To leave the country we needed an export license. To get an export license we needed an import license, and since they hadn't given us one when we entered we were stuck. Mentally I cursed the customs man at Turbo. Remembering his confused mutterings about a car navigating the Gulf of Darien or a boat driving up to the customs house, I understood why we'd had such an easy entry. He hadn't known what papers to give us.

By that time it was eleven o'clock. Slowly I explained once more that it was obvious that we were leaving the country. "Look at the direction the jeep is pointing. And how can we sell it in Colombia if we're going to Ecuador?"

"Rules are rules," he answered adamantly. "You have to have papers. Are you sure you don't have any other papers?"

I fumbled through our stack of documents, which included everything from extra passport photos to postage

stamps to a check for a short beer. In desperation I handed
him the only other thing we had connected with the jeep,
the Panama Canal tonnage certificate. Across the top it said
Motor Ship LA TORTUGA. I showed it to him, explaining
that our remarkable vehicle was also registered as a ship. To
my amazement—and relief—his face brightened.

"You're registered as a ship? Why didn't you say so?
There's nothing in the rules about ships." He lowered the
chain. "You may pass."

Chapter Eight

It was just a few yards to the arch and Ecuador, and we were hoping that the welcome sign meant what it said. The difficulty in leaving Colombia had come as a surprise—proof of ownership had been sufficient to take the jeep across the borders of seven countries. We were convinced that the Colombian official had made a mistake, and when the Ecuadorian officials passed us with but a cursory glance at our passports we were sure of it.

"There are still a few minor formalities to take care of in Tulcán," they said, "but you have time to get there before the offices close."

Every few hundred yards of the four miles from the border to Tulcán there was a chain across the road, and a guardhouse that lacked only a crescent moon to make it a perfect Chic Sale. At each we stopped while the guard examined our passports and walked around the jeep several times before lowering the chain. It was still a few minutes before twelve when we arrived but both the immigration and customs offices were already closed. It looked as if we would have to wait until Monday, and Tulcán did not appear to be the most desirable weekend stop.

Traffic was slight in Tulcán—in fact, when I heard a whistle there wasn't another car in sight. "Halt." A hefty policeman waddled over to the jeep looking as if he were loaded for bear. In Spanish that made a machine-gun sound like a dripping faucet he accused us of going the wrong way on a one-way street. I looked around for a sign—there wasn't any, but I apologized for doing such an obviously stupid thing. Five minutes later he was still lecturing us when another gentleman made it a foursome. The newcomer said a few words to the policeman, who promptly left.

"Thanks," I said fervently. "I was beginning to think we would spend our first weekend in Ecuador in jail."

"It was nothing. I'm the immigration officer. May I help you?"

How lucky could we be? Along with several others of the watching crowd, we followed him to his office, where he unlocked the door, stamped our passports, and inscribed the usual information in an immense book. When he was finished he rubbed his hands and said, "That will be ten sucres for overtime work, please." Ten sucres was about fifty cents U.S. Fortunately we had procured some Ecuadorian money in Bogotá before leaving. He was pocketing the money when a youth with a whiny voice and black stringy hair asserted that he was the assistant to the customs officer and was authorized to take care of the rest of the "minor" formalities —in exchange for overtime pay.

In another office the assistant looked at our passports and opened another huge book.

"May I see your Libreta de Pasos por Aduana."

I looked at him blankly. "My what?"

"Your Libreta de Pasos por Aduana, the document issued by the automobile club guaranteeing that you won't sell your vehicle in Ecuador."

I had never even heard of such a document. Perhaps, I thought, it was for commercial travelers.

216

"There must be some mistake," I said. "We're tourists. Is this document absolutely necessary?"

"Oh no," he replied. I breathed a sigh of relief. "Instead you may post a cash deposit equal to the customs duty on your vehicle." He consulted his book and named some astronomical figure in sucres. Reduced to dollars, it was still more than we had for the rest of the trip. There *had* to be some mistake.

"Quito," I said, "is just a day's drive from here. We'll straighten this out there."

"You won't get past the first guard," was the gloomy reply.

The first chain was just out of town. Inside the usual little outhouse of a guard station was a soldier, the end of his rifle sticking out the window. Walking slowly from his cubicle and around the jeep, he leaned against the door. "Your credentials?" he asked.

With a self-confident and assured air which I didn't feel I gave him every document we had. Most of them were in English, but he scrutinized each one carefully, some upside down, nodding and grunting approval. Handing them back, he gave us a slip of paper and lowered the chain. "That will be one sucre please."

I was so relieved I would have given him a hundred sucres if he had asked for them. It was several minutes before we relaxed enough to look at the paper which read, "As a driver you have contributed to a fund for a drivers' mausoleum."

The road to Quito was of fine cobblestone construction, a pleasure after the chuckholed one in Colombia. We would have enjoyed the drive if it hadn't been that every few miles there was another chain or a wooden bar like a railroad barrier. At each we sweated while the same ritual was performed and we were allowed to pass. The fund for a drivers' mausoleum apparently had only the one solicitor.

From Tulcán at almost ten thousand feet elevation the Pan American Highway rose and fell, the afternoon sun glaring from the smooth cobblestones. In one place was a bit of transplanted Africa with tiny Negro children playing in the dust before conical-roofed grass huts. The tropical valley was green with banana palms and the sound of a river diluted the whistling wind from the surrounding barren hills. But except for that brief dip into the tropics the route led through the cool highlands, through Ibarra and Otovalo, where the Saturday market was dispersing. Hundreds of Ecuadorian Indians trotted along, the color of their hand-loomed cloths contrasting with the amber-colored terrain. In bright full skirts, bowl-shaped hats like halos, and shawls loaded with babies or other produce, women urged their men home. As the afternoon waned, the air grew crisp and the graceful folds of red ponchos covered the loose blouses and short white pants of the men, but always their thick queues of blue-black hair hung outside under their floppy felt hats.

Ecuador, named for the line that girds the globe, was a paradox. It was far from our conception of an equatorial climate as we stood huddled in our *ruanas* straddling the center of the world while the sun tinted the snow-capped peak of Cayambe. Beside the road was a concrete replica of the earth and an obelisk inscribed *Linea Ecuatorial oo° oo′ oo″*.

Quito was busily preparing for an important event when we arrived. It seemed that we were always entering a city on a holiday, but this time it was something special. Everyone was cleaning or repairing. Sidewalks were freshly patched, public buildings were newly painted, grass was being transplanted, the streets were swept, signs were being erected, and along the main street a grandstand was partly constructed. The occasion? President Rojas Pinilla of Colombia was paying a visit to Ecuador.

The festivities had resulted in a housing shortage in Quito. There were available rooms but they were either too expensive or very much too cheap. At one of the former class we asked the young lady at the desk if she knew of a more modest place.

"Why, yes," she said, "my family has an extra room."

It was another bit of extraordinary luck. Within the hour we were happily ensconced with the Vega family in their comfortable stucco and tile home a few blocks from the American Embassy. It was fortunate that we were close to the latter—we were to spend a great deal of time there.

Señora Vega was a kindly woman who rarely wore anything but black. She had raised twelve children and two more in her home didn't bother her a bit. Although we were paying guests, she treated us as part of the family. Even Dinah was welcomed by their huge dog. Señor Vega was a suave mustached gentleman who usually wore a Homburg, as did most of the professional men of Quito—probably because the Indians used the more conventional soft felt hats. Only three of the children still lived at home; about our age, they were all ardent lovers of American jazz and Italian opera. Although Pepe, the youngest son, knew some English, for our benefit only Spanish was spoken. And also for our benefit each day Señora Vega prepared a different Ecuadorian dish: avocado baked in whipped eggs; *humitas,* a savory mild form of tamale; *locro,* potato and cheese soup;

baked bananas; and always the refreshing beverage of cooked pineapple and *naranjilla*, a pulpy fruit like an orange.

The first thing on the agenda was to determine the truth about what was required for travel by car in Ecuador. After picking up our mail at the Embassy we made an appointment to see the vice-consul, Mr. Allan McClean. Mr. McClean was filling out a complicated form when we entered. A fine-featured man with dark hair graying at the temples, he sat back in his chair and relaxed.

"Now then," he said, "what can we do for you?"

"We would like to know what is required to enter Ecuador with an automobile." I went on to describe the difficulty at Tulcán. As I spoke, Mr. McClean grew less and less relaxed. By the time I had finished he was sitting straight up in his chair.

"Smugglers," he declared, "that's what you are, smugglers. Bringing an automobile into the country illegally is one of the most heinous of crimes here."

Martians, circus performers, and now smugglers. What next? Previous name calling had provided many a laugh, but there was nothing humorous about this situation. With grave face Mr. McClean went right to work on the problem.

He called the chief of customs. The chief of customs wired Tulcán. How had we passed a dozen guard stations without documents? Tulcán wired back. They had no record of us, had neither seen nor heard of us. We visited the customs chief, the police chief, and the automobile club. Then we visited them all again. At the end of a week all we had seen of Quito was what we saw between government offices. Finally, thanks to Mr. McClean, the last paper was signed. The customs chief waived the bond requirement, entered us legally in the country, and gave us a letter of authorization to leave. One thing still bothered us—what would we encounter in entering Peru?

At the Automobile Club of Ecuador we learned the sad news. The man at Tulcán had been correct. The only alternative to a Libreta de Pasos por Aduana was a large cash deposit varying from 50 to 110 per cent of the value of the vehicle. Furthermore, all tourists with automobiles were subject to this requirement. And, what was worse, the requirements in the rest of the countries along our route, Peru, Bolivia, Chile, and Argentina, were even more stringent. With the Libreta, however, the tourist could travel freely across the borders. In effect a bond, the Libreta protected the governments against illegal sale of the vehicle and loss of customs duties.

I felt like a prize sap. Of all the oversights of which I was guilty the worst was neglecting to join an auto club in the States. All this trouble could have been avoided; the Libreta could have been issued before we left. But one thing was certain—unless we could obtain this magical document our trip was over. How ironical—to pass all the physical obstacles only to be stopped by a legal one. The manager of the auto club was sympathetic but he said:

"I'm sorry. Our rules prohibit the issue of a standard Libreta to anyone who is not a resident of Ecuador. However, perhaps we can bend those rules a bit and give you a temporary one good only for Peru. The auto club there has had much more experience in these matters. Maybe they can help you."

We went back to see Mr. McClean. Before the Ecuadorian auto club could issue even a temporary document, we needed a letter stating that the Embassy would be responsible should we fail to live up to the agreement. We both knew that the Embassy couldn't possibly assume that responsibility. Why should they? But we underestimated Mr. McClean. In a short time we had a letter stating that he would do all in his power to assure that we fulfilled the agreement. It was an ingenious letter since Mr. McClean's power in such matters was decidedly limited, but it accomplished its purpose. With our one-country reprieve safely tucked away with the letter from the customs chief and a letter of introduction to the president of the Automobile Club of Peru, we went back to the Vega house to pack. As we left, Pepe Vega joked, "Next time you come to Quito I hope you can find time to see the city."

Guayaquil was not on our planned route, but the Vega family extolled the virtues of Ecuador's principal port to such an extent that we felt compelled to go there. Besides being fascinated by seaports we thought we might be able to sell the outboard motor. Before we left, a friend of the Vegas gave us a letter of introduction to a member of the Guayaquil yacht club. Just as in Colombia all business was done through friends, in Ecuador apparently it was through letters of introduction.

We got a late start from Quito. Perhaps it took longer to pack in the nine-thousand-foot altitude or perhaps it was because we were unconsciously reluctant to leave the friendly atmosphere of the Vega home. In any event, we traveled only thirty miles before making camp between the marshmallow-topped peak of Cotopaxi, a perfect cone over nineteen thousand feet high, and Iliniza, a seventeen-thousand-foot fang piercing the blue sky. Off the road several hundred yards we prepared supper while little shepherdesses watched shyly from the midst of their flocks, smiling winsomely, timidly sharing our dessert of Life Savers. The next morning our hipbones were bruised and our joints stiff—both air mattresses had gone flat. Ah, the trials of camping. We were spoiled by too many comfortable beds.

The precipitous descent to the hot coastal area was memorable. The road was a spiraling, crater-filled trail which knocked off the covers and overturned a can of Spry and a can of honey. The spilled honey inside the cabinet was bad enough, but the heat melted the Spry too. And then there was a rather rude introduction to the *mixto*, the half cargo truck, half third-class passenger bus that is the terror of the Ecuadorian roads. The first contact, a gentle caress along the side, left La Tortuga with three dented gas cans, a bent spare tire rack, and a nasty crack in the wood paneling of the cab. The driver didn't even slow down. A half hour later the driver of another *mixto* was a little more considerate. He stopped and looked at the gaping hole he had put in La Tortuga's bow before driving off without a word.

We were sick. The jeep was no longer amphibious, and ahead of us was still the Strait of Magellan to cross. The whole front was battered in; she would never be the same. And it would be an expensive repair job just to make her watertight again; the hole was big enough for Dinah to crawl through.

Guayaquil, too, was preparing for some important event —we encountered the same difficulty with rooms as in Quito. And after the accident there was an even greater need for economy. After lunch in one of the many sidewalk cafés I asked the waiter if he knew where we could get an inexpensive room. With a sly wink at me he pointed to a building across the street.

"You might find a room up there," he said.

In a shaky groaning elevator we rode to the top floor of the building where a small peephole in a door opened to my knock and a carrot-topped middle-aged woman peered out.

"My wife and I would like a room," I said.

"Your wife?" She raised her eyebrows doubtfully. "Yes, of course, your wife," she repeated, smiling at Helen. "I have just one vacant room. Come in."

Looking as if she had stepped from a Toulouse-Lautrec canvas, she was shapely for her age—the silk dressing gown made that evident. We had never been greeted by a concierge in a dressing gown before, but then it was hot in Guayaquil. Following along the dark corridor, she showed us the room. Even in the obscure light the color was startling —a passionate shade of red. And there was a full-size double bed. That in itself was rare in Latin America.

"How long will you be?" she asked.

"Perhaps four days," I replied.

She seemed surprised. "Well, I don't usually rent for that long, but I guess it's all right."

The waiter had told us it was a boardinghouse, but when I asked about meals the landlady corrected me:

"I serve only breakfast, and I'm sure you'd prefer to take your meals out. We eat rather late around here."

We had been in rooming houses decorated in better taste but certainly none more colorful. Done in pink and baby blue, with turquoise satin drapes, only the perpetually drawn shades kept it from being blinding. After two days I concluded that the other residents were all women, and very popular ones judging by the number of male visitors they had. Dressing gowns seemed to be the accepted attire day or night, and there were always men sitting in the living room or enjoying a drink over their game of cards. By the end of our stay I was sure that either the waiter had misunderstood my intentions or I had misunderstood his Spanish.

It was too late to do anything about the outboard motor or the hole in the jeep the afternoon we arrived, so we strolled lazily through the streets taking advantage of every bit of shade. The sticky heat clung, rose from the sidewalks in shimmering waves, changing reality to fancy, fantasy to entity, until both became fused, and that first day in Guayaquil became a fleeting series of dreamlike impressions:

A waterfront town, a mile and a half of river, ships anchored in the middle with lighters attached to their sides like pilot fish to a shark. Tiny dots that scurried under the watchful eyes of customs officials, loading, unloading, bananas, coffee, automobiles, rice, machinery, hats. Wooden boats rubbing together, rudders askew, sails patched and dirty. A bell rings, "Cast off," and brawny arms heave with a bamboo pole, the reflections golden in the muddy water. A breath of blessed breeze, the sails flutter, then droop listlessly like the ragged children who hung over the gunwales watching others play with pretty toy boats while maids kept a wary eye on their charges.

From columns supporting the iron rail along the river an overpowering stench of urine mingled with the smell of newly milled lumber, of fish, of flowers, and of garbage floating to the sea. Men sleeping in corners, rolling blindly into more protected shade as the sun stabbed at their faces. And on the terrace at the yacht club, men in white sipping cool drinks; on the walk in front, men in tatters wandering aimlessly. The excited buzz of sidewalk gamblers as they watch the gaudy designs of the whirling wheel, the disappointed moan of the losers, and the smile of pleasure as the winner opens the pack of Luckies and slowly takes a puff from the prize.

That evening we sat under the striped canopy of a sidewalk café enjoying our first taste of that Guayaquil delicacy, *ceviche de corvina*—raw fish and pink onions pickled in lime juice. The air was cooler and there was almost a music to the noise of traffic, but Helen's mind was somewhere else.

"Estrada," she repeated again and again. "Estrada. That name's familiar."

"It should be. We've seen it plastered on every building in town. Emilio Estrada, Mayor of Guayaquil."

"No, I mean before that."

Later, back in the room, Helen dug out the letter from Quito to the man in the yacht club. It was addressed to a Señor Estrada.

"But that doesn't mean it's the same man," I said. "Estrada in Ecuador could be like Jones in the States."

But when we inquired for the gentleman the next morning at the yacht club we were directed to the City Hall.

The Mayor of Guayaquil was a handsome man in his thirties, tall, robust, and with a passion for sports cars and boats. La Tortuga could hardly be called either, but the fact that she was a sporting compromise aroused his interest. He received us warmly, speaking perfect English, and after reading the letter from his friend wanted to know all about the trip, and then asked to see the jeep. He spotted the hole in the bow immediately.

"What happened here?"

"Those *mixtos* are murder," I said. "We were hit twice in less than an hour."

"Well, we can't have her leaving Guayaquil like that. My

226

brother and I own the Ford agency. I'll call my boys and tell them to take care of you."

I was still thanking him when the conversation ended with an invitation to a Lightning-class regatta at the yacht club the next day. The next day was a dead calm—there was no regatta, but we were invited below decks of several luxury yachts and had an unequaled opportunity to meet people who might be interested in an outboard motor. The answer was always the same: "No, this is off season. But it will bring a better price in Peru anyway."

Three days later La Tortuga was ready. Mayor Estrada's men had done a good job; she was watertight again, but there was no mistaking her *mixto* mar even with new paint on the bow. We hadn't accomplished our main objective in going to Guayaquil, that of selling the outboard motor, but we had met some fine people, and even with La Tortuga's disfigurement we felt the side trip was worth it as we headed for Cuenca and the Peruvian border.

There was one bridgeless river to cross on the road out of town, but regular service was provided by a mobile bridge, a decrepit barge that looked as if it had fought all the battles of the Pacific. La Tortuga was surrounded by curious people, and we were avalanched with questions: "If that thing is really amphibious, why don't you go in the water?" I gave up trying to explain that we always used bridges when available, and finally offered an explanation they understood—that I was too lazy. After even a short immersion it would take a full day to clean and relubricate the differentials and wheel bearings.

Honking loudly on every curve and moving well to the side for anything larger than a bicycle, we climbed steadily to the highlands and the Pan American Highway again. The road was a tortuous repetition of the descent—bumps, steep grades, and rapidly changing vegetation from mirrored rice paddies and extravagant fans of banana palms to the cold wind-swept *paramos*. A giant checkerboard of green and gold, the fields of waving grain rippled like a breeze-ruffled lake at sunset. Moving endlessly as in a circus ring, horses flayed wheat with their hoofs, and on the crests of the rolling hills sheep and goats were tended by red-ponchoed Indians in sheepskin chaps, the wool long and matted. Near Cuenca, the center of the so-called Panama hat industry, women in flame-colored skirts shuffled to market balancing towers of semi-finished hats on their heads.

Between Cuenca and the Peruvian border there was supposedly a fifty-mile gap in the Highway, but it was rumored that a trail through the military zone was passable in dry weather. Closer to the border the trail dwindled to a path through tall ceiba trees and low shrub. In the rainy season

228

it would be a quagmire, but that time of year—August—we had no trouble except with the suffocating clouds of brown dust. As a result of a border dispute the military zone was well manned and guard stations were numerous. In that fifty miles we were stopped fourteen times to show our credentials. We were happy to have some to show.

The entry into Peru was effortless. Neatly uniformed officials stamped our passports and Libreta, and we silently blessed the auto club in Quito. At Tumbes, the border town, there were a few extracurricular questions when Peruvian Army Intelligence learned we had passed through the Ecuadorian military zone. When he was through with us, I'm afraid that the interrogating officer had a low opinion of Yankee powers of observation.

La Tortuga speeded along the black ribbon of asphalt through the moonlike terrain of Peru's arid north. By "speeded" I mean a fast thirty-five miles per hour. From the Pacific port of Tumbes, where some four hundred years earlier Pizarro began his bloody conquest of Peru, the Pan American Highway replaced the ancient Incan road that had stretched for thousands of miles to the south. Undulating yellow sand had covered the early thoroughfare, but there was bleak evidence of the past near Trujillo, where hundreds of acres of mounds pimpled the countryside. Chan-Chan, imperial city of the pre-Incan Chimu empire, remained as mud-and-pebble relics of temples, palaces, and a canal that brought water from the coastal range of the Andes. Some of the mounds had been excavated, exposing yellow ochre reliefs to the depredations of weather and man, but at nearby Chiclín, a vast irrigated sugar cane plantation, owner Señor Larco Herrera had guarded antiquity in his private museum. In the dim interior were mummies of warriors curled like fetuses in death, wrapped in millenium-old fabrics, the intricate designs still brilliant, preserved by the rainless atmosphere. Surrounding them were their copper knives, bone combs, wooden war clubs, and ceremonial masks. Spanning time, we wandered from room to room, but one piece of pottery brought me with a smile back to the twentieth century—a potbellied little man that was a perfect likeness of the Nearsighted Mr. Magoo.

Trujillo was founded by Pizarro, who apparently left there a few ruthless descendants. When we returned to the square from a browse around the quiet town we found that it hadn't been so quiet around La Tortuga. Scores of uniformed youths from an elite academy were climbing on top, prying open the windows, and making liberal use of their pocket-knives to carve their names on La Tortuga's wooden stern. I was disgusted. Helen was rabid. With Dinah's assistance she pinned one of the culprits against the side of the jeep.

"But"—he shrugged innocently—"it's our custom." With that weak excuse for vandalism he ducked away.

"Modern barbarians," Helen whimpered, running her fingers over the deep gouges in the smooth surface she had so painstakingly sandpapered. In ten countries La Tortuga's only scars had been acquired in travel, which was to be expected, but in Trujillo the precedent was set. Thereafter the jeep became public property, to be adorned with names, phone numbers, and lovers' hearts, using anything available for the inscription—bottle caps, broken glass, wire or, rarely, the more conventional pencil or pen.

Lima was covered by a low-hanging overcast that symbolized our gloomy prospects. While other tourists chattered of bargains in Peruvian silver, or worried about smuggling out of Peru their forbidden vicuña rugs, or pondered how they could carry a case of pisco on their sixty-pound airline luggage allowance, we were faced with the pressing problem of peddling an outboard motor, the desperate need of acquiring a new Libreta, and the mundane matter of mattress hunting. What a way to see sophisticated Lima, City of the Kings, one-time capital of Spanish South America and cultural mecca of the Pacific.

Near the center of town, off the Plaza San Martín, we checked into a pension, once a fashionable private residence. With high ceiling ornately trimmed with baroque designs in plaster, our room was big enough to hold a ball. The landlady was inordinately proud of the new modern conveniences, a beautifully tiled bathroom with sparkling fixtures of purple, pink, and black. But the plumber who installed them got his pipes crossed. Water draining from the sink filled the tub, and when the commode was flushed there was an echoing gurgle from the bidet.

Lima, near Callao, the starting point for Kon-Tiki, was alert for anything new in the way of aquatic conveyances. Spotting La Tortuga in front of the pension, a newspaperman requested a photo of her afloat. Later that day La Tortuga filled the front page of the afternoon paper along with news of church burnings in Buenos Aires by Peronistas, the followers of Argentina's dictator Juan Perón. But there was no room for headlines and a photo caption too. Under the picture of La Tortuga and crew, in bold type it read, **PERONISTAS IN ACTION.**

With that announcement to Lima society the small white envelope among our mail came as a great surprise, an invitation to dinner from Ambassador and Mrs. Ellis O. Briggs.

At the bottom was written, "Dinah is invited." Two days later, with complete nonchalance, Dinah entered the black limousine that brought us to the large residence on Avenida Arequipa.

Ambassador and Mrs. Briggs received the three of us graciously and informally in the library. Dinah said "Thank you, no," to the martinis and "Yes, please," to the appetizers, tiny cheese cornucopias. A Lord Calvert gentleman in a green tweed suit, Ambassador Briggs smiled amiably at Dinah, who immediately recognized in him an indulgent friend. Lying at his feet on the thick pile rug, she watched with persuasive eyes, an optimist to the last bite.

What could have been a cheerless Spanish colonial mansion was instead a warm and friendly home reflecting the personalities of Ambassador and Mrs. Briggs, and the air of cordiality pervaded the sunlit dining room. White-gloved *mozos* poured wine into crystal goblets and served black mushroom soup, delicate white fish, dainty hot breads, filet mignon, and spears of buttered asparagus. From the adjoining alcove Dinah sniffed appreciatively. To our embarrassment she reverted to the customs of her feudal ancestors and took her place beneath the table. Despite our stern reproofs there she stayed, knowing we couldn't gracefully disrupt the congenial atmosphere with more severe forms of discipline.

After dinner the conversation turned to the southern end of the continent, Tierra del Fuego, an area the Ambassador knew well. Over a liqueur in the library he spoke of the terrific winds, the barren treeless plains, the gigantic sheep *estancias* on this island mass of land across the Strait of Magellan.

The most urgent problem confronting us in Lima was that

of acquiring a new Libreta de Pasos por Aduana. Without that magical passport to motoring we would never reach Tierra del Fuego. At the Automobile Club of Peru, the assistant manager, Señorita Mariluz Injoque, a slim attractive brunette, listened with interest to our winded account.

"And so," I concluded dismally, "now La Tortuga's wheels are more deeply bogged in red tape than in any marsh we've encountered."

Calling the manager, Señor Ricardo Palma, she sympathetically related our difficulties, adding, "I hope we can help these people. The story of their journey could do much to promote interest in the Pan American Highway."

Then followed an interview with the president of the auto club, Señor Eduardo Dibos, a dedicated man who had spent much of his life in actively boosting road construction and nurturing the ideal of Inter-American travel. Several days later we were issued a Libreta, valid for all of the remaining countries on our route. With it was a friendly admonition—normally the Libreta is issued only in the country where the motorist is a resident. It was a great concession, one for which we are extremely grateful.

With headache number one relieved things were looking up. But sight-seeing was still limited to mattress factories, outboard motor dealers, and whatever lay between. We were having little success on either score. Our air mattresses were flatter than yesterday's soufflé, the imported ones in the stores were thirty-five U.S. dollars apiece, and sponge rubber was sold by the troy ounce. We saw a good bit of Lima that was never included in a guided tour searching for someone to make straw pads, from the old Rímac section across the river where secondhand mattresses were renovated to an ultra-ultra place where the manufacturer disdainfully replied, "We make nothing but king-size." Back in the room I was gluing patches on the patches of our old ones when Helen burst in with the startling news that she had sold the outboard motor. I forgot about mattresses. After two weeks of trying the Colombian method of friends, the Ecuadorian system of introductory letters, and the more familiar means of conducting business—the classified sections of the newspapers—I had given up on the motor and was resigned to carrying it to Tierra del Fuego. But my enterprising wife discovered there was still another way of doing business in Latin America—by luck, charm, and a dog. In one breathless sentence she explained:

"Dinah stopped to sniff in front of a bicycle shop and I saw bicycle motors in the window and there was a friendly young man behind the counter and since I had nothing to lose I asked if they bought outboard motors and he said 'Yes' but Papa said 'No' so the young man escorted me to another shop where the man behind the counter said 'No' but a customer smiled and said 'Yes.'"

Except in Mexico our itinerary in all the countries thus far had been dictated by the Pan American Highway—there was only one route. But from Lima we had a choice. The most direct was the official route of the Highway along the coast of Peru and then across the copper and nitrate desert of Chile to Santiago, the capital. But this route bypassed what to us was the most interesting aspect of Peru, the land of the Incas, the Altiplano, and Cuzco, center of the flourishing Incan culture until the Spaniards despoiled it in the 1530's. Accordingly, we discussed with the auto club an alternate. We decided to head east from Lima over the highest motor road in the world and then along Peru's Central Highway to Cuzco and Lake Titicaca, across Bolivia and the northern part of Argentina. From there our route would take us back across the Andes to Santiago, Chile, through the pass where Aconcagua thrusts its snowy crown higher than any other mountain in the Western Hemisphere and the Christ of the Andes spreads his arms in benediction. From Santiago we planned to travel south to South America's Switzerland, across fifty miles of lakes to enter Argentina again, through desolate Patagonia, across the Strait of Magellan to Tierra del Fuego and Ushuaia, the world's southernmost town at the tip of the continent. From Ushuaia, where the trip would actually end, we planned to head north to Buenos Aires and catch a freighter home from there.

Before leaving Lima I serviced the jeep and installed a high-altitude jet in the carburetor. La Tortuga had never been higher than twelve thousand feet and I wasn't sure how she would perform at altitudes where the Air Force recommends oxygen for its pilots. At first the ascent was gradual, winding through the valley of the Rímac River, but then as the road climbed higher and higher walls of rock rose in sheer cliffs. At Infiernillo, or Little Hell, bridges hung suspended from the maws of tunnels, and three times the road crisscrossed back on itself in one awesome canyon. Wheezing and panting, the 60-horsepower motor moved La Tortuga's five-thousand-pound bulk slower and slower. Repeatedly I advanced the distributor and dropped to lower gears. At the crest, 15,665 feet above sea level, the jeep gave a relieved little cough, and we stopped to let her cool. A few snowflakes touched our faces, then melted to join the rivers flowing to both the Atlantic and the Pacific.

For much of the next six hundred miles to Cuzco we traveled above ten thousand feet, across the Altiplano, where tumbled masses of rock punctuated the somber rolling plains. Shying at our approach, shaggy wild ponies and even wilder vicuña fled over the clumps of wiry grass. In places remnants of the Incan road system were still visible, a system that had carried Incan armies from Cuzco north to Quito and as far south as the center of Argentina. After more than five hundred years short stretches of Incan road looked better than parts of the Pan American Highway, but what amused me more was that the ancient foot couriers traveled faster than we did. Running in short relays, the *chasquis* carried to their Incan lords news, fresh fish, and delicacies from the far reaches of the empire, covering as much as a hundred and fifty miles in a day. Our daily average through this rugged terrain was less than a hundred miles.

One reason we made little progress was La Tortuga's lack of power at high altitudes. But equally retarding was the llama. Intrigued by this distant cousin to the camel, we couldn't pass one by without stopping. Ornamented with necklace of bright wool and ear brands of streaming colored ribbon, she haughtily returned our stare. Supposedly a beast of burden, she carried her tiny bundles with condescension, moving with mincing steps, her tail prissy, like a bustle on her generously rounded rear. Vanity, thy name is llama.

When we arrived in Huancayo, the Sunday-morning market was already buzzing with activity. The highway ran through the main street, which was blocked off for Indian commerce, and every foot for ten blocks was filled with little stalls of red-and-white striped canopies. Parking the jeep in a side street, we joined the throng, but somewhere in the shuffle I lost Helen. When I found her twenty minutes later she was breathless again. I sensed some new portentous development.

"Now calm down, take a deep breath, and tell me. What's all the excitement?"

"I found someone to make some mattresses for us. He said he could finish them today."

That *was* good news. We couldn't travel any more that day anyway since traffic over the one-way road for a hundred and fifty miles south of Huancayo alternated in direction every other day. The day for our direction was Monday. Together we went to make final arrangements. For the equivalent of ten U.S. dollars the Indian craftsman would make two pads to fit the jeep. He showed us the materials, arresting pink ticking for the cover and a gray-black vegetable fiber for the stuffing. The fiber had the resiliency of damp spaghetti, but it was softer than the hard boards we were almost accustomed to.

The market in Huancayo was unique in one respect. It was surprisingly sedate. Especially the hat bazaar, where Helen, unconcerned at being out of vogue in her faded culottes, was just as interested in the Daché creations of Huancayo as were two fashionable barefoot Indian misses. Dressed in full skirts of sunflower yellow and scarlet, aqua satin blouses, bibbed and tucked, they were as intent on their selection as any lady on Fifth Avenue. And similarly, with hundreds of hats to choose from, they couldn't make up their minds. Renoir types with taffeta ribbons, shallow-crown derbies, pale gold sailors of straw, they tried them all, very particular about the fit, which was a bit ludicrous since it was obvious the hats had no fit at all. And finally, like any lady on Fifth Avenue, they left without having bought one.

After a night of squirming the appropriate hollows into our new mattresses we left at dawn to cover the hundred and fifty miles to Ayacucho before dusk. The road was one

238

way with good reason. A precarious shelf scratched from the side of a deep gorge, it twisted high above the Mantaro River, a milky turquoise froth in a cleft of multicolored rock. Plummeting to green valleys, straining wearily to where eagles circle, La Tortuga crept toward Cuzco, through Ayacucho, Andahuaylas, Abancay, towns spaced along the Central Highway as evenly as the hostels of the ancient Incas.

Pisac, near Cuzco, was off the main route. Like nearly every other village, it slept six days out of seven and began to stir early for the Sunday morning market. The winding dirt trail was queued with Indians; some of the more prosperous used burros or llamas to carry their produce, but for the most part the beast of burden was the Indian himself. A few miles from Pisac we came upon an Indian carrying nothing but a silver-capped staff. Sitting jauntily on his head was a red hat, like a felt-covered salad bowl. He was wearing the usual bright striped poncho, and his black knee-length pants, cut up a few inches on each side, were reminiscent of the dress of the Indians of Chichicastenango, Guatemala. We recognized him as a tribal chieftain and asked if he would like to ride with us to Pisac. We didn't speak Quechua and he didn't speak Spanish, but our gestures toward him and then to the jeep conveyed the idea. He nodded, smiling beneath the long straggly hairs that hung from his upper lip, and very gingerly climbed in. Dinah could have been more hospitable, and if we had known how long the sour smell of stale *chicha* would cling to the inside of the jeep we might have been less so. As La Tortuga bounced down the steep descent to Pisac, our guest sat stiffly erect in the seat, clutching his staff of office and trying vainly to maintain his jiggling hat and his dignity at the same time.

Unlike Huancayo, there were no individual stalls at the Pisac market. In the square near the ruins of an old church the vendors sat at random on the ground and spread their wares before them. One of the busiest sections was the pharmacy, where fifty or more little cloth sacks, rolled halfway down, revealed herbs of all classes, powdered glass, and bits of hide and cloth. To the side were bulging bags of dried llama fetuses. For the hypochondriacs among the old lady doctor's patients there were primitive placebos—pink and blue sugar candy in heart and diamond shapes.

We left Pisac late that afternoon. Just eight miles from Cuzco, with the ominous crack of rending steel, the wheels locked, and we were thrown against the windshield. Dazed, I crawled beneath the jeep and removed the cover of the rear differential. What was left of the gears was piled in a mound of metal chunks. I removed what pieces I could and disconnected the rear drive. Using front-wheel power, we limped into Cuzco.

I was baffled. There had been no warning whine to indi-

top—View of Machu Picchu from the lookout point 2,000 feet above the silent city. Machu Picchu, Peru. center—The watchtower at Machu Picchu, Peru, exhibits the precise stonework of the Incan artisans. left—Festival in Ilave, Peru, near Lake Titicaca.

ABOVE—Reed boat of Lake Titicaca in the process of being constructed. CENTER—Llama-power at 14,000 feet in Bolivia was better than horse-power. BOTTOM—The Gate of the Sun at Tiahuanaco, Bolivia, the oldest known ruins in the Western Hemisphere.

ABOVE—The guitar and folklore group of Carmen Cuevas Mackenna accompanies these three Chilenos as they dance the *jota* near Santiago, Chile. The *jota*, like the cueca, is a dance of courtship, and in this case is an imitation of two roosters courting a hen. BELOW—La Tortuga crossing Lake Todos los Santos, at the base of Mount Osorno in Chile.

ABOVE—Sheep on their way to be shorn on Estancia Leleque in Argentine Patagonia. RIGHT—Argentine gauchos having their morning asado on Estancia Leleque. BELOW--Penguins near Port Deseado in Patagonia.

ABOVE—La Tortuga and crew looking across the Strait of Magellan at Tierra del Fuego. BELOW—Workers of the Argentine Road Commission help La Tortuga over the tail end of the Andes in Tierra del Fuego.

ABOVE—La Tortuga and crew on the outskirts of Ushuaia, the world's
southernmost town. BELOW—Destination—Ushuaia.

RIGHT—Buenos Aires cemetery, a city of the dead complete with trash can, street lights, and water faucet. BELOW—Battered La Tortuga in front of the statue of Christopher Columbus, Buenos Aires, Argentina.

A short rest near Uspallata, Argentina, before the last climb to the Christ of the Andes pass.

Trail's end—the Christ of the Andes on the Argentine-Chilean border.

cate a misadjustment, there was plenty of lubricant, and the differential wasn't hot. There was no obvious reason for it to fail. With dismay I realized there could be only one answer. Metal fatigue. With five thousand miles left to go, faithful La Tortuga was wearing out.

True to form, we arrived on a holiday, this time on the eve of a three-day holiday. There would be no repairing of La Tortuga until the festivities were over. Cuzco, city of the Incas, of pageantry, and of the most unmelodious bells in the world, was celebrating the Day of La Merced, patron saint of the Army.

We became accustomed to the hourly tolling of the giant bells, and they didn't bother us much during the day—that is, if you consider the day as commencing at 5:00 A.M. But on the Day of La Merced they began ringing at midnight, each boy trying to ring his bell louder and faster than his partner. The resultant dissonance made a boiler factory sound like a symphony.

From our second-story room opposite the church we had a grandstand view. The Army marched in full regalia, its band adding to the din, followed by hundreds of demurely veiled young girls, and the city fathers, stiff shirts, tails, white gloves, furry cocked hats, and all. Ceremoniously gathering in front of the cathedral, they silently filed inside through the watching crowd of awe-struck Indians. Voices were raised briefly in singing, and to the thunder of drums the priests filed out, the archbishop robed in white, his assistants holding the corners of his brocaded cape to display its dazzling gold lining. And then, borne by thirty men, appeared the life-sized Virgin of La Merced, resplendent in a glittering gown selected for the occasion from her extensive wardrobe. Dramatically the procession began its methodical pace through the streets, followed by the same city fathers, young girls, soldiers, and black-draped figures of the well-to-do. Solemnly—with popping firecrackers strewn by altar boys —the calvacade continued around the square. The image on its weighty pedestal tipped precariously as the bearers crouched to avoid sagging power lines. But once they didn't crouch quite far enough—with a crackle of sparks and a wisp of smoke a short circuit consumed the Virgin's tinsel halo.

As we walked through the streets of Cuzco I had the feeling that the curtain was rising on an archaeological play. In the program of tiered walls, layer upon layer of time, I read Act I in the wall's foundation, the archaic art of the Inca, colossal stonework of mosaic precision. Act II, enter the Spaniard with his mud and straw construction. And at the top, Act III, the machine age, corrugated iron roofs. Center of Incan rule and religion, it was in Cuzco that the greatest temples were built, to the moon and the stars, handmaidens to their highest deity, the sun. On the plateau above the city were other Incan monuments: the huge fortress of Sacsahuamán, Kencco, the underground chamber of meditation carved from living rock, and the baths of the Incas, where crystal water flowed from an unknown source. All bore witness to the ingenuity of a race that worked without benefit of steel and moved stones larger than the jeep without beasts of burden.

The guidebooks say that no trip to Cuzco is complete without a visit to Machu Picchu, the mountain stronghold of the Incas. Since it was accessible only by rail, we bought our tickets—but not for the exclusive eight-passenger Autocarril, or even the de luxe thirty-passenger rail bus recommended by the tourist agencies. Early the next morning we clambered aboard one of the antiquated wooden cars with our fellow passengers—Indians, chickens, and pigs. Delighted at not having to ride in a baggage car, Dinah quickly made herself comfortable—on the poncho of a passenger who rebuked us for making her move. A few minutes later the Toonerville Trolley began what might be the slowest train ride in the world, six hours for the seventy-mile run. After creeping up the side of the valley we were soon clacking over flatter country at a breath-taking fifteen miles per hour.

The first little town was less than an hour away, but some of the passengers were already hungry when we arrived. The villagers provided dining car service. Through the open windows passed handfuls of popcorn, chunks of bread, and little fried cakes of corn. Dinah aloofly refused the dog biscuits we offered and managed to coerce an Indian woman into sharing a bit of off-colored meat. About halfway to Machu Picchu the engineer, too, developed an appetite, and the train stopped at another village for his lunch hour. Perhaps it was the swaying rick-rack ride, or it could have been the altitude, but, though relished by the others, the squinty-eyed whole roast heads of pig didn't tempt us.

After three hours more the conductor finally called Machu Picchu and pointed straight up. From the canyon bottom I looked at the green wall of mountain and the dirt road that snaked up its side. Across an old iron bridge a truck was waiting to carry us two thousand feet up the Hiram Bingham Highway to the small inn at the base of the ruins.

Two days later, overwhelmed by the mystery of Machu Picchu, we sat again on the rock throne of the Incas. Alone with the silence that had enshrouded Machu Picchu for centuries, we looked down on a dead city, a gem of architecture on a pillow of green velvet grass. Across the valley rose a lookout point, a spiked peak like a minaret over the mountain dome on which the city was built. In the late afternoon light terraces were delineated; temples, towers, and walls stood out in bold relief. Once roofed with thatch, they were now vined with wild blackberries and an occasional primrose.

As the air grew crisp the rock throne was still warm beneath us, and we tried to imagine Machu Picchu as it might have been perhaps ten centuries ago—the workers cultivating terraces where yucca, potatoes, and corn grew, the fountains of clear cold water channeled from distant springs, the Virgins of the Sun in their gardens of orchids, begonia and lupine, the priests performing their daily rituals in the Temple of the Three Windows or in the observatory, where the prismatic pointer of the giant sundial still casts its shadow. And we could almost see the Incan sovereign as he climbed the chiseled steps to the same rock throne where we sat watching his god slide behind the misty crags.

A few dud firecrackers and one dangling wire were the only remaining signs of the three-day fiesta when I began work on La Tortuga. The jeep agency, which was also the noodle distributor, was the logical place to start looking for parts. They had star-shaped noodles, alphabet noodles, long skinny noodles, and short fat noodles. But they were fresh out of jeep parts. I tried the auto parts stores, the garages, and the salvage yards, but the parts stores had no gears, the garages had no parts at all, and by the time anything reached the salvage yards it was too worn out even for scrap iron. At the Cuzco office of the Peruvian auto club, in Ecuadorian tradition, I presented my letter of introduction from the office in Lima. In the Colombian tradition Mr. Guzman, the director, had a friend, the chief of the road commission maintenance shop, who just might have some parts.

Señor Escobedo was a calm rugged man with a weathered face. He showed me a dismantled jeep.

"If there is anything you can use, you're welcome to it."

Everything I needed was there and the parts were in good condition. Relieved, I thanked him and said that I would order new parts from Lima to replace them. "But," I added, "I don't know how long they'll take to get here."

"No," he said, "don't bother. I'd rather you help someone on the road and consider the debt paid."

He said it as casually as if he had loaned us a cup of sugar. The real Good Neighbor policy in action.

With La Tortuga on her second wind, we left Cuzco for Lake Titicaca, an inland sea on the 12,500-foot Altiplano.

The dirt road bordered the azure water; on the horizon reed boats under reed sails appeared like a golden flotilla of Chinese junks. Converging on Ilave, a village near the lake, were streams of Indians coming from the surrounding hills to celebrate the feast day of San Miguel. On the outskirts of town white tents like the first flakes of a snowfall dotted the sterile landscape.

The main street was as tightly packed as ears of corn in a bushel, but slightly less static. Nudging La Tortuga through the surging crowd, I tinkled the doorbell we had installed for that purpose. Above the bedlam it made absolutely no impression. Pulsating around us were dancing devils, the Indian version of Old Nick himself, with pointed ears, red nose, forked tail, and a long whip that cracked out at anyone who got too close. To the beat of drums women in fringed shawls of neon hue swirled their skirts in a petticoat pin wheel of color. Strumming ukuleles of armadillo shells, men in crimson-striped ponchos weaved in a short shuffling hop while others shrilled on reed pipes like so many mythical Pans. It was the first day of a five-day fiesta, and the dispensers of *chicha* were doing a flowing business. I could see it was going to be quite a party before it was over. Resorting to our bellowing horn, usually reserved for blind mountain curves, we gently pushed our way through the revelers. As we left the merriment behind we could still hear that half-savage, half-lilting music, its rhythm as elusive as the condor.

The rhythm was still haunting us as we continued along the shores of Titicaca to the Bolivian border, where, thanks to having all our papers in order for the first time, we made an uncomplicated crossing. A few miles farther a symmetrical mound pushed up from the Altiplano. At its base was the cradle of pre-Columbian civilization, a South American Stonehenge. Crumbling, inscrutable, uncared for, the tall stone fingers of Tiahuanaco thrust from the ground in an acre-sized rectangle. At one end stood the granite Gate of the Sun, a solid block of stone incised with mystic ciphers

246

and geometric patterns, and pocked with holes from where silver and gold inlays had been pilfered. Nearby was a six-foot monolith with bulging eyes and folded hands. Like La Tortuga, it was held together with baling wire, the only sign of restoration. A mile away over the stubbled hills was an even sadder monument to an enigmatic race. Older than Machu Picchu or Mexico's Monte Albán, ponderous slabs of stones lay tumbled like a house of cards.

It was less than sixty miles from Tiahuanaco to La Paz, Bolivia's 12,400-foot de facto capital. With the rate of exchange pathetically spiraling to four thousand bolivianos to the dollar, for the first time we could afford the best. But the Sucre Palace had no vacancies, so we parked La Tortuga in front of the second best, where the doorman assured us that under his watchful eye she would acquire no new inscriptions.

Amazingly enough, there was no fiesta in progress—but they were getting ready for one—October 12, celebrating the discovery of America. Whole families sat like cross-legged tailors in their cluttered little workshops sewing spangles and bits of glass on silver-brocaded jackets or painting horned papier-mâché masks with bizarre colors. Grinning diabolically from the walls were finished masks, mouths sparkling with pointed teeth of mirror.

There wasn't a single level street in La Paz; even the Prado, statue-studded center of social promenading, was several hundred feet higher at one end. After several hours of puffing through the crevasse-like streets of this stratospheric city I would have felt more comfortable in a space suit. Not only was I giddy, but I was famished as well. Helen, less affected by the altitude than I, was preoccupied with the current trend in ladies' hats, the derby—black derbies, white

derbies, yellow derbies, and even pink derbies. I would have been glad to see the Brown Derby, but settled for a restaurant on the Prado.

"*Quiere un bebi biff?*" asked the waiter.

I got the first two words, but the last two stumped me. He repeated them while I mentally sifted through my whole Spanish vocabulary. I finally realized that the last two words weren't Spanish at all, but were his pronunciations of English "baby beef."

"Yes," I said, "a steak will do just fine." In this stratospheric city of astronomical exchange, the waiter appropriately returned with the literal translation of "baby beef" —two monstrous steaks that overhung the plates. What we couldn't eat Dinah enjoyed for the next two days.

Back at the hotel the doorman had done his job well. Although someone had left a name, it was not in the usual manner. Tucked in the door was a neatly folded note that read:

"I hope you will be coming to Chile. If so, when you reach Santiago you are welcome to stay with me."

The note was signed Carmen Cuevas Mackenna. We had heard much of Chilean hospitality, but we never knew it came looking for you.

In this land of extremes the Bolivian part of the Pan American Highway was no exception. Zooming skyward through the tin and platinum mining regions, it was a corkscrew trail fit only for mules equipped with oxygen masks. At one place the map read 18,300 feet, no doubt a topographical error—a hurdle even for Pegasus. In any event, we were seldom under twelve thousand feet, and some of the gradients were so steep that even in the lowest of the six gears it was necessary to back down and get a fast run at them. Those six hundred miles across Bolivia to Argentina were a succession of stops for chassis tightening and carburetor cleaning. The constant pounding from the rutted chuckholed road did what even the railway tracks in Costa Rica hadn't done—popped the heads from the spring shackle bolts.

That week in the rarified air had its effect on the three of us as well as on La Tortuga. Helen and I lost interest in everything except getting to lower altitudes. Only a near emergency could stir any of us to the slightest activity. At night, with the cold knifing through our down sleeping bags and Dinah trying to snuggle in with us, we slept fitfully and awakened logy, entombed in a frost-encrusted jeep. Our lukewarm, high-altitude coffee did little to stimulate or thaw us.

La Tortuga was just as difficult to get started as we were, and one morning the battery went dead. After five minutes of pushing, the jeep was still immobile—so was I. For several hours we sat on the lifeless Altiplano until a truckload of barrel-chested Indians came to our aid. With unbelievable ease they pushed La Tortuga while I could only lean futilely against the stern. Tongue hanging out, searing pain in my lungs, I marveled aloud at their energy. Reaching into his furry goatskin pouch, one of them helpfully offered me a handful of coca leaves to chew.

"This will make you strong too," he said.

Thanking him, I declined. Although coca, from which cocaine is made, is a mainstay of Altiplano life, I preferred to be a ninety-seven-pound weakling rather than a bleary-eyed Samson with blackened stubby teeth.

Chapter Nine

ARGENTINA was celebrating too—of course. We concluded
that either every day's a holiday or that we had an uncon-
scious affinity for festivity. But this was a new twist—the
celebration of the elimination of a holiday. Until three weeks
before we arrived, for ten years October 17 had been glorified
as the day of General Juan Domingo Perón, ex-President of
Argentina. But with the ousting of Old John Sunday, as the
English-speaking residents unaffectionately called him, the
day was stricken from the list of national holidays as completely as his name was being obliterated from the rocks and
buildings along the road. There was, however, a Jekyll and
Hyde atmosphere—with the gaiety was an air of tension. The
new government feared a counterrevolution by the followers
of Perón, and on October 17 took appropriate measures to
prevent it.

A nearly bang-up assault on us was one result of these
measures. With machine guns leveled, a cordon of soldiers
halted us on the road. With visions of wanted posters—that
picture in the Lima paper labeled PERONISTAS IN AC-
TION—I started in alarm.

"I'm a Yank!"

"Not a tank?" quipped an amused young officer. "Then
do us—and yourselves—a favor and get off the road."

We gladly complied and spent the rest of the day in nearby

Río Cuarto eating meat tarts and drinking good Argentine beer.

With October 17 behind us we relished the freshness of spring below the equator. Well-fed cattle and horses grazed placidly on the broad pampa. Fruit trees were blossoming, rows of grape vines corrugated the fields, and buckboards and surries rumbled along the dirt paths beside the fine paved highway.

In Argentina the age of the horse was far from past. Government restriction on the importation of automobiles had kept the carriage builders in business, and there were few late-model cars on the road. Anything newer than 1946 was almost certain to bear an official license plate, the comparatively new 1938 models were driven with pride by their well-to-do owners, and Model T's were rolling briskly along. Enjoying the bounce-free ride, fourteen-year-old La Tortuga rolled briskly along too, no doubt spurred to a youthful vigor by the cars she passed so many years her senior.

All through the trip keeping pace with the seasons had been a vital factor in our being able to get through the roadless areas: southern Mexico, Costa Rica, Panama, and Ecuador. It came as a surprise to learn that even where there *were* roads the weather would continue to affect our travels. From the equator our southerly course was taking us to colder climes, where snow, not rain, would be our problem.

Revived after almost a week of breathing the rich low-altitude air, we headed westward from Mendoza into the highlands again to reach Chile. Near the foot of the first range of the cordillera the paved highway changed to a gravel road. At Uspallata, an Argentine Army garrison about sixty miles from the Chilean border, we were told that a late snowfall might still block the pass. It seemed that for the first time we were out of step with the seasons. However, previous experience had shown that the only way to be sure was to see for ourselves. If we couldn't get through we would return to Mendoza and continue south through Argentina to Ushuaia, seeing Chile on the way back.

As we climbed higher and higher the road narrowed, and closer to the snow line the damage from the spring thaw had not been repaired. But at Puente del Inca, only fifteen miles from the border, we were encouraged to learn that a truck had passed just a few days before.

Higher yet we went, to eight thousand, then nine thousand feet, where drifts and slides covered the road and dingy snow sagged menacingly from the slate-gray sides of the canyon. Following the tracks of the truck, we detoured down embankments, across shallow streams, and past places where the driver had shoveled away snow. We followed the tracks to Las Cuevas, the Argentine border post, where they stopped. No car had crossed into Chile since the previous fall.

The rustic log and stone buildings of the frontier settlement were quiet. While we warmed ourselves in front of a blazing fire, friendly officials told us that the road through the Christ of the Andes pass, twenty-seven hundred feet higher, was definitely blocked with snow. There was, however, an alternate route through the International Tunnel, which, although principally for trains, was also used by automobiles. But there was one hitch. It wouldn't be open officially for another month, and planks had not yet been placed on the ties.

The officials didn't know the condition of the road on the Chilean side, but they thought we had passed the worst. Once through the two-mile tunnel, it would all be downhill.

However, after Costa Rica the thought of tackling even two miles of railroad tracks seemed out of the question. But after we inspected the first half mile it looked as though it would be a smoother ride than anything we had encountered in Bolivia. The ties were flush with the ground; I could see no necessity for planks—except possibly to raise low passenger cars enough to clear the rails. Since no train was scheduled that day, we decided to go on.

Once we were inside the tunnel, the circle of daylight from the entrance faded quickly. A brief twilight and we were in the blackest night. Boring two holes through the emptiness, our headlights flared from ice stalactites, reflected from roaring streams of water, and transformed the rails into twin silver lines. A half mile, then a mile, a sign proclaimed the international boundary, and we were in Chile. As we slid over patches of ice I tightened my grip on the wheel. Depressions between the ties became more marked, and too late I understood the need for planks. By the mile-and-a-half point the wheels were jumping from tie to tie—shades of Costa Rica. With a quarter of a mile left to go we stuck in the ice between two widely separated ties.

I was disgusted with myself for not having first inspected the full length of the dank tunnel. With a deep drainage ditch on either side and less than three feet between the jeep and the tunnel walls we couldn't turn back. As we rocked free, a noise from the transmission punctuated the echoing sound of the exhaust. Fifty yards from the entrance the noise grew to the metronomic evenness of a missing gear tooth.

Just outside the mouth of the tunnel was Caracoles, a small switch house of the Transandino Railway. Standing in the door, a man stared at the clanking apparition that appeared. In a canyon of blinding snow-peaked crags La

Tortuga lurched off the tracks; the metronome reached a crescendo, and the motor thudded to a halt.

The nightmarish hike that followed to Portillo, seven freezing miles of ice-filled tunnels, the arrangements we made there for a special flatcar, and the disappointment we felt as we watched La Tortuga pushed up the ramp at Caracoles all formed a chain of events that brought about still another change of plans. Even if the transmission had not gone out we could not have continued: the "downhill" road we had been going to take was covered with piano-sized rocks and five feet of snow. But as we swayed in the caboose of the freight train that carried us forty miles to the Chilean town of Los Andes we resolved to cross this pass under our own power. Instead of shipping home from Buenos Aires we would cross the continent again to reach Chile and ship home from Valparaiso.

In the back yard of a Los Andes hotel I was faced with the same problem as in Colombia—how to get at the transmission without removing the motor. Since the baling-wire repair job had proven so successful, I thought I'd try another shotgun method. With a hack saw I enlarged an inspection plate in the floor boards to a foot-square opening.

Working inside the cab, feet hanging from a sky hook, I disconnected drive shafts, propeller shaft, bilge pump, and sundry other bottlenecks in the mechanical maze, and two days later I jiggled free the transmission. The damage was considerable—chips of broken gear teeth had ruined almost every moving part. And there wasn't a replacement in Los Andes. Leaving the jeep there, we boarded a train for Santiago, fifty miles away.

The railroad terminal in Chile's capital was a nineteenth-century version of Grand Central. Hailing a cab, we found that Chile's hospitality did not extend to dogs. After five taxis slowed, looked at Dinah, and sped off, we finally tricked one into stopping by hiding her behind a pushcart. And we soon learned that the hotels were just as fussy. Starting in the middle, we descended the ladder of hotel quality until, near the bottom, we finally found one that would admit Dinah—with reluctance.

After getting comfortably—more or less—settled, we telephoned Carmen Cuevas Mackenna to thank her for her invitation. Above a background of strumming guitars an effervescent voice streamed from the receiver, and in English spiked with Spanish she charmingly but emphatically declared that she was very offended to find us in a hotel. "I've been expecting you for weeks," she said.

Carmen was Chile's foremost teacher of guitar and folk music, and her studio home was a constant happy turmoil. Even after a week of unsuccessful searching for jeep parts we couldn't be dejected around buoyant Carmen. She always had something planned, and one Saturday afternoon, along with seventy of her students, we accompanied her to her country place near Santiago. In a setting of green hills a whole lamb roasted over glowing coals while pink-sashed *huasos*, Chilean cowboys with four-inch silver spurs, basted the meat with sprigs of laurel dipped in wine. Leafy salad, French bread, and several large pitchers of *borgoña*, red wine with fresh strawberries, completed the *asado*, and for those few who were still hungry there were *empanadas*, moon-shaped turnovers of meat seasoned with raisins and olives. Later, in American hay ride fashion, about twenty of us rode through the countryside on the back of a truck. Singing spirited Chilean songs to the accompaniment of guitars, concertinas, and tambourines, we saw a Chilean motto come to life—"The house is small, but the wine jug is big." As we stopped at each little farm along the way, the master of the house swung open the gate and welcomed us with a large *chuico* and as many glasses as he had. With red wine flowing, dancing followed. In pairs everyone joined in the *cueca*, a

lively folk dance of subtle meaning in which waving hand-kerchiefs and raised eyebrows told the story of shy courtship.

Santiago was a city of late hours and even later dinners, and an appointment in the afternoon could mean any time up to seven. The cocktail hour stretched till ten, the dinner until twelve or after; with dancing and more cocktails whetting the appetite again the party broke up after breakfast. We soon learned it was wise to eat something before leaving for a dinner engagement, but after one experience we abandoned that practice—eager to please us, one considerate host served dinner at eight, and we couldn't eat a bite.

During the day—what was left of it after recovering from

these nightly sorties—we finally tracked down all the parts needed for the jeep except one. This, a simple round shaft, a machinist agreed to make for us. It would be ready in a week, he said. I should have known he meant Chilean time. I promptly returned on the seventh day to find the part made, but since his heat-treating equipment was out of commission —had been for a year—he didn't know just when the shaft could be hardened. Exasperated at his nonchalance, I took the job to another shop, where another mañana-minded machinist procrastinated. Salvation came in the form of a taxi driver who informed me that some Nash transmission parts were similar to those of a jeep.

There remained one detail to take care of in Santiago. We made arrangements for passage home on a Grace Line ship leaving from Valparaiso, Chile, for San Pedro, California. Then, just before leaving for Los Andes to repair La Tortuga, we said thanks and good-by to hospitable Carmen. After a smothering embrace for the three of us she winked, shook her finger in mock sternness, and affectionately said, "*Hasta pronto,* and remember, when you come back, *no* hotels."

In comparison with the silent glide of today's fin-propelled automobiles La Tortuga's was a hubbub, but to me her normal thrashing-machine medley of rattles and rumbles was like music. After so many thousands of miles I was in tune with her every sound, and as we headed south once more the characteristic gear whine from beneath the floor boards was reassuring. However, despite this comforting sound we babied her along. Ushuaia was still more than two thousand miles away, two thousand miles of rough dirt roads broken by lakes, the Strait of Magellan, and the tail end of the Andes. Some eight hundred miles south of Santiago the road in Chile ended at Puerto Montt, where, in order to continue south, we would first have to turn eastward across three Andean lakes to reach Argentina again.

But there was another reason for driving slowly. We had taken this circuitous route especially to enjoy the gentle beauty of Chile's lake region, and it was a restful ten days to Puerto Montt, winding through daisy-filled meadows and ferned woods, past foaming waterfalls and under overhanging willow trees, camping at night beside crystal brooks or one of the varicolored lakes that dot the countryside.

A fishing village of glinting corrugated iron roofs, Puerto Montt was settled by German immigrants, and blond, blue-eyed children played along the shores of the muddy bay. Beyond the haze to the south stretched fifteen hundred miles of fiords and glaciated cliffs, and to the east was Chile's Fujiyama, Mount Osorno, at the base of which was Todos los Santos, the first lake we would cross to reach Argentine Patagonia.

When we arrived at Lake Todos los Santos a light rain was stippling the surface of the gray water. Of Osorno only the black lava moraine of its lower slopes was visible beneath the ceiling of clouds. But early the next morning more fitting than Todos los Santos was the lake's other name, Esmeralda. Mirrored in the emerald water was a second Osorno, a perfect cone with snow two thirds of the way down. In La Tortuga's wake the reflection disappeared in a myriad of specular flashes of light. With none of the apprehension we had known off Costa Rica, none of the qualms we had felt in the storms off Panama, we traveled at an easy three knots over the placid green water, calmed by the steady throb of the motor and the heat of the sun on our backs. Each revolution of the propeller turned the kaleidoscope as peak after snowy peak came into view—Puntiagudo, a needle in a pin-cushion of clouds, Tronador with its three jagged crags like teeth in a broken comb. Six hours after entering the lake we pulled out at a boat landing near Peulla, where we went through Chilean customs.

Several miles away over a narrow road lined with dense forest was the Argentine customs house at the edge of Laguna Frías, the second lake we were to cross. After waiting a day for the customs chief to make his appearance we crossed the tiny link in less than an hour, and another few miles through more dark forest brought us to the third lake. While smartly dressed Argentine tourists watched from the deck of a two-hundred-passenger steamer, La Tortuga dipped into the water for the third time in three days.

The narrow arm of Nahuel Huapí, one of Argentina's largest lakes, was a thirty-mile watery corridor to the road leading south through Patagonia. The one-day delay at Laguna Frías had brought the brief spell of fair weather to a close, and when a brisk breeze ruffled the Prussian blue of the water I increased our speed to four knots. Dashing against small rocky islands, the waves grew higher, and I looked for a place to get ashore, but on either side the granite walls dropped steeply into the water. With whitecaps racing by and the stern lifting with a following sea I floored the throttle. When a large tree-covered, steep-shored island loomed, Helen consulted the map.

"I think that's where we change course to go ashore," she said.

"It can't be. We've been under way only two and a half hours, and it's twenty-five miles to the island where we turn. Remember, mate, that's a road map. It wasn't meant to navigate by."

But as we breasted the island I saw the mouth of a bay. Helen was right. With a quick full rudder we headed for the gravel beach, the wind hitting us broadside and the jeep heeling heavily to port. When we landed we had covered the thirty miles in less than three hours. The wind had almost doubled our top speed. I was glad we weren't heading the other direction, and I wondered what the stormy Strait of Magellan would be like.

San Carlos de Bariloche, Argentina's favorite mountain and ski resort, was fifteen miles from where we came ashore. Wooded almost all the way, the road bordered the main body of Nahuel Huapí, now a deep purple with sea-sized waves. At Bariloche, a colony of luxury hotels and Swiss-style homes, we spent two days repacking the wheels and changing the lubricant in all the gear boxes after our transit of fifty miles of lakes.

As we continued south early in the morning, clouds swept across the sky, casting soft shadows on the gravel road. Tall trees laced their branches overhead, the limbs vibrating in the wind that was to be our constant companion for the duration of the trip. Edging the shores of smaller lakes, winding through forests of oak and pine, we descended slowly and the vegetation thinned. By midafternoon we were rolling over the bleak grasslands of Patagonia, mile after mile of solitude with rain turning to sleet on the windshield. The wind became a physical force, the jeep swayed from side to side, but even over the scream of the gale I was conscious of a slight increase in the whine from beneath the floor boards. I tried to ignore it. It was only a little louder, I reasoned, and with La Tortuga getting older by the mile I had to expect that. Helen noticed it too as the whine became a growl, and I slowed to ten miles per hour, hoping to reach the closest town, Esquel, sixty miles to the south. But a few minutes later power fell off and a curl of acrid smoke rose from the floor boards. Quickly I pulled to the side of the road. Neither of us spoke as we waited for the floor boards to cool before trying to locate the trouble. When I found it, I was stunned. This time it was the transfer case. Located just behind the transmission, it was every bit as difficult to repair. And even if I'd had the parts, repairing it beside the road would have been like working in a wind tunnel.

Even in Alaska I couldn't remember being as cold as we were that night and all the next day. And it was almost mid-summer in Patagonia. I would gladly have traded my poncho for a parka. Huddling in the jeep, we tried to warm the inside with the motor, but the starter jammed. I thought coffee might help, but the wind blew out our windproof stove. In twenty hours not a soul passed until late the next afternoon, when, during a lull in the wind, I heard the hum of a motor. I jumped out to flag the small truck, but it wasn't necessary. True to the unwritten law of Patagonia, the driver was already stopping. When I told him what had happened, he spoke of an *estancia* a few miles down the road.

"I'll tow you there. Just ask for Señor Pienay."

In the office of the *estancia* a gentleman with reddish-brown hair and a neat mustache looked up from behind his desk. In my best Spanish I asked to speak to Señor Pienay. In my poncho, half frozen, I probably didn't present a very good picture, but I didn't think my appearance warranted a frown. It must have been my Spanish.

"Whom did you say?" he asked:

"Señor Pienay," I repeated, and then explained our difficulty.

He smiled, and then in British English with an Irish accent he said, "You mean Mr. Paine, the manager. He's not here right now. I'm Pat Wilson, the accountant. Won't you come in and have a spot of tea?"

It wasn't until then that I saw the sign on the wall—Argentine Southern Land Company, Limited. We were on one of the huge British sheep farms that spread over all of Patagonia.

Sheltered from the wind by staggered rows of slender poplars, the staff house of Estancia Leleque was a rambling one-story brick building. Inside Mr. Wilson introduced us to the rest of the staff, a miniature United Kingdom with representatives from Ireland, Wales, Australia, and the Channel Islands of England. A roaring fire and hot tea soon had us warm again—something I didn't think was possible—and we discussed the problem of getting parts. The consensus was not encouraging, but the friendly reception they all gave us was at least heartening. Mr. Wilson made us welcome with the guest room, and later Mr. Paine, a jaunty Englishman in polished boots, riding pants, and a soft tweed cap, offered a place to work on La Tortuga.

"But don't be too surprised if you don't find the parts in Esquel," he said. "They'll probably have to be ordered from Buenos Aires, and you may have quite a wait." Then Mr. Paine countered this dismal forecast with a warm invitation. "Why don't you plan on spending the holidays here with us?"

For a moment I couldn't think what holidays he meant. Then I remembered. It was a week before Christmas.

That night in the sitting room of the staff house Helen and I became acquainted with *mate*. Mr. Wilson, despite his Irish accent, was Argentine-born, and a connoisseur of the art of preparing this hot herb brew that was as universal

264

in Argentina as tea in China. After spooning some of the green flakes into a small pear-shaped gourd he added boiling water, and an aroma like new-mown alfalfa rose from the mouth. Sipping the brew through a silver straw, he added more hot water, then handed the *mate* to Helen.

"*Gracias*," she said, reaching for it.

With a mischievous smile he withdrew it. "To say *gracias* to *mate* means 'No, thank you,' *not* 'Thank you.'"

The next morning I went to work on the jeep. I was getting quite proficient—this time it took only a day to remove the unit. No gears had been damaged, and I was relieved to see that all I would need were two bronze thrust washers, a shaft, and a couple of bearings. But after taking a bus to Esquel and scouring all the stores and garages in the little town all I came up with was the by now familiar reply, "No *hay*." Packing the worn parts with a note requesting fast service, I shipped them by air to Buenos Aires and returned to Leleque.

Our room in the staff house was a cheerful one, with

bright Araucano Indian rugs on the floor and soft beds with warm guanaco fur covers, but we didn't spend much time there. More often we were by the fire in the sitting room learning about *estancia* life or, when the rain stopped, playing tennis on the poplar-protected courts. And many times we took tea with the Paines.

The British seem to take their customs with them wherever they go, and the red brick home of Mr. and Mrs. Paine, with its spacious gardens and flowered walks, looked as if it had been transplanted from an English countryside. Even after twenty-seven years in Argentina afternoon tea was a ritual with the Paines, and promptly at four the table was set with hot scones on lacy doilies, butter balls, English marmalade, and tea cakes.

One morning at breakfast Evan Thomas, the Welsh-Argentine foreman, asked if I would like to see the sheep sheared. While Helen visited with Mrs. Paine, I went with Evan to the corral, where he pointed out my horse, a big Roman-nosed beast named Picasso. My previous experience with horses had been limited to carrousels, and I eyed the black animal with apprehension, but Evan said he was the gentlest horse on the *estancia*. In fact, Angela, the Paines' lovely eighteen-year-old daughter, had learned to ride on him as a child. Reassured, I climbed aboard.

The high sheepskin saddle was soft, and as long as Picasso stayed at a walk I had no trouble. But when he broke into a trot I bounced up and down like a yo-yo. Evan said it was just a hop, skip, and a jump to the shearing shed. I found that distance was relative—it was five miles, but then he thought in terms of hundreds of miles. Leleque covered more than four hundred thousand acres, and it took a month just to patrol the fences.

It was, however, a hop, skip, and a jump—with Picasso doing all three with equal facility. Having a warped sense of humor, he looked back at me and leered, and then tried to rub me off on the flanks of Evan's horse. And fences were his special delight—he loved to scratch his sides on them. Sensing my insecurity, Picasso maliciously took advantage of it, but I was not to be browbeaten. Gradually I gained confidence. I even managed to stay on at a canter. The only trouble was that I didn't want to canter. That was Picasso's idea.

When we arrived at the shearing shed, the sheep had already been brought in from the corral, and the men were busy relieving them of their fleece. Entering at one end of the shed, each was bundled in his wool like a 1920 college student in a raccoon coat. At the other end he emerged pink, naked, and bewildered.

Just before lunch we headed back for the staff house. Confidently I grasped the wisp of mane on Picasso's neck and swung my leg over his broad back as I had seen Evan do. Picasso snickered. I didn't know that the horses were accustomed to galloping back to the corral for their special treat of oats, and Picasso was a creature of habit. Moreover, he was like a Sunday driver who can't bear to be passed. Off we went like a shot. Man o' War would have hung his head in shame. The starters at Hollywood Park wouldn't have believed it. Eddie Arcaro—look to your laurels. Picasso and I just couldn't get together. He went up, I came down, and the meeting was painful. Evan said I spent all my time in the air, but I disputed that statement. I had proof that I had spent sufficient time in the saddle—two dollar-sized blisters on my stern.

Three days later I was healed enough to think of going

to the shearing shed again, this time to join the Gauchos for their morning *asado*. Arranged in a tepee around a fire that had already burned to glowing coals were ten iron stakes stuck in the ground. On each was skewered a whole side of mutton, roasted a golden brown, juices snapping into flame as they dripped. Wearing baggy *bombachas*, pants that looked like the opaque counterpart of a harem girl's filmy costume, the egg-shaped cook was pouring a sauce of wine and garlic over the meat. The tangy aroma made me hungrier by the minute, and I wasn't the only one. More men rode up and tied their horses to the nearby hitching post, and then sat on their haunches around the fire. Most of them wore accordion-pleated boots, *bombachas*, and berets, the only kind of hat that would stay on in the Patagonian wind. When the mutton was done, there were perhaps thirty men waiting. Out came long knives from the back of their wide sashes, and each man sliced off a chunk of meat. Placing a corner of it between his teeth, with vigorous strokes he sawed off a bite-sized piece perilously close to his nose. In a few minutes the skewers were bare, and after tasting it myself, I could see why the men averaged daily four pounds of meat apiece.

Each day we looked for the parts to arrive; each day the bus passed without leaving a package for us. And then it was Christmas. Even in Patagonian summer there was a blanket of fresh snow on the foothills of the Andes west of Leleque. Christmas Eve, along with the staff, we tied white handkerchiefs around our necks and paraded to the kitchen, where, with apple champagne, we toasted to the cook before sitting down to the feast she had prepared. It was a gay evening with Argentine *empanadas*, English plum pudding, and two huge tender stuffed turkeys. But behind our gaiety was a little nostalgia as we thought of the previous Christmas around the fireplace in California.

In the days that followed, Picasso and I came to an understanding, Dinah frolicked with a pair of pet lambs, and was bullied into relinquishing her bone by a tame ibis. Evenings in the cozy sitting room we thumbed through copies of *Punch* or *Blackwood's Magazine*, or just sat quietly sipping *mate*. No one agreed as to whether *mate* was a sedative or a stimulant, but one thing was certain. It was a favorite way to pass the time, a companionable, meditative custom, almost like passing the peace pipe.

New Year's came, just one year to the day since we had left California. Still no parts, but there was another turkey, more apple champagne, and "Auld Lang Syne" in Spanish. Then, like a late Christmas package, the parts finally arrived. Made in Argentina, the replacements looked fine, but after checking the hardness with a file it was with misgivings that I reassembled La Tortuga. I had no choice, and I figured they would surely last the rest of the trip. After almost three weeks we said good-by to our friends of the poplar oasis in the Patagonian desert.

The sea of land that was Patagonia stretched endlessly, undulating, the sparse shrubbery only a few inches high, shorn by the devastating shears of the wind. Occasionally there was a higher clump of bushes, as if nature, having repented her cruelty, had given a little shelter to the sheep that huddled in the lee. But that same shelter was a death trap to more than one animal ensnarled in the sharp branches. Whitened bones stood grimly upright like Halloween skeletons. On the few scattered lakes fire-winged flamingos colored the sky like a premature sunset, plovers and

the rapier-beaked, orange-necked ibis flapped effortlessly in
the wind. And La Tortuga purred her even song, shuddering
once in a while when a sudden gust slowed her progress or
the gravel from her wheels overtook us and rattled over the
top. The passing of another car was as much of an occasion
as the passing of a ship at sea, and even the lone Gaucho
on the horizon was strangely out of place in this land that
seemed made for no living thing.

For four days we continued almost due south. The rain
that had been intermittent for so many weeks became a
steady unending thing and the dirt road ran with rivulets.
Wild guanacos gazed curiously, but at any change in La
Tortuga's speed they bolted and ran leaping away like an-
telope. As we passed, drab brown ostriches made their ungainly way through the brush, breaking into a wabbling,
wing-flapping gait in the open spaces.

Toward the afternoon of the fourth day the road forked.
Hugging the foothills of the Andes, the right branch was

the most direct route to the Strait of Magellan—and the most deserted. Pointing to the left branch, the coastal route, a sign listed the more important cities in southern Patagonia, still hundreds of miles apart. For several minutes we sat there. The jeep was running fine. We had planned to take the shortest route, but without knowing why we turned into the left branch. Three days later, one week and eight hundred miles south of Leleque, the transfer case went out again on the outskirts of a one-street town.

Piedrabuena was like the river that flowed beside it, silent yet moving. With the transfer case emitting a grating clunk we limped through the muddy streets to the Chevrolet garage. Sympathetically the owner-mechanic, Señor Cardenas, cleared a place for La Tortuga amid Model T's and decrepit trucks and offered all of his facilities for her repair.

Three blocks away, at the other end of town, we entered a single-story building that said "Hotel." The lobby was a deserted saloon with a rococo mahogany bar and a big mirror that echoed the green pallor of the walls. Side-stepping the open cellar trap door, we followed the proprietor through a dimly lit hall.

"You may have our best room," he said.

We watched the rain dripping from the ceiling onto the center of the bed. The damp room smelled musty and old, and the high narrow window made it only a little less dungeon-like. Making her customary inspection, Dinah promptly put her foot through the linoleum where it covered a hole in the floor.

Just in time for dinner, we gnawed on tough mutton in the dining room that sloped like the dizzy room of a carnival. With a grandfather clock that didn't tick and a caged canary that didn't sing, we ate to the accompaniment of kitchen clatter and the discordant drip, drip, drip of water falling in buckets placed in strategic spots on the floor. In short, the hotel did nothing to alleviate our depression.

Glad to get out of the gloom, we went back to the garage and began the dissection. With each bolt I removed, and each time a tool fell into the thick black grease of the bilge, I thought of the last time at Leleque and the time before that in Los Andes. I was in a bitter mood, but I had had enough practice so that the job progressed more rapidly. By evening the transfer case was out. It took only a few minutes to locate the trouble, but more than an hour to clean out the pieces of what had once been two bearings, a shaft, and two thrust washers—exactly the same parts I had replaced at Leleque.

I asked Señor Cardenas, the philosophical mechanic, where I might find parts.

"*Muy difícil.*" He shrugged. "Possibly in Río Gallegos or, if not there, in Punta Arenas on the Chilean side."

The next morning I left Helen and Dinah molding in the kitchen, the only warm place in the hotel, while I stood outside waiting in the rain for the bus to Santa Cruz, where a plane would take me to Río Gallegos, two hundred miles to the south. Helen gave me a pathetic smile when I told her not to expect me for a week—what a miserable sentence, a week in Piedrabuena.

The ancient International truck, with improvised body jammed with bucket seats, was already full, but I talked a mother into letting me hold her child on my lap for the two-hour ride through muddy ruts to Santa Cruz, twenty-five miles away on the coast. Santa Cruz boasted one new building, an impressive paneled wood and fieldstone post office built during the reign of Perón. Covering a whole city block, it would have served nicely for a city twenty times the size of diminutive Santa Cruz. The street that ran in front was a quagmire, as indeed were all the streets in town, and the drivers of the few cars and trucks had to know the way as well as a pilot knows a harbor to avoid sinking axle deep in the many mudholes.

The airport was three miles from town. The car that the airline office provided had no windshield wiper on my side —for which I was grateful. Zipping up the winding road, skidding sideways harrowingly close to the bank, we arrived in much too short a time at the grassy plateau that served as a landing strip—only to wait two hours for the plane.

Also waiting was a woolly sheep that passed the time by scratching her ears against a nearby post. Before anyone was aware of it she raised her head and stared northward at the distant speck in the sky. When the DC-3 landed the sheep was the first one there, climbing up the ladder before it was even in place, to receive her customary handout from the crew. After that the passengers could climb aboard.

In less than an hour I was in Río Gallegos, with its clean paved streets and good hotels. But I felt guilty sleeping so comfortably when I thought of Helen back in Piedrabuena under soggy covers in her funereal hotel.

As soon as the shops were open the next morning, I started making the rounds. I had learned long ago never to ask for parts for an amphibious jeep. This immediately invoked the answer "No hay." Instead I solemnly placed the parts on the counter and asked if they had anything that looked remotely like them. The answer was still "No hay." But at the second place a phenomenon occurred. They had the bearings! After trying every other place in town for the shaft and thrust washers with no success I was entering the airline office to book passage for Punta Arenas when a man came running after me. I couldn't believe it. A shipment had arrived on the same plane with me. Although the parts weren't exactly the same, I thought that with the help of Señor Cardenas, a genius by necessity at improvising, they could be made to work. And with still more luck I was able to catch the same plane back to Santa Cruz.

It was still raining when the plane took off, and it seemed as if it were forever gaining altitude. As a matter of fact, it never did. All the way back we skimmed over the tops of waves close enough to see the foam on the whitecaps and over land so low that sheep scattered and giant hares scampered for their holes. With the plane shuddering and shaking in the gusts at least half the passengers made frequent use of the paper bags in front of them. Casually the copilot explained why we were flying so low. At that altitude the wind was blowing only seventy miles an hour. None too soon for me the Santa Cruz strip came in sight, and it was a perfect landing—until the brakes were applied. The plane did a complete turn, slid two hundred yards through a barbed-wire fence, and ground to a stop. The sheep was a bit confused, but recovered in time to still be the first to greet me as I stepped with relief from the plane clutching my little package of parts. Mission completed.

The next day and the day after we spent honing, grinding, and cutting to make the odd pieces fit. With pieces of tin can we made the thrust washers thicker, and with emery powder and elbow grease made the shaft thinner. In a record week, thanks to Señor Cardenas and a lot of luck, we had La Tortuga ready for the last two laps: two hundred and fifty miles to the Strait, and then 335 miles to Ushuaia.

With the green water lapping at La Tortuga's wheels Helen and I stood on the shingle beach at the narrowest part of the Strait of Magellan. Staring across the three miles that separated us from Tierra del Fuego, we could dimly see the beach opposite, where an oil refinery road led south, and, above that, the glow of burning natural gas that made this truly a Land of Fire. Our phenomenal luck was still with us; for the first time since we reached Patagonia there was no wind, the sun was warm and bright, and the stormy Strait didn't seem stormy at all.

Yet we hesitated. Without warning the wind could return, changing the calm water to a maelstrom in minutes. And even though it was calm, a few hundred yards offshore we could see the warning eddies that marked the fast current in the central channel. According to the chart, it was as high as six knots, about the maximum we could hope to tack against—if the motor held out. But everything else in La Tortuga had already broken down, and if the motor did fail we would be carried downstream to where cliffs lined both sides.

But those were chances we had been determined to take. There was another reason for our hesitation. In Río Gallegos we had been told that the 335 miles of completed road over Tierra del Fuego was just Perón propaganda, that twenty-five miles of it was nothing but a horse trail, that no car had ever crossed the tail end of the Andes to Ushuaia. If we couldn't reach our goal anyway, should we risk crossing the Strait? Yes. We both agreed. We wouldn't be satisfied until we had at least gone as far as we could.

Pointing La Tortuga upstream, for several hundred yards we stayed in the slack water close to shore. Then, sighting on a point of land across the Strait four miles above our intended landfall, we headed at a 45-degree angle to the current. Our plan was to hold that course until mid-channel, where we would come about and use the current to aid us in making the beach.

Pitching in the eddies, the jeep swung downstream, and I countered with left rudder as we entered the fast current. With the jeep tossing and swerving I jockeyed her back on course, keeping my eyes on the sight. A few minutes later a sharp jolt rocked the jeep. With a forty-fathom bottom we couldn't have gone aground. A bombardment of jolts followed, and from under the jeep streaked a school of porpoises, arching in unison a few feet ahead of the bow. From the top Dinah's head switched like a spectator's at a tennis match as the eight-foot porpoises zigzagged and crisscrossed around the jeep, filling the air with their watery snorts. We were so intent on these black-and-white aquatic clowns that we were in mid-channel before we realized that we had pivoted downstream as if at the end of a string compass. We were still headed toward the point of land we had been sighting on, but we were head on to the current instead of at a 45-degree angle to it. Still worse, we were almost opposite the cliffs, far below the beach where we were to come ashore. I tried to conceal my alarm. The current must be more than six knots, I thought. All I could think of was to get to the other side as fast as possible, hoping there might be slack water near shore. Letting the bow swing around, I floored the throttle and headed directly across current.

Slowly the cliffs of Tierra del Fuego loomed closer. I thought I could feel the force of the water lessen. About twenty feet from the brown furrowed walls I changed course to head upstream. Nothing happened. The jeep stood still in the current, and though I hated to push La Tortuga I

276

floored the throttle again. Shuddering under full power, almost imperceptibly she began to creep back along the shore. I steered closer until the right wheels were almost touching the steep sloping face of the cliff. We could begin to measure our progress.

Motor straining, La Tortuga crawled with agonizing slowness the several miles to the end of the cliff. In the slower water near the gravel bank I could let up on the gas, but at each point that jutted from shore it took full throbbing power to get around it. While two wild guanacos peered from a rise and hordes of red-beaked shore birds squawked into flight, we chugged upstream to the beach three hours after leaving the other side.

High and dry on the beach where we landed, left there by a thirty-foot tide, was a battered surplus LCT belonging to the oil company. Standing nearby were several men. One in particular seemed very perplexed.

"What made you think you could cross the Strait in that thing? Don't you know there's a ten-knot current?"

I swallowed hard. "Ten knots? I thought it was six."

"Six average, but where you crossed, the First Narrows, it runs ten. Where're you going, anyway?"

Still shaken, I almost stuttered, "Ushuaia," and then explained where we had come from.

His face softened. "You're really determined, aren't you? I'm sorry to tell you that the road is not finished. The road commission is still working on it. But when you've gone as far as you can go, come back here. We'll take you back across the Strait in a barge."

Through the courtesy of the oil refinery we serviced the jeep in their maintenance shop and continued south over the same rolling barren plains as in Patagonia. Split down the middle by the Argentine-Chilean border, Tierra del Fuego was the home of some of the largest sheep farms in the Western Hemisphere. After the worst onslaught of rain in sixty years the fences were strung with the half-decayed carcasses of hundreds of sheep that had been caught and drowned in the flooded hollows.

To reach the First Narrows on the continent we had first crossed into Chile, but once on the island, in order to continue south, we had to enter Argentina again. In accordance with tradition, the connection between the two countries was abominable. In this case we were not even sure it was a road. After we left the Chilean customs house, a muddy trail turned into a pair of grassy ruts, and then disappeared entirely in the middle of a mushy meadow. Turning around, we went back, positive we had followed the wrong cow. But, no, that was the international highway between Chile and Argentina in Tierra del Fuego. Just head off across the meadow, we were told. We did, and promptly bogged down. In just a few minutes a jeep threaded its way through with a practiced manner and towed us out. When we thanked the driver, he said it was his job. "Everyone gets stuck here. But it's better ahead. Except for a bridge on the Argentine side, that is; it washed out in the last rain."

Helen looked at me. Apparently our adventures were not over yet. At the first Argentine police station—where we went through Argentine customs for the fifth time—we asked about the bridge. It wouldn't be repaired for a month. How about the road on the other side? It was good to Río Grande, and from there to Lake Fagnano, seventy miles this side of Ushuaia. But beyond the lake it was bad, with a twelve-mile gap of horse trail still remaining over the Andes. We were

278

encouraged. A twelve-mile gap was better than a twenty-five-mile one.

We weren't too concerned about getting across the bridge-less river—until we saw it. It wasn't a river. It was a swampy lowland, flooded by the rains. Built on a fill, the road was interrupted by a crumbled concrete bridge. To one side was a flooded ditch about a half mile long. It looked just deep enough to float La Tortuga. The driver of a marooned truck on the other side looked on enviously as we slid down the embankment.

With wheels churning and propeller spinning we moved forward slowly to within fifty yards of where we could again climb to the road. Progress stopped. The water was too shallow to float us and too deep for the wheels to get traction on the soft bottom. I was picking out a fence post to winch to when our friend made it much easier. Tossing us a cable, he put his truck in reverse and, like a fish on a line, he hauled us out.

At Río Grande, halfway across Tierra del Fuego, we heard more encouraging news. The road crew had widened all but eight miles of the horse trail.

Excitedly we hurried south. Shortly out of Río Grande the country changed. The rolling plains became sharper, the valleys deeper, low shrubs became higher, and a few rocks showed through yellow-brown tundra. The shrubs became small trees; valleys became arroyos. And then as we crested the top of a hill we saw the white cordillera running east and west, the Andes, majestic right to the end. On the other side of the range lay Ushuaia.

Around the edge of Lake Fagnano, a sixty-mile finger of water on the north slope of the mountains, the jeep jolted over log corduroy fills and slipped through mudholes that gradually became worse. Through a heavy rain we started climbing. The trees were larger, some more than a hundred feet high and three feet in diameter, an unspoiled wilderness except where the bulldozed road left ruin in its wake. Incongruously among dense forests of spruce flitted green parrot-like birds.

It was almost dusk when we reached the last road camp on the north side of the range. From a log house strolled several men. Puffing on their pipes, in silence they walked around the jeep. When I asked about the road, they answered with indifference:

"This is as far as you can go."

Through the trees we could still see road ahead, and until it stopped we were going on. As we drove off, they were calling after us:

"You'll never get up that first *subida*."

About a mile farther we came to that first grade. Spiraling like a snail shell, it looked almost straight up. We left the jeep at the base of the incline and hiked ahead to see if we had any chance of getting up. The rain was still falling; our rubber boots slipped on the hard but ice-slick clay surface. The road wound two miles up to the crest, but the first quarter mile was the steepest. It would be a hard climb, and risky, but if I stayed close to the bank I thought we could make it.

Putting La Tortuga in the lowest gear and four-wheel drive, while Helen and Dinah stayed outside, I slowly engaged the clutch. Keeping the wheels just on the verge of spinning for maximum traction, I gently worked the throttle, and the jeep moved forward. With darkness approaching rapidly I impatiently fed more gas to the engine. The wheels spun, the jeep momentarily stood still, slid backward, and

I lost all the ground I had gained. With Helen ready to push a rock under the wheels I tried again. Tensely I kept a light foot on the throttle, and La Tortuga inched painfully up the *subida*. Past the steepest place, I congratulated myself on my skillful driving and looked around for Helen. A breathless figure staggered from behind the jeep. She had been pushing all the way.

At the crest we made camp in the dark while a howling wind from the Antarctic brought with it clouds of snow that soon coated the bow of the jeep. To keep the motor from freezing I left it running most of the night.

By morning the weather had cleared somewhat, but the sky was still gray and overcast. While Helen straightened the inside of the jeep, I walked ahead to where the road crew was working. The foreman told me that the eight-mile gap had now been reduced to three. I really got excited when he said that just two days before the road commission jeep had broken through.

"But," he added, "that was before the all-day rain and last night's snow."

For more than an hour I studied the trail, weighing the possibility of getting through. Barely six feet wide in places, the trail sloped to the valley below, and was a maze of chunks of blasted rock. Just twenty-five miles beyond this three-mile barrier was Ushuaia. I asked permission to try.

To my surprise, the foreman was enthusiastic. "Permission?" he said. "Why, if you're willing to take the chance, we'll even help you. It would be a thrill for us to see the first tourists reach Ushuaia by car."

I returned to Helen with the news, and we began the roughest overland travel of the trip.

After the first half mile it took all of the twelve-man road crew to keep us going. They put down logs, filled in holes, and pushed while we winched through foot-deep mud. Through the rocky part the wheels clawed over the slippery stone, the jeep pointed its bow straight up and came crashing down on a huge boulder, balanced there with wheels spinning until the men shoved her off. I crawled out to look at the damage—a broken spring, shattered rear window, and a giant dent in the hull.

With the trail tipping toward a hundred-foot canyon, we made the winch line secure to a tree and crept up the short grade. La Tortuga fishtailed, the wheels slipped sideways, and I heard the men yell, "*Pare, pare.*" But I couldn't stop! I felt the right rear wheel drop over the edge. From outside Helen screamed, and inside Dinah jumped wildly over me through the window. The winch line snapped taut, and all twelve men pulled sideward, braced the wheels with logs, until, with the winch, we crept back on the trail.

For the next two hours it went like that, sometimes with mud over the wheels, sometimes the wheels hanging over a trembling log bridge, sometimes dragging bottom over sharp rocks. And then the men surrounded the jeep. Grinning with satisfaction, they said, "*Que le vaya bien.* You're past the last bad spot."

Dazed, we drove those last twenty-five miles. We could scarcely believe that the uncertainty was over—until we saw the deep blue of the Beagle Channel, freckled with whitecaps, the protected harbor with its several small ships and, at the foot of the white-topped Andes, the red tin roofs of Ushuaia. To the south lay only a few scattered islands and the Antarctic.

I'M NOT sure what I expected to find in Ushuaia, but I knew one thing—for us the streets would seem paved with gold. I didn't expect to find the hearts of the people that way too. And although I was almost sure that a celebration would be in progress for one reason or another I had no idea that we would be the guests of honor. Ushuaia was feting Don Bosco, patron saint of sports.

Things started happening the same afternoon, January 23, 1956, that we first drove through the graveled streets of the world's southernmost town. A station wagon pulled alongside La Tortuga, and a white-gloved cavalierish Argentine Naval officer leaned out the window. In excellent English he asked where we had come from and invited us to join him the following evening for dinner. Captain Lopez de Bertodano was commandant of the naval base which was Ushuaia's *raison d'être*.

The same day we paid a visit to the road commission headquarters to thank the chief for the help his men had given us in getting through. We were invited to stay at the camp rather than go to the one hotel in town, El Gran Parque, alias Los Tres Mentiras, The Three Lies, since it was neither grand, nor parklike, nor could it qualify as a hotel.

A dubious distinction of Ushuaia was that its penal colony had been recently reactivated to accommodate the bigwigs of Perón's deceased government. One gentleman was of sufficient notoriety to warrant a visit from an American newspaperman, who, in passing through Río Gallegos, had heard that two crazy Americans had drowned while crossing the Strait of Magellan. He was quite disappointed that we hadn't because, he said, "It would have made a much better story."

The next evening at dinner with the commandant we were totally unprepared for what followed. "We would like you to be the guests of the Argentine Navy on a cruise to Buenos Aires. I expect the ship to dock within the week."

We were literally speechless—but managed an eager nod!

In jest Captain Lopez de Bertodano addressed me as Captain. "You know," he said, "I've been aboard almost everything that floats, but never an amphibious jeep."

"Well, sir," I answered enthusiastically, "as captain of the M.S. *La Tortuga,* I invite you to come aboard for a cruise around the harbor—after I've checked her for holes."

"Fine," he smiled. "Shall we meet your ship, *Les Eclaireurs,* when she comes into port?"

At the end of the week the A.R.A. *Les Eclaireurs* was sighted and we called for the commandant. With a duet of La Tortuga's horn and the ship's whistle we steamed out to meet her. There was a stiff wind, and the commandant asked if we were sure La Tortuga could weather the sea. I assured him that what we had been through made Ushuaia Harbor look like a millpond. With all due respect to La Tortuga, he smilingly intimated that he would prefer to stick to his regular command.

The following day, Sunday, the day of Don Bosco, we gave a public demonstration of La Tortuga's aquatic ability, making eleven turns around the harbor with most of the children in town aboard. We were slightly embarrassed, however, when, by the time we had taken the last group for a ride the tide was out and we were stuck. But with half the townspeople good-naturedly pulling under the direction of a jolly priest it was no trouble getting out.

One of the most heart-warming things of all was the way the men from the road commission came to the dock to see us off, each one giving us a vigorous embrace.

That night, as we lay in our cabin with the ship pitching and rolling beneath us, we felt a quieting strangeness. We had reached our goal. There was no more wondering what the jungles and the mountains and the sea would hold for us. La Tortuga was securely lashed on deck of the first ship she had ever been on. For the first time we could feel the power of the sea without fear, and yet, in the dark, while we listened to its roar, our experiences in reaching Ushuaia were still vivid, especially the pounding surf of the Pacific, the storms and reefs of the Caribbean, and the compelling current of the Strait of Magellan. But by morning we were well adjusted to being at sea as passengers rather than crew, and for the first time we were heading north.

Les Eclaireurs was not as we had expected either. She carried forty passengers. Since Perón had been a general and not an admiral, the Navy had suffered when it came to appropriations, with the result that, in order to make both ends meet, it had been forced to become a merchant fleet—at least part of it. A new ship, *Les Eclaireurs* had first-class accommodations, and the passenger list included a host of Argentine lovelies on vacation from their jobs in Buenos Aires. With the ship's officers and a score of midshipmen on a training cruise Helen and I looked forward to learning something we had never had time to learn while traveling—to dance the mambo, tango, rumba, samba, and maybe even the cha-cha-cha. But what was the craze? Dixieland!

Buenos Aires, second in the hemisphere only to New York in size and sophistication, was a busy metropolis. Stores even stayed open during siesta. Modern, progressive, clean, yet it had an Old World beauty in its statues and parks and mansard roofs. We were in a mood to celebrate, and all three of us walked into the first-class City Hotel. When we registered, the clerk informed us that Dinah would be there "with pension." That was a new one! An American-plan hotel for dogs! Luxuriating in endless hot water, with piles of clean towels, soft music, and even softer beds, our one regret was that their American plan extended only to dogs. At eight that night Dinah's waiter appeared. With black pants, white jacket, crisp napkin draped over one arm, he entered balancing a silver tray stacked high with whole broiled steaks —more than I had ever seen outside of a butcher shop.

The 985 paved miles across Argentina from Buenos Aires to the Chilean border took more than a week. We crawled at a turtle's pace trying to save La Tortuga's failing strength for that last climb, that last challenge to erase the miles by flatcar over the pass to Chile. And it was well we did travel slowly. Between Mendoza and the border the second gear sheared a tooth. In low gear we kept going, climbing, climbing, climbing to Las Cuevas at the frontier. Seven miles and twenty-seven hundred feet higher stood the statue of the Christ of the Andes. We moved up so slowly that Dinah walked beside us. An hour passed, two hours, the transmission held, and four hours later we reached the Christ, literally on a gear and a prayer.

In the shadow of the outstretched arms we felt an exultation tempered by a humble gratitude. There, at the foot of the Christo Redentor, we said thanks to the people all along the way without whose friendship we could not have realized our dream.

Behind us was a year and a half of travel, more than twenty thousand miles, backed by nine years of striving. We had come to look on La Tortuga as our home, a rolling, floating home that had taken us where no other car or boat had ever gone.

And Dinah? Well, she was her usual blasé self, unaware of her dubious accomplishment in contributing to the confusion of archaeological knowledge. Perhaps someday, high in the Andes, scientists will discover a corroded metal tag. They will treat it with chemicals, polish it, and read: "My name is Dinah. I live in Anchorage, Alaska."

www.ingramcontent.com/pod-product-compliance
Lightning Source LLC
Chambersburg PA
CBHW070745160726
48004CB00001B/51